Differently Literate

Dedication

To my husband, Leslie

to my sons, Jon and Chris

to Douglas Tallack

and to all the boys who ever discussed their books and comics with me.

Differently Literate
Boys, Girls and the Schooling of Literacy

Elaine Millard

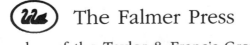 The Falmer Press

(A member of the Taylor & Francis Group)
London • Washington, D.C.

UK Falmer Press, 1 Gunpowder Square, London, EC4A 3DE
USA Falmer Press, Taylor & Francis Inc., 1900 Frost Road, Suite 101,
Bristol, PA 19007

First published in 1997

**A catalogue record for this book is available from the British
Library**

ISBN 0 7507 0660 0 cased
ISBN 0 7507 0661 9 paper

**Library of Congress Cataloging-in-Publication Data are
available on request**

Jacket design by Caroline Archer

Typeset in 10/12 pt, Garamond by
Graphicraft Typesetters Ltd., Hong Kong.

*Printed in Great Britain by Biddles Ltd., Guildford and King's
Lynn on paper which has a specified pH value on final paper
manufacture of not less than 7.5 and is therefore 'acid free'.*

Contents

Contents

Contents

List of Tables

Acknowledgments

There are many people whom I wish to acknowledge for their help, support and encouragement in what has been for me a significant new learning process. First, Les, Jon and Chris, the men in my family, who were the earliest to share my interests in reading and difference, and enter into debate with me; secondly, students on the PGCE course at Sheffield University from 1991–95 who participated in the research process, and; thirdly my colleagues in the Literacy Research Group at Sheffield University, Ann Finlay, Peter Hannon, Cathy Nutbrown, and Jo Weinberger, who not only modelled and refined the research process for me but have also taken a keen interest in my writing. I wish also to thank especially Bernard Harrison and Jo Weinberger, who made time to read my work and provide helpful commentary when they were particularly busy with their own lives.

Introduction

This book is the result of the bringing together of several strands of enquiry that have engaged my interest over the past ten years. The first of these is a sustained interest in the gendered nature of reading, which began as the work for an MA dissertation in Critical Theory, and which was subsequently published with the title *Reading as a Woman* (Millard, 1985). This pre-occupation subsequently widened into an interest in gendered differences in the acquisition and uses of literacy at all stages of education. I began this phase of research by questioning the nature of literacy and its relationship to contemporary social practices, in order to understand what tensions might be generated in the manner in which reading and writing are presented to pupils at home and in school. I sought to understand how we, as both teachers and parents, convey to pupils what we consider it is to be literate, both as part of a particular family and as a member of the wider social community and its institutions.

The second is a pedagogical concern for the development of effective methods of encouraging all pupils' reading during the middle school years, age 8–14, based both on classroom experience and developmental work as an Advisory Teacher in Nottinghamshire for the early implementation of the National Curriculum in English, during the period 1989–90. Again, this interest widened when, during the first investigations into school-based reading habits, I became more and more conscious of the continuing influence of the home in shaping pupils' orientation towards reading in school.

It is not the first occasion on which Sheffield Division of Education has been involved in investigating home influences on children's reading. In 1975 Frank Whitehead prefaced an interim report to the Schools Council on *Children's Reading Interests* with the provocative question, 'Why bother to spend time and money investigating what children choose to read in their leisure time?' Whitehead, with his colleagues, Capey and Maddren, were reporting on a survey conducted in March 1971, by means of two written questionnaires for pupils and schools in which just under 8,000 children, in a stratified random sample, had been questioned on their tastes in reading. From this research, teachers were alerted to the steady decline in the number of adolescents who chose to read any book for leisure. One of the findings they chose for comment, but to which, however, little attention was subsequently given, was the fact of boys' lesser enthusiasm than girls' for reading and, in particular, for reading works of fiction. The survey had found that by the age of 14, 36 per cent of adolescents recorded that they no longer read any kind of book as a leisure activity. Forty per cent of the boys and 32 per cent of girls fell into this category, revealing a significant gender difference (Whitehead, Capey and Maddren, 1975, p. 47). Whitehead answered his own questioning of the need to investigate these matters by suggesting that English held a 'very special and unique position' in education, because the greatest bulk of the learning appropriate to the subject took place outside of school in 'the home, the neighbourhood, the play ground and the street' (p. 7).

Twenty years on, my own endeavour to find out more about young people's reading has been driven by many of the same concerns that had motivated the Schools Council to fund Whitehead's national survey; that is, to understand some of the constituents of the kinds of attitudes and experience that pupils bring to the classroom from their homes. Whitehead's team had argued that in 1969 when the Schools Council Project began its work it seemed important 'to attempt to set reading in its context in the social and cultural life of the children concerned' (Whitehead, Capey, Maddren and Wellings, 1977, p. 18). It was a concern I wished to develop further, so I began a small scale survey in which I had asked children in their final term of the junior school (10–11 years) to talk to me about how they saw themselves as readers and from which I had begun to form a picture of some of the cultural and social factors that influenced their reading choice.

This age group is of particular interest to literacy researchers as it is positioned at the transition stage in education, marked by the move from primary to secondary school. The main strand of this earlier enquiry was provided by interviews with sixteen 10 and 11-year-old pupils, from five primary schools, recorded on two separate occasions, once at the beginning of their final primary school year and again in their first year at secondary school. I also interviewed the four primary teachers and four secondary English teachers responsible for each class. My intention on this occasion had been to identify and report on those features of teachers' practice in both sectors that encouraged children to see themselves as strong readers. In fact, the outstanding finding was the wide variation in each of the schools between boys and girls, in both attitude to reading and their willingness to share books with others. This was subsequently published in 1994 as a chapter in *Developing Readers in the Middle Years*. It is this work from which the research reported in the following pages was developed and expanded.

Further impetus was given to the extension of the research project by the Ofsted (1993) publication, *Boys and English*, which reported a particular strand of the last inspections conducted by Her Majesty's Inspectorate, prior to Ofsted. The report endorsed what many teachers and academics had suspected for some time, that imbalances in educational achievement were no longer being created by the relative failure of girls in school subjects such as mathematics and science, but through boys' under-achievement in every aspect of the language curriculum. This fact had hitherto attracted little critical attention, although previous reports by the Assessment of Performance Unit (APU) had already recorded significant differences in both performance and attitude between the sexes (Gorman, White, Brooks, Maclure and Kispal, 1988).

Under the sub-heading, 'Boys' Performance in English', the Ofsted report drew attention to the following:

> 5. Boys do not do as well as girls in English in schools. There are contrasts in performance and in attitudes towards the subject. The majority of pupils who experience difficulty in learning to write are boys. Boys' results in public examinations at 16 are not as good as girls', and many more girls than boys continue to study English beyond 16. (Ofsted, 1993, p. 2)

In public examinations at 16, in both English and English literature, boys' results compare unfavourably with girls'. In General Certificate of Secondary Education (GCSE) English in 1991, the proportions of boys and girls gaining a graded result were similar, but fewer boys were entered for the examination. Almost 15 per cent more girls than boys gained a grade A–C. Many fewer boys than girls attempted GCSE literature examinations and the contrasts between girls' and boys' performance was similar to that in English. The main findings reported included the following detailed comparisons:

> 11. Where classes were organised according to ability, there were more girls in the upper ability groups and more boys in the lowest in almost all the schools.
>
> 12. In all year groups, girls read more fiction books than boys and tended to have different tastes in reading. Few teachers monitored differences in girls' and boys' reading experience. (Ofsted, 1993, p. 2)

Further, over half the lessons that the inspectors reported seeing had been concerned with the reading and studying of literature, primarily modern narrative. Responses to reading, therefore, seem to be clearly implicated in the gender differences reported. The publication of the report confirmed that this was an opportune time to follow up the initial work and to focus in particular on those aspects of the interaction of reading and gender that had become increasingly significant during the development of the previous research. To an initial interest in reading, I added at a later stage in the enquiry a focus on its interaction with the writing process, in order to draw wider conclusions about the nature of gendered literate behaviour.

All the national studies I have cited above — including the Schools Council survey of 1971, the APU surveys conducted between 1979 and 1983 and the 1993 Ofsted Report — reveal a range of differences in achievement between boys and girls, without situating the evidence within a theoretical frame that can offer some explanation of the relative weakness of the boys. For example, the Ofsted Report made the following comments:

119. The reasons for boys' poorer achievements in English are not identified easily. There is no firm evidence that the differences in boys' and girls' performance reflect difference in innate linguistic ability. Research studies on the existence of possible biological sex differences in language ability are inconclusive . . . Research has also shown that there are contrasts in boys' and girls' attitudes towards writing and reading: girls are more likely than boys to be enthusiastic about these aspects of their work in English. (1993, p. 27)

The statement draws attention to a need to focus specifically on attitudes that separate the sexes and to investigate more thoroughly how each group constructs for itself a notion of what it is to be a reader in particular social contexts.

There are, therefore, three strands to the research work described in the following pages. The first seeks, through critical analysis of the history and nature of the teaching of literacy, and of the English curriculum in particular, to establish patterns in the social construction of a reading population in order to establish what is understood by literacy and expected of it by the general public. This strand also tracks the influence of gender difference on attitudes to reading, approached initially through feminist research in this area. The second strand considers the current context for literacy development as evidenced in a research into the interests of first year pupils in nine comprehensive schools (age 11–12). It focuses on pupils' attitudes to their reading and writing, concentrating in particular on the individual responses of boys. The third strand draws these two together to make inferences about the main influences on current reading habits and writing preferences in order to assist teachers and educators to review their current practice in relation to individual reading, particularly in relation to the boys in their classes, who can, but do not choose to read. Practical suggestions arising out of consultation and work with teachers are provided in the final chapter.

The first section of this volume covers two key areas of critical enquiry from which the analysis of the data collected in the fieldwork ultimately developed. Chapter 1 describes how attitudes about the relevance of reading to their lives is differently relayed to boys and girls and considers the role gender might play in the outcomes of the education process. Chapter 2 discusses how particular methods of instruction reinforce cultural norms and determine the ways in which readers are expected to behave. The consequences of promoting individual preference and pleasure in reading in the secondary phase of schooling are also considered.

The second section consists of a detailed account of the investigation conducted in the schools and the outcomes of this, relating the data back to the theoretical concerns that were raised in the first section. Chapters 3 and 4 analyse the pupils' responses to reading identified both through a questionnaire and a number of individual interviews. Chapters 5 and 6 describe textual methods of analysis used to draw comparisons between reading preferences and narrative writing style. Chapter 5 considers the implications for teaching and learning of three books typical of those read by the age group and Chapter 6 identifies gender differences encoded in the written narratives of a section of the group surveyed.

The third section draws all these strands together to discuss their consequences for the literacy curriculum. Chapter 7 returns to a review of the key elements of the theoretical debate and examines the need for a revision of the principles for developing literacy in schools in the light of the practices identified by the enquiry. Chapter 8 uses the outcomes of the empirical study in order to make practical recommendations for the development of more 'boy friendly' reading and writing policies and strategies for developing more flexible literacy practices throughout the school curriculum.

Section 1

Considering Gender and Literacy Research

Chapter 1

The Influence of Gender on Schooling

WAR

*A group of eight-year-olds
follow me into a room.
Three boys, three girls.
'Let's move the table.' I say.
We all move the table.
'Who's going behind the table?' I say.
'Me,' says one boy —
'Get away from the girls,' he says.
After eight years alive in this world
we have taught him to be at war
with half the people in the world.*

Michael Rosen

Gender and Early Schooling

From the beginning of the social interaction that comes with full-time schooling, girls and boys in the same classroom have been shown to create quite different educational experiences for themselves (Arnot and Weiner, 1987; Walkerdine, 1989; Delamont, 1990). Research data reported in the past twenty years have shown that boys occasion more discipline problems for their teachers (Clarricoates, 1978; Brophy 1985; Swann and Graddol, 1988) and that attempts by teachers to give girls an equal share of classroom attention are actively opposed by boys (Goodenough, 1987; D'Arcy, 1991; Jordan, 1995). In mixed group settings, for example, it has been shown that boys claim more teacher time, even when teachers are making a conscious effort to be even-handed (Clarricoates, 1978). Boys learn at an early age to control both the girls in their class and the women who teach them by adopting a 'male' discourse which emphasizes negative aspects of female sexuality, and embodies 'direct sexual insult'. This has been characterized by researchers as 'slagging off' (Lees, 1906, Walkerdine, 1981). Boys act as if the very fact of working with girls will demean them. For example, D'Arcy (1991) has described how a boy in primary school, who had

9

been asked to share a table with a girl, pushed her things away with a ruler so as not to be in contact even with her belongings and then refused to sit on a chair previously occupied by other girls in the class.

Children bring the knowledge that they are differently gendered, along with the need to display their difference in particular ways, into the earliest stage of schooling. What constitutes sex role appropriate behaviour is confirmed by, and negotiated through their interaction with other children. Paley (1984) begins an account of a year of life in her kindergarten classroom by emphasizing the differences she observed:

> Kindergarten is a triumph of sexual self-stereotyping. No amount of adult subterfuge or propaganda deflects the five year old's passion for segregation by sex. They think they have invented the differences between boys and girls and, as with any new invention, must prove that it works. (p. ix)

Later she recounts a typical story told to the class by a boy:

> We sneaked up in the house. Then we put the good guys in jail. Then we killed some of the good guys. Then the four bad guys got some money and some jewels.

And juxtaposes to it this one told by a girl:

> Once there were four kittens and they found a pretty bunny. Then they went to buy the bunny some food and they fed the baby bunny and then they went on a picnic.

She comments:

> Every year the girls begin with stories of good little families while the boys bring us a litany of super heroes and bad guys. Language development and creative dramatics may be on my mind but the children take over the story-plays for a more urgent matter: to inform one another of the preferred images for boys and girls. (p. 3)

The differences in the story themes chosen vividly illustrate both boys' and girls' use of story telling as an element of contrasting gender display. Jordan (1995) has described boys' cooperative fantasy play as re-enactments of ' "warrior" discourse a discourse that informs epic narratives in a tradition stretching from Hercules and Beowulf to Superman and Dirty Harry' (p. 76). These plays, she suggests, are used to determine the hero roles available to boys, while creating a further masculine identity which is designated 'not female' (*ibid.*).

Primary teachers in England have also reported significant differences in boys' and girls' reading interests, often citing this as one of the major factors in boys' weaker all-round performance in the literacy curriculum (Osmont, 1987; Pidgeon, 1993). Osmont reports that children brought to the classroom their perceptions of what adults at home were reading describing considerable differences between men's and women's reading matter. She reports that a majority of mothers were observed reading mainly fiction, whereas fathers read newspapers, information books and documents brought back from work (Osmont, 1987 p. 160).

Pidgeon (1993), reflecting on the gendered responses of her 5–7-year-old readers, was prompted to ask herself why the books that she had shared with equal pleasure with boys and girls only a short while before, suddenly became marked as more appropriate to the interests of one particular gender. She asks specifically:

> We know that by the age of seven, marked differences between girls' and boys' reading abilities and reading preferences can be identified. These differences are perpetuated and become more obvious through- out school and into adulthood. How do these differences emerge and why? Can it be that right from the beginning of children's reading experiences, they are linking these experiences with what they know about gender?' (1993, p. 21)

Later she argues that at five, just when the majority of infants are learning to read, gender role becomes increasingly important. Further she suggests that a gender-related study of children's reading behaviour at home reveals their understanding of marked differences in their parents' habits of reading (1993, pp. 30–2).

Minns (1993) has also described differences in orientation towards the use of texts in her account of three 10-year-old boys and their reading. Boys, she demonstrates, not only read different texts but they read shared books differ- ently. In particular she records how one boy, Clayton, chooses to read the same journals as his father, who is a farmer (p. 62). Later, discussing his rather factual response to a well-loved reader, *Charlotte's Web*, where he has ex- pressed a special interest in the life cycle of the spider, Minns suggests that this is a newly acquired defensive gesture:

> It is as if Clayton is transforming what could be a totally aesthetic experience into a factual exchange of data, and making them a part of his theory of how the world works.

> Clayton's sense of himself as a reader appears to be related to his own developing masculine identity. Two things are of key importance to him: his father and the world of farming. They are the pivot on which his life turns, and, although he demonstrates a sensitive response to fiction, at the same time he feels pressured to construct a stereotyped masculine role in his public response, often on his guard against cer- tain ways of reading. (1993, p. 65)

She concludes that Clayton has adopted a view of reading from his father which is concerned about 'finding out' (in this instance, about the behaviour of spiders) so that he treats *Charlotte's Web* as he would a natural history text. Despite a school environment that values and fosters an interest in the reading of stories, his individual reading interests at the end of his primary education are turning away from fiction, to the kinds of information books that he identifies with his future adult role, a fact Minns obviously regrets. Hers is a concern that I have encountered in large numbers of teachers of this age group. They experience the change in boys' reading habits as a kind of denial of their own values and interests. Mothers similarly find the change in their sons' reading unsympathetic and attempt to win them back to the old ground.

It is not only in the choice of reading matter and ways of reading it in which boys differ markedly from girls. The whole area of reading for leisure holds less interest for them throughout schooling. In a range of English-speaking countries, larger surveys and cross-cultural studies confirm the data provided by case studies of individual readers. Gender differences in the primary school are reflected not only in differences in book choice, but also in the amount of time and enthusiasm given to reading (APU, 1987). Moreover, particularly in the United States, research has found that reading is increasingly seen by pupils as an activity more appropriate to girls than boys as they progress through schooling (Wallbrown, Levine and Engin, 1981; Kelly, 1986; Shapiro, 1990). Although earlier cross-cultural studies found this trend to be more noticeable in the United States (Downing, May and Ollila, 1982), later studies have shown that differences in attitudes to reading are now widespread in Britain (Davies and Brember, 1993; Millard, 1994; Benton, 1995); Australia (Patterson, 1986) and New Zealand (Bardsley, 1991). Parents and librarians, as well as teachers, have reported a growing disinterest in boys for the reading that is expected of them both at home and in school (Wheeler, 1984; Nicolle, 1989).

Where the uses and gratification that pupils take from their reading have been considered, boys have been found to be more likely to read for utilitarian purposes; girls for their own intrinsic pleasures (Clark, 1976; Wheeler, 1984; Greaney and Neumann, 1983). Clark's classic study, *Young Fluent Readers* (1976), showed that even at the pre-school stage there were noticeable differences in the reading materials chosen by boys and girls:

> The children read a variety of print . . . sports news and television programmes were two of the sources of interest in the newspapers to the boys in particular. The girls tended to be interested in reading for themselves stories they had already heard, or stories of a similar level. The boys on the contrary . . . were inclined to show interest in the print in their environment and use their reading skill to extend their knowledge. (p. 49)

Clark's study also highlighted the different induction of boys and girls into the world of print. Children kept records of their reading in diaries, and her analysis of these records showed significant differences. Particularly noticeable in boys' accounts were the inclusion of daily papers, comics, annuals and collections of stories, whereas the girls' records featured fairy tales, Enid Blyton mystery stories and books on horses, ballet and wild flowers. Clark further suggests that the girls were more content with the kind of work they were given to do in school than were the boys in her study (1976, p. 86). Boys therefore, experienced a dissonance between the literacy they practised skilfully at home and that demanded from them by teachers.

Content Difference in Reading Choice

More recent studies of reading attitudes in English primary schools have concluded that the major difference in reading attitudes for Year 2, Year 4, and Year 6 children is similarly located in the content of what was read rather than in a lack of interest in reading itself (Davies and Brember, 1993; Stables *et al.*, 1995). It has also been repeatedly recorded that gender differences in reading interests widen as pupils progress through school. An Australian survey of 194 16-year-old students found that 41.6 per cent of the boys chose not to read fiction, as compared with 19.3 per cent of the girls and that there were wide differences in the kinds of genre chosen by the sexes, with girls of all abilities reading large numbers of romance titles (Patterson, 1986, p. 46). In a comparative study of readers in England and the United States, Fisher and Ayres (1990) found significant differences in the reading choices of boys and girls.

Individual studies also highlight gender bias in choice of texts. Bissex (1980) who documented the reading and writing history of her son Paul from the ages of 5 to 11, characterized his reading interests as a liking for: 'science fiction, adventure stories, humorous stories, and informational books with an emphasis on remarkable facts and scientific kinds of information' (p. 168). Although Bissex reported that Paul was able to follow his own interests widely at home, she found, as with the boys in Clark's (1976) study, that this was not the case for his work at school. Such evidence suggests that there is less provision for boys to exercise their reading interests within the school environment than those that are seen as appropriate by girls.

The differences in reading choice is also mirrored in the way that the two genders report responding to the reading they choose. In the reading of novels, for example, Brownstein (1982) has argued that although boys and men often fantasize about the narratives they read, it is largely girls and women who tend to 'live longer in them' (p. xv). She discusses what it means for a woman to search for the significance of her life by reading stories about women who are doing just that:

> The marriage plot most novels depend on is about finding validation for one's uniqueness and importance by being singled out among all other women by a man . . . For a heroine is just that, an image; novel

heroines, like novel readers, are often women who want to become heroines. (p. xvi)

A student teacher, writing an account of her own reading development as part of an autobiographical reflection on learning for a teacher training course, described the quest to become the heroine as motivating her own adolescent reading:

As a young girl I would search out books which dealt with women often set apart from the rest of society. I would imagine myself in their situation and almost come to believe I was a heroine, for I was able to understand, empathise and appreciate their dilemmas, their distress and their internal dialogue. It is perhaps why *Jane Eyre* remains one of my favourite books.

In comparison, a male student, on the same course, offered a quite different account of the development of his interest in the subject:

It was definitely the writing element I enjoyed most in English. Looking back I can see that my reading was not as involved. Some of my early writing is typified by petty authorial intervention (so unnecessary), more often than not to make sure that 'Miss' did not miss the joke . . .

I was probably responding to the sort of literature I was influenced by outside school. At the age of 14 I loved Terry Pratchett's *Disc World* which lead me to value literature on the basis of how funny I found it.

The contrasts of interest are sharp and the gendered differences expressed here have been found as often in the accounts of postgraduate students training to teach English as they are found in the reading and writing preferences collected from pupils which form the subject matter of later chapters.

Large Scale Surveys of Reading Interests

That the trend away from voluntary reading was most acute amongst adolescent boys was signalled twenty years ago. The Bullock Report (DES, 1975) drew on the first report of the School Council Project, directed by Whitehead, Capey and Maddren (1975) which identified a strong tendency for older boys to display a preference for factual books. Furthermore, Department Education and Science (DES) research at that time indicated that one-third of 14-year-old boys of average intelligence read nothing at all for pleasure. Subsequent surveys have reproduced the findings of Whitehead's team, which show that there is a steep falling away of interest in reading at adolescence and that this is particularly marked in boys. This decline is also documented in the reports of the Assessment of Performance Unit (APU) produced between 1979–83, which consistently show boys to be at a disadvantage in the literacy curriculum. Comparable results to those of Whitehead, Maddren and Capey have also been reported recently by Peter Benton, whose 1995 survey, using a similar questionnaire to Whitehead's team, showed that a third of boys aged 13+ chose not to read at all for pleasure (Benton, 1995, p. 102). The Ofsted Report, *Boys and English* (1993), using evidence drawn from the inspections of secondary schools and following the introduction of the National Curriculum (1989–92), gives a current national perspective. The opening statement is unequivocal:

> Boys do not do as well as girls in English in schools. There are contrasts in performance and in attitudes towards the subject. The majority of pupils who experience difficulty in learning to read and write are boys. Boys' results in public examinations at 16 are not as good as girls', and many more girls than boys continue to study English beyond 16. (Ofsted, 1993, p. 2)

It further reported that:

> In all year groups girls read more fiction books than boys and tended to have different tastes in reading. Few teachers monitored differences in boys' and girls' reading differences. (*ibid.*)

One major cause of this difference may be the way reading is presented in schools. At an age where teachers want pupils to begin to progress from children's stories towards fiction for older and adult readers, a large number of pupils stop reading altogether. Many of those who do continue to read for pleasure move into a gender-related selection from the best seller shelves: girls choosing horror and popular romances, boys opting for action and science fiction. Further, many boys read as little in school as they are allowed to get away with.

Gender Differences in Writing

The picture is much the same in writing. In large scale studies, girls have been shown to be more enthusiastic about their writing from the outset of their schooling. The APU surveys carried out between 1979–83 found that a greater number of boys agreed with the statement 'I hate writing' with more girls endorsing 'I like writing' (Gorman, White, Brooks, Maclure and Aspel, 1988, pp. 176–7). At 16+ more girls opt to study English as an 'A' level subject and express an interest in careers that have writing as a central activity (Gorman, White and Brooks, 1987, p. 58). Many more girls were also found to have engaged in writing activities before they started school. A tour around any toy shop, or early learning centre, is sufficient to confirm that desks, toy briefcases, and much of the paraphernalia associated with writing, are targeted at girls rather than boys. Boys are directed by illustrations on the packaging to construction and action toys: and this, despite more than two decades of international campaigning for equality of treatment.

Girls' enthusiasm for writing activity is illustrated in the work of Steedman (1982) who documented three working-class girls' extended story writing in the primary school. She ends her detailed study of the texts they produced with a discussion of 'sex and stories', in which she comments:

> Every instinct possessed by those who grew up in the culture that produced the *Tidy House* insists that it must have been written by little girls and that it could never have been written by little boys. In the classroom where Lindie, Melissa and Carla worked, little boys did write, certainly not with the alacrity displayed by the girls, but sometimes at great length, frequently producing episodic, epic adventures with lone male heroes moving through time and space. As a group, the boys in this particular classroom (and in many others) demonstrated far less competence in reading and writing than did the girls. Several of them were only just beginning to read at the age of eight and did not have the means to produce extended pieces of writing. (1982, p. 135)

Steedman echoes other primary teachers' recognition that early differences in boys' and girls' attainment is related to classroom choices. Girls often choose to 'do literacy activities'; their male peers often do not. Some early years teachers now vary the scene of writing in their classroom — including it as part of a larger role-play area rather than providing a simple writing corner — in order to attract more boys to experiment with writing. Nor is girls' interest in writing always to their own best advantage. Steedman's subsequent analysis of the three girls' stories, reveals their obsessive concern with marriage, child-care and other domestic themes — a preoccupation that acts to limit their educational aspirations. In other words, both sexes' literacy practices are determined by their gendered identity.

The grater willingness of girls to write outside of school has also been recorded by the APU (1987a):

> . . . over one-third of girls (from a random sample of 100) replied that they wrote letters, either to relatives or to pen friends. One girl maintained a correspondence with seven pen friends, another with five. Only six girls in this sample expressed a reluctance for undertaking more writing . . .

> By contrast, a comparable sample of boys' responses showed that a third of them did no writing at home, or wrote very little. (p. 9)

These findings are striking in their resemblance to those cited by Newbolt in 1921, related to the education of Victorian girls. He quotes from the report of the Schools' Inquiry Commission (1867) — one of the first occasions on which differences in boys' and girls' achievements were noted — to the effect that:

> A cultivated young lady would read and write well, would be faultless in her spelling . . . she would posses a facility of expression and composition in her own language, greater than that possessed by most men of her class of life. (Board of Education, 1921, p. 100)

White (1987) has also recorded marked gender differences in the themes that were chosen for writing by older pupils. She reported finding that given a free choice, boys wrote about such things as plane crashes, war exploits and murders, while girls continued to prefer writing which was self-reflective or empathetic (1987, pp. 9, 12). In all these cases, each sex is shown to be limiting both the range and variety of their writing repertoire, but it is boys who remain most reluctant to engage willingly in writing of all kinds.

By the end of their compulsory secondary schooling, large numbers of boys achieve poorer results in GCSE English than girls in the same class. The Ofsted Report, *Boys and English* (1993), cited the 1991 examination statistics support this:

> Amongst those taking GCSE English in the last year of compulsory schooling in 1991, 98.9 per cent of boys and 99.4 per cent of girls gained a graded result, however, a smaller proportion of boys than girls was entered. 45.5 per cent of boys and 60.3 per cent of girls gained grades A–C and 7.9 per cent of boys gained a grade A pass compared to 12.4 per cent of girls. Many fewer boys than girls attempted GCSE English Literature examinations: 47.5 per cent of those taking English literature were boys and 52.5 per cent girls. (Appendix B)

It is, therefore, important to look more closely at the cultural practices that create differences of attitude and that have persisted, and to some extent intensified, during a period when teachers have made special efforts to counteract gender bias, particularly in English teaching, and when there have been many LEA initiatives to redress inequalities of achievement.

Gender Differences in Academic Achievement

The findings in the early 1980s by the APU that girls were falling behind in mathematics, resulted in a series of projects to render the subject more girl friendly (Joffe, Foxman and Jordan, 1988; Walden and Walkerdine, 1982; Walkerdine 1989) and textbooks and mathematical tasks were successfully redrafted to reflect girls' interests. There has been no similar focus on the relative under-achievement of boys in the language curriculum. On the contrary, feminists have illustrated that books chosen for reading with classes in school are biased towards boys' lives, suggesting alternatives with positive role models for girls (Stones, 1983; Baines, 1985), including feminist rewriting of fairy stories (Lurie, 1990). It is, of course, perfectly understandable that feminists have focused on girls' needs, particularly as in their own academic careers they have found male academic institutions resistant to change (Rudduck, 1994, p. 9). However, this concern has created a lack of equity in a focus that considers the performance and interests of only one sex.

Before analysing in detail how the construction of English as a subject is related to gender difference, I shall consider different ways of theorizing that difference, turning first to the repeatedly discredited, but stubbornly persistent, notion of biological or inherent genetic difference.

Biological Explanations of Gender Difference

Boys' under-achievement in the literacy curriculum was first made an issue during the period when the 11+ was a decisive factor in secondary school selection throughout the country and not simply an out-dated practice retained in some Local Education Authorities. Superior performance in the language tests by girls were sufficiently marked for it to be necessary to weight test scores in favour of the boys to ensure 'equality' of provision. Boys, it was argued, had greater 'spatial' ability, less detectable by school tests. Evidence of the existence of sex difference in reading ability could be deduced today, for example, from the much bigger proportion of boys who are referred as having special educational needs. Biological explanations have therefore attributed such differences in boys' intellectual growth to their slower physiological and psychological maturation. It was fashionable in the heyday of the 11+ to talk of 'late developers', who were more often than not male.

In 1927 the American, Lincoln, posited a theory that boys' slower skeletal growth caused difficulties in adapting to the auditory and visual demands of reading (Lincoln, 1927, quoted in Shapiro, 1990, p. 241). On the other hand, arguments that boys' brains seem to be more specialized in visuo-spatial ability have been used to argue for boys' 'natural' advantages in science, mathematics and technological subjects.

Feminists have themselves used arguments grounded in biological determinism to theorize the continuing oppression of women, based on their reproductive role and its commitments (Firestone, 1970), and the body and its difference remains a central focus of feminist debate with an insistence on the 'sexualisation and embodiment of the subject' as the key to understanding the 'politics of ontological difference' (Braidotti, 1989, pp. 89–91). Current research using electronic imaging has claimed to have revealed differences in men's and women's brain function related to their processing of language. How these differences are theorized remains contentious, however, and they have been used contradictorily in the popular press to argue both for women's greater facility with language skills, while supporting the contradictory view of a 'biological ceiling' to their attainment.

Gender as Socially Constructed

It is now, however, more common for gender theorists to look to the ways in which social interaction shapes individual and group expectation of what men and women should be. Instead of the biological sex of an individual determining his or her nature through genetic predisposition, it is now recognized that a major influence on behaviour is that of gender identity — where gender refers to socially constructed maleness and femaleness — as opposed to biological sex. Simone De Beauvoir put the case most memorably for feminism in her formula that 'one is not born a woman, one becomes one' (1984, p. 295). Gender studies with a sociological perspective, therefore, look towards cultural distinctions to explain the differences they find between the sexes.

One of the earliest of the explanations of ways in which boys' and girls' interests begin to separate out, each from the other, in the early years of schooling was looked for in the concept of sex-role stereotyping. According to social learning theory, children shape their behaviour in response to the ways in which significant others in their lives expect them to behave. From the outset of learning, long before they enter schools, different models of the kind of behaviour that is appropriate to their role are given to boys and girls, both by the adults who surround them, and by their friends who willingly police the boundaries of gender difference. Schools, which both openly and covertly embody society's values, actively reinforce the differences by the subject choices they offer and the career paths they recommend each sex follow (Marland, 1983). Take, for example, the question of girls being encouraged into science and technology when there has been no matching emphasis on more boys being attracted in the humanities and languages. The model, therefore, implicitly suggests that it is girls' education that is deficient and that girls need to become more like boys in their aspirations. The evidence that schools expect boys and girls to have different educational aspirations are, as I suggested above, well documented and evidenced in collections of research data from both primary and secondary schools (Delamont, 1990; Minns, 1991; Weiner, 1994).

It is an important factor that English-speaking countries represent reading as an activity preferred by girls. Girls are more likely to be portrayed as readers in the illustrations in children's books, given books as presents for birthdays and Christmas and to describe themselves as devoted to their books (Willinsky and Hunniford, 1993, p. 92). The Canadian researcher, Cherland (1994), describes something she labels the 'greeting card phenomena', identified in a collection of pictorial representations of people reading. From a sample of thirty notecards she found only two representations of males reading: one the illustration for a bookmark produced by the Canadian Children's book centre; the second an advertisement for the Canadian Literacy Guild. She comments:

> Certain images were chosen for these greeting cards for the reason that these cards represent certain cultural ideals. And the cards sell because they represent something lovely and desirable, something that, for the women who buy them, reverberate with meaning . . . They provide yet another textual framework in which women are positioned as peripheral to the work of the world, and in which women of color and poor women are made invisible. (Cherland, 1994, p. 201)

The image of the reader is here shown to be linked to a construct of a feminine identity. In previous work I have suggested that a flexibility in adapting to the variety of roles presented in their reading can be expected of girls far more than it can of boys:

> Activities that are seen as girl preferred are surrounded with far more taboos for boys than boy preferred activities are for the girls. Dressing in 'male attire', acquiring boys' toys, and 'trying on' a male role is part of most girls' early experience. The role models they encounter reinforce the positive aspects of masculinity, whether these are represented by dramatic roles, such as Shakespeare's or Shaw's St Joan or those suggested by the casual adoption of jeans, tee shirts and boots. The female role on the other hand is always an area that acts as transgressive for boys, an area for disquiet or ridicule. (Millard, 1994, p. 102)

Further, in the incidents reported by D'Arcy (1991), cited above, boys are shown to behave as if contact with anything remotely associated with femininity will contaminate or 'pollute' them and the fear in such response is borne out by anthropological studies that have demonstrated men's fear of women in general and of menstruation in particular. This is an area that I will return to in discussing psychoanalytical interpretations of sexualization.

Gender Role as Social Display

Goffman's sociological constructs of gender roles in everyday life may similarly be used to throw specific light on the social role that reading plays in marking gender difference. He describes rituals and highly conventionalized representations of masculinity and femininity in American society, such as, for example, having one's cigarette lighted, or the space one chooses in a crowded room, so that each subject is caught up in an enactment of gender identity in every aspect of social behaviour (Goffman, 1976). Reading and the associated behaviour of sitting quietly or becoming absorbed in a book can also be understood as gender marked behaviours. Nursery school children rapidly fall in line with what they conceive to be gender appropriate aspects of such display, whether it is behaviour in the play corner or the reading area. Reading itself, as portrayed in books and paintings, has an element of display in exactly the way that Ophelia is sent reading a prayer book, to meet Hamlet, as an appropriate display of feminine piety. The visual images, which Cherland (1994) describes on her greetings cards, frequently feature women reading as a leisure activity, their clothes decoratively arranged as they appear absorbed in a book (p. 202). The act of reading, therefore, comes to the new reader with an overlay of encrusted cultural dispositions, roles and attitudes that suggest it is a more appropriate activity for one sex than it is for the other.

Gender Regime

Harris, Nixon and Rudduck (1993), however, suggest that the concept of sex role modelling is lacking in sufficient complexity to account for the contradictory aspects of gender relations and the competing views given to adolescents by schools, parents and the wider community. As a way into interpreting their own data relating to schoolwork, homework and gender, they proposed instead adapting the framework of gender regime (Kessler *et al.*, 1985) to describe the ordering of the practices that construct various kinds of masculinity and femininity in schools. They explain that their 'data led us to see young people as caught in overlapping gender regimes — the regime of the community, the regime of the peer culture and the regime of the school' (Harris, Nixon and Rudduck, 1993, p. 5). They further suggest that although challenges were offered to each external regime by the school, to some extent the residual effects of the other influences were still strong. Perhaps the most powerful influence of all was the pressure of peer culture, particularly that of the gender appropriate peer group.

Actions performed in similar contexts on a daily basis have the effect of reinforcing the dominant (patriarchal) structures of society and uniformity of gendered behaviour. The idea of a 'regime' is central also to Giddens' (1991) concept of 'cyclical practices', in which a routine of social actions and attitudes are repeated and recreated. By analysing such practices, Giddens emphasizes that gender is a 'matter of learning and continuous work', work, which is underpinned by regimes that:

> . . . centre on gratification/deprivation and hence are a focus of motivational energies — beginning, as Freud made clear with the earliest unconscious developments of the reality principle. The types of regimes individuals build up as habits of behaviour, therefore, remain as unconscious conditioning elements of conduct, and are tied into enduring motivational patterns. (1991, p. 62)

It is the linking of behaviour, motivation and the unconscious in psychoanalytical theories that are particularly useful in explaining why gendered differences are so resistant to rationalization and change.

Bourdieu (1990) similarly accounts for the residual effect of older cultural practices on current social routines in his concept of the 'habitus': that is, the body of traditional practices in which individual difference is structured into practical activity:

> The habitus, a product of history, produces individual and collective practices — more history — in accordance with the schemes generated by history. It ensures the active presence of past experience, which deposited in each organism in the forms of schemes of perception, thought and action, tend to guarantee the 'correctness' of practices and their constancy over time, more reliably than all formal rules and explicit norms. (Bourdieu, 1990, p. 54)

What the 'habitus' creates, in effect, is an unexamined common-sense or practical way of proceeding within any repeated social routine that rules out, as extravagant or unconventional, other kinds of behaviour. Bourdieu demonstrates exactly how practical activity is resistant to change because we carry within us the organizing structures of the past, internalized as second nature and therefore their arbitrariness and their historical basis have both been forgotten. A familiar example that demonstrates the workings of the 'habitus' in relation to early gender differentiation may be detected in the way in which active toys, that encourage boisterous play, are most often given to a boy child, while a little girl will be encouraged to sit and colour-in pictures or look at books. Subsequently, boys may be described as 'naturally' more boisterous, girls more self-contained and reflective. This ensures that children continue to be presented with the kind of gifts 'most suitable' to their sex. The 'habitus' therefore legitimates the activities of boys and girls who fit the conventional norm, those who behave differently may find themselves marked as deviant, and in the later stages of their development attract the label 'tomboy' if an active girl, or 'sissy' if a more passive and gentle boy. But, as Thorne (1993), who made a study of playground name-calling, has argued, these terms do not carry equal force:

> 'Sissy' like 'tomboy' alludes to gender deviance, but with relentlessly negative connotations. The major contemporary definition 'an effeminate boy or man' has eclipsed the word's earlier more neutral use as a term of address for girls ('sissy' was originally derived from 'sister'). Put simply, a sissy is a person whose character, interests and behaviour partake too much of qualities, such as timidity, passivity and dependence, that are stereotyped as childish and as female. (pp. 115–16)

Thorne explains that convention works to stigmatize the 'sissy' boy, who is seen to have failed as a male, whereas a tomboy girl is allowed to retain a positive self-image. In later life, women are happy to acknowledge a tomboy-ish girlhood, whereas male graduates, questioned by Thorne, recalled the experience of being labelled 'sissy' or 'wimp' as very painful (1993, p. 117). Engaging tomboys abound in children's stories, but there are far fewer literary examples of sissies. Where such boys are portrayed, they are usually endowed with superior strengths of moral courage, or persistence, as in the popular class novel for 11–12-year-olds, Betsy Byars' *The Eighteenth Emergency*, where the 'hero', Mouse, stands up alone to the school bully, Hammerman. Thorne comments on books written in the 1970s to combat gender stereotyping, and which featured 'sissies', such as *Nobody's Family is Going to Change*, (a book for this age range that features a black boy who wants to be a ballet dancer):

> Unlike literary tomboys, who often have male and sometimes female companions, literary sissies remain relatively isolated as they pursue their interests and successfully weather criticism from their fathers and other boys. But while fictional sissies triumph and gain some accept-ance for who they are, fictional tomboys experience eventual loss and resignation. (Thorne, 1993, p. 118)

The implication is that a boy who is a 'sissy' will always be positioned outside the mainstream social group. Girls, on the other hand, are permitted to journey through and out of their tomboyhoods, as in the example represented by Jo March of *Little Women* (arguably the most famous tomboy of all), to marriage and maternity, with only a few pangs of regret. Boys who act like girls are therefore construed by the logic of the 'habitus' as far more deviant than girls who act like boys.

Psychoanalytical Theory, Freud and Gender

Some psychoanalytical theories stress the impact of sexual development both on the individual's sense of self and on intellectual growth. They emphasize the ways in which the individual's response to bodily change patterns their response to their gendered identity. Traditional Freudian theory has focused on negative aspects of femininity and its problematic position in western cul-ture, embodied in the famous Freudian question, 'What do women want?' Women have been considered to be at a disadvantage in a patriarchal culture that privileges the phallus and ascribes status and power to the phallic male. Within the Oedipal system, to be a girl is to lack something and, in relation to the male, they appear castrated and therefore impotent. Boys know that the possession of a penis puts them in the power position (despite the reminder that it is the symbolic power of the phallus that is at issue, not the physical organ) but continue to fear its loss and despise the women, including their mothers, whom they perceive to be castrated. The implications of classic Freud-ian analysis is that femininity is predicated on girls surrendering a common identity shared by children of both sexes which is 'masculine' in nature.

There are, nevertheless, other ways of looking at the question of gender differentiation. Far from being an uncertain state for most girls in western societies, becoming a woman is a well-recognized occurrence, even marked in the United States by a special celebration at the onset of menarche. With her first period a girl's entrance into womanhood is assured and older women may still ask a young girl's mother 'has she become a woman?' A biological event brings with it a future promise of a well-established social role, that of mother-hood. For boys, there is no similar, simple, recognizable event, only a network of signs and social behaviours to reassure them of their arrival at manhood. Researchers have suggested several physical markers that might equate to girls' development; the breaking of the voice, or the beginning of the growth spurt or even the occasion of the subject's first nocturnal emission (wet dream). None of these events have the same socially accepted significance or import as the girls' first period. Indeed, discussion of the occurrence of wet dreams is so tightly bounded by taboos, other than in the company of other boys, that it is indeed a most unlikely signifier.

Later feminist interpreters of Freud, such as Chodorow (1978), have there-fore argued that it is masculinity rather than femininity that is the less clearly defined state, with ensuing anxieties and attendant insecurities for the male. Chodorow's theories are an adaptation of Karen Hornsey's idea of the male perception of the feminine as a threat or pollution, which results in dread of all things female. Her main argument is that in order to establish a secure core gender identity, thereby ensuring ontological security, the infant boy has to reject some of the powerful primary unconscious identification with his mother, making maleness more problematic for him:

A boy must learn his gender identity as being not-female or not-mother. Subsequently, again because of the primacy of the mother in early life and because of the absence of concrete, real, available male figures of identification and love who are as salient for him as female figures, learning what it is to be masculine comes to mean learning to be not-feminine, or not-womanly. (Chodorow, 1978, p. 45)

Chodorow proceeds to argue that it becomes more important for men than it is for women to have a clear sense of gender difference and to maintain rigid boundaries between the sexes. Further, she suggests that it is men who treat their sons and daughters more differently and enforce gender role expecta-tions more vigorously than do their mothers, emphasizing a difference rather than a commonality between themselves and women (1978, p. 48).

With the knowledge brought by postmodernism of the multiple subject positions created in competing discourses, Freudian theories now appear to be over deterministic and Chodorow's theories have been particularly criticized by other feminists for her equation of sexual with an essentialist cultural iden-tity which suggests fixed personality traits for the sexes adapted to unchanging cultural practices such as female nurturing and mothering. Yet, sociological theories have also pointed to the lack of positive male role models as instrumental in creating an identity problem for the adolescent during the formation of social groups. Child-care is still largely the province of mothers, whether or not they are living with the father of their child, and the fact of absent fathers, either through working patterns or marriage breakdown, create social conditions in which boys often have to test their masculinity against that which they already know — the feminine. Chodorow's analysis of the problems that arise from the different ways in which boys and girls achieve autonomy can then be seen to have relevance to particular social contexts and cultural practices. Although it is difficult to accept that masculinity presents a problematic position for *all* young males, it is also necessary to avoid assuming that patriarchy confirms all of them in a privileged and confident position of uncontested power — a position that is implied in early feminist analysis of difference.

Jordan (1995) has a more convincing account of how gendered subjects adapt to particular views of what it might mean to be either masculine or feminine in a particular historical context when she divides a concept of core gender identity from that of an appropriate gender role. A gender identity is adopted quite early on, at around the age of 2, and for the vast majority of subjects this remains stable throughout their life; gender role evolves more slowly and its meaning is negotiated through social interaction with others (Jordan, 1995, p. 73). Jordan suggests that, rather than taking on board passively the definitions of gender offered by society through role modelling, children become active agents in constructing gender positions through their interactions with adults and with each other. For boys, one of the established ways of doing this is to define their masculinity by using femininity as a subordinate term. It follows that the disdain growing boys need to show towards girls, and which is embodied in the Rosen poem reproduced at the opening of this chapter, can be attributed to boys' defensiveness about their masculine status, rather than fear of women themselves. Lacking a positive feature with which to identify, boys appear anxious to declare what they are not — not a 'puff' or a 'sissy', not 'wets' or 'boffins', but above all else not girls. The problem for education and literacy learning is that in co-educational settings 'being good at school work' is more often constructed as an attribute of girls; a fact acknowledged in the prevalent stereotype of the 'girlie swot'.

Mac An Ghaill (1994) has provided us with persuasive evidence of how older 'macho' boys within a particular school setting, with an agenda other than that of the school management, not only reject academic attainment as inappropriate for themselves, but also actively strive to undermine schooling for other males. These dominant 'macho' figures became:

> . . . a pivotal group within the school creating an ethos in which the academic/non-academic couplet was associated with a feminine/masculine division for a wider group of 'ordinary' male students who were not overtly anti-school. (Mac An Ghaill, 1994, p. 59)

From a fairly early age, most boys can be shown to fear the 'contamination' of femininity and all the evidence related to language learning that I have cited so far, points to the fact that in school the subject English, and the activities associated with being good at it, work to position the successful learner on the feminine side of the cavernous divide they are creating through their peers' policing of gender difference.

The tendency, until recently, has been to see the advantage of a gender division to be located all on the side of boys. Patriarchy has been characterized as able always to position 'woman' as the second term and by this to confer power and control within the grasp of every male. However, some recent studies have concentrated on the difficulties that the changing position of women has brought for boys in heightening rather than ameliorating gender difference. In *The Trouble with Boys*, Phillips (1993) suggests:

> For a girl, being more boyish means being more powerful in the world. For a boy, to be more female is to be less powerful. The pursuit of equal rights with men has inadvertently confirmed the pre-eminence of traditional masculinity by seeking to emulate it. In doing so it has actually narrowed the options available to boys. To be better than a girl a boy has to be more of a man. The only way out of being a masculine man is seems to be becoming a failed masculine man or separating yourself from notions of normality. (p. 59)

Jordan similarly argues that middle-class men who have no physical work to do define their masculinity as being 'not female' in order to avoid the social opprobrium of being seen as employed in effeminate occupations. To support her argument, Jordan further suggests that clerical resistance to female priests occurs because the men need the confirmation of the label 'not female to affirm their identity as males' (1995, 80). The result of such male insecurities is to heighten the need for difference and Jordan concludes that in Australian schools 'the current pressure for non-sexist education thus increases the contradictions experienced by boys during their school year' and argues that it explains why non-sexist policies have done little to 'modify the virulence of the antagonism towards girls found in many schools' (p. 82). In fact, recent studies of young middle-class men suggest that non-sexist policies have significantly increased their hostility to the feminism expressed by their liberal parents (Mac An Ghaill, 1994).

Gender, Language and Subjectivity

The third arena for the explication of sexual differentiation is that of language and the realm of the symbolic. Closely related both to Freudian views of gender differentiation and theories concerned with constructs of gender is the postmodern emphasis on the nature of subjectivity, constructed identity and the relationship of the individual to language. This focus is particularly strong in the work of the French theorists Lacan, Kristeva and Foucault. Lacan (1977) has emphasized the constitution of the subject in language and the power of its pre-existing system to shape consciousness. In the beginning the child does not experience itself as separate from either mother or the world. At the mirror stage, faced with its image, it becomes aware of itself as a separate entity and the 'I' which is observing becomes divided out from the self which is observed. At this point the child also enters the realm of the symbolic through language which is already dominated by 'the word of the father' and in which the subject must take its place in a pre-existing order as a gendered subject. Patriarchal language ensures that the discourse frames this identity in a particular fashion, ascribing particular gender attributes, as well as subject positions and places from which to speak. Characteristically in the Lacanian frame 'woman' is symbolically positioned in the place of the other and defined in terms of absence and lack while the phallic position is male. Feminists who adopt a Lacanian perspective stress that both men and women can take up the phallic position — that no one has the phallus. However, the tie between symbolic phallus and physical penis persists and the male appears 'essentially' the more powerful as well as symbolically.

Kristeva's (1984) work on modernist poetics provides an interesting additional insight into the relationship of ways in which the 'feminine' is shaped in relation to language. 'Femininity' she defines as that which has been repressed by the dominant phallo-centric culture with its associated emphasis on logic and order. The repressed feminine impulse erupts in language, expressive of pleasure and anarchic excess and is located in the play of signification in avant-garde 'poetic' language. It is related to the unconscious, a memory of the ebb and flow of pulsation in the womb (the chora), which was the first communicative bond with the mother. It is embedded in the realm of the semiotic, before the institution of the symbolic order by the word of the father which inscribes the individual a position within patriarchal culture. The semiotic is not, however, itself the feminine, it is more than this, encompassing in the pre-Oedipal mother all aspects of masculinity and femininity together. The semiotic embodies no gender divisions and remains repressed, discernible only in the rhythms, intonations, gaps and textual disruptions of language. Kristeva's theories position 'woman' as that which has been repressed within patriarchal culture, rather than as the label for a biologically determined subject. Men can occupy the subject position that is ascribed to this 'other' but only at the risk of accepting for themselves marginality in relation to the symbolic order (as in Thorne's, 1993, account of the 'sissy' and 'wimp' discussed earlier and Kristeva's own identification of the avant-garde poet). Femininity and womanhood are discreet entities, it is only patriarchy that identifies them as the same, and positions women on the boundary between the symbolic order and imaginary chaos.

Kristeva's theory which unites concepts of the creative impulses and the feminine may also help theorize boys' reluctance to identify with the play of language that features so strongly in the English curriculum. The request to identify with a creative stimulus in the classroom may awaken subconscious feminine impulses that most males have learned to find threatening and disruptive of their core gender identity.

Foucault's theories also concern themselves with the institutionalization of attitudes and meanings through the establishment of specific discourses within society which create consent to dominant patterns of power and control. Central to Foucault's thought is a definition of discourses as 'practices that systematically form the objects of which they speak' (1973, p. 49). The importance of his work for this study is his linkage of discourse with the framing of meaning around social practices and the exercise of power.

What all three theorists disclose are the ways in which the gender differences of a particular cultural group are inscribed in its language, so that the 'habitus' is reinforced and positions created within discourse which appear more 'naturally' available to one gender than to the other. Authority, it is argued, is located within male culture; on the other hand, the creative process maybe inscribed within the feminine, particularly in its most expressive and experimental forms.

This perspective has central importance for the discussion of difference in performance in reading and writing, for, as I shall set out in greater detail in the next chapter, English teaching, which is the main vehicle for developing literacy in schools, particularly in shaping reading, has as its central proposition the growth of the individual through the extension and development of language. Certainly, the concerns of the English curriculum, particularly in the focus on uses of expressive language and varieties of narrative that explore what one girl interviewed for this study called 'emochens', can often be stereotyped as a more feminine concern. The Ofsted Report, *Boys and English* (1993), picked out this area as one in which boys appeared particularly disadvantaged, having found 'little evidence of boys discussing the affective aspects of experience or of their writing with conviction about personal feeling' (p. 9).

Gender and the Teaching of English

Traditionally, English is a subject in which girls achieve more than boys and which in state comprehensive schools is more often taught by women. There is currently talk about the feminization of the whole teaching profession with larger numbers of women in post throughout the system. Teachers in the early years, where reading and writing activities are key elements in learning, are overwhelmingly female. It is therefore the case that reading and writing may appear to learners to be the sole concern of women, throughout the state school system.

Constructions of gendered identity, and the ways that these mesh with the teaching of literacy are the twin perspectives from which I have therefore begun to consider the nature of pupils' reading and writing preferences in school. In

Chapter 1 I outlined the demands society makes on the individual to become literate; in this chapter I have considered pupils' reaction to pedagogical practices which position them in particular relationships to literacy events offered at home and in school. I have argued that it is boys' need to establish a masculine identity in relation to these activities that creates the greatest barrier to equal access to literacy as it is currently presented in the curriculum. In the next chapter, in order to develop this line of argument further, I examine in more detail some of the practices which have become established round the teaching of literacy, illustrating how these contribute to pupils' views of themselves as readers and writers.

Chapter 2

The Teaching of Reading and Writing in School and Its Legacy

I passed English all right because I had all that Beowulf and Lord Randal My Son, stuff when I was at Whooton School, I mean I didn't have to do any work in English at all, hardly, except write compositions once in a while. (J.D. Salinger quoted in Bullock, 1975, p. 124)

The Importance of History

The fact that boys and girls position themselves very differently in relationship to the literacy experiences provided by schools is central to my argument. Therefore, in order to theorize how certain versions of literate behaviour gain a validity, this chapter considers the role that literacy occupies in the current school curriculum. To understand the process fully it will be necessary to consider the development of English as a school subject and trace the versions of literate subjects thus produced.

Teaching itself is essentially a practical activity and as such has gathered around it a set of practices whose original underlying theories, or social and political imperatives, have become lost or hidden and which now appear to the users as the products of common sense or even 'natural' behaviour, and remain unexamined as part of the 'habitus' (Bourdieu, 1990) of school life. For example, within the English curriculum, to teach reading through an immersion in stories of one kind or another is so well established in English-speaking countries that cultures which favour other genres for teaching their children — using religious texts, as in Punjabi schools, for example, or political and moral tracts, in the Chinese system — appear strange and lacking in an understanding of children's 'natural' approaches to learning.

In the previous chapter I used the concept of Bourdieu's 'habitus' in order to theorize how gender differences become ingrained in the social practices separately adopted by boys and girls. I now intend to consider how methods of teaching reading and writing in the early years, and the structure of the English curriculum in the secondary school, have become naturalized particular versions of the literate individual in school. I shall divide my discussion of this influence into three sections: the first focuses on the teaching of reading and the development of writing in the primary school; the second on the role of the secondary school English curriculum; and the last on the effect of an insistence on personal responses to literature in the later years of schooling.

Methods of Teaching Reading

Reading, defined as the ability to make sense of written words on the page of a book, is considered by both parents and teachers alike to be the prime marker of the literate individual. So much so that educationalists frequently slip from discussions of standards in literacy into discussions about the teaching of reading itself. This is understandable in the context of the importance of reading as a learning tool, and particularly with the current emphasis on a continuous learning society where adults need frequently to up-grade their skills and are encouraged to dip in and out of the learning environment for much longer periods of time. The corollary of this is that a suggestion of a fall in reading standards attracts immediate critical attention and moral panic, particularly from the popular press.

A widely held popular belief that learning to read requires more formal methods continues to be supported by one branch of reading specialists who, starting from an analysis of the underlying patterns that govern language production, advocate that reading itself is best taught systematically. From this perspective it is argued that children should be first taught to 'build' words (c–a–t) and then to move to short practice texts where they are able to identify the 'simplest' words of the language and by 'sounding out' phonic elements and blending the sounds acquire the skills necessary to decode unfamiliar words. The main instruments used for such instruction are reading schemes organized around phonic analysis with supporting workbooks (Morris, 1979; Chall, 1983; Adams, 1990). Other schemes, based on 'look and say' methods, seek to gradually introduce children to a controlled sight vocabulary through repetition and practice of the most frequently used or 'key' words. The texts convey a message to the learner that, in school, reading is something to be worked at and that school books may not always have a relevant meaning, unlike the books that are shared at home.

Other commentators have stressed that all written forms of the language are structured by conventions with more complex rules which determine the patterns that are appropriate for a wide variety of instrumental and expressive purposes (Clay, 1979; Smith, 1983). The latter place more emphasis on the nature of written discourse, considering all language activity as a social construct whose elements are governed by social as well as linguistic conventions. Each written format, whether it is a bank statement, a letter of application for a job, or a three part Victorian novel, is governed by rules that determine the appropriate register, vocabulary, syntax, length and printed format. This analysis suggests that children learning to read should first understand the purpose that print plays in their environment and the different functions writing serves in the context of their lives. The former approach has been labelled 'bottom–up' and contrasted with the latter approach labelled 'top–down' (Pumfrey, 1991, pp. 114–23). The first asks the learner to build up knowledge of the reading process from recognizing the smallest units of meaning, such as the phonemes and graphemes, towards a full 'decoding' of a text; the second introduces learners to the larger purposes for reading from the outset. Both models can be seen at work in literacy-related pedagogies, influencing attitudes to the teaching of reading at particular points in the history of education.

It is currently widely held that the use of 'real books' — that is, a method that focuses on teaching reading as meaning through good quality story and picture books — is a new phenomenon that has only recently gained favour in schools and has widely displaced the teaching of phonics. The available historical research data do not, however, support this. In fact, a careful study of early accounts of reading instruction reveals that both the 'alphabet method', with its emphasis on learning sounds, and the 'direct method', with instruction from interesting stories, have a long history of peaceful co-existence in schools. In 1862, Laurie recommended in his *First Steps to Reading* that lessons should not only 'introduce the learner by easy stages to the phonic and orthographic difficulties of language' but that a child's first books should also 'contain matters which shall be interesting to him and that the words that occur in them should be within the compass of his vocabulary' (quoted in Vincent, 1989, p. 85).

An oscillation between teaching the mechanics of decoding and an emphasis on the importance of meaning in reading has been a repeated cause of debate, but what is also true is that major changes of emphasis in the pedagogy of literacy are frequently precipitated by factors other than educational ones. Prior to the Education Act of 1870, which established elementary school education, there already existed a wide range of institutions catering for the education of working-class children. These ranged from the much maligned dame schools (a Victorian equivalent of child-minders), to private day schools run for profit, and the charity schools run by the National Society of the Established Church and the British and Foreign School Society of the Dissenters. These last two used a monitorial system; such as the system described in *Jane Eyre* (1847), where older pupils worked under the supervision of a trained teacher to hear younger scholars repeat their lessons prior to becoming teachers themselves. Rote learning, repetition and a heavy dependence on reading primers were essential props for the monitors, who were frequently only a small step ahead of their charges. As the century progressed, the 'professionalization' of teaching encouraged the imposition of more formal methods of instruction, largely as a way of structuring a reading curriculum.

Foucault (1979) has described how the development of a profession depends on the introduction of a discourse that confers particular status on the group and whose methodology excludes others from its practices. Methods used for teaching reading in school are, in this process, frequently presented as different from methods used in the home. At the beginnings of schooling, therefore, instead of making use of the attractive collections of little fables and cautionary verses that publishers were already providing for children, the teachers in the British and Foreign School Society returned to methods introduced by early eighteenth-century schoolmasters, such as Thomas Dyche and William Markham, based on patterns of sounds and their representation. Primers were produced, which, after the introduction of the alphabet, presented pupils with lists of disconnected syllables — ba, ab, ca, ac — to be used in word-building. These were followed by lists of monosyllabic words, which were then grouped into sentences each conveying an improving message. The use of the name 'primer' is a marker of how distant such methods had grown from the act of reading a story book. Reading was taught by rote and school monitors conducted repetition sessions where the content of primers were chanted out loud on the model of the catechism.

By the late 1840s, the school inspectorate, set up in 1839, had become critical of the 'synthetic and analytic' methods of teaching early reading (an early phonic approach) and their reports began to encourage more reliance on methods now known as 'look and say'. The inspectors recommended that instead of commencing with meaningless syllables the pupil was to be presented with whole words in short sentences. They also advised the use of a mixture of methods, suggesting that practice in recognizing the alphabet and chanting syllables should be set alongside more meaningful reading. In practice, however, more well-to-do parents had never abandoned the practice of providing their children with the equivalent of 'real books', whose production had rapidly increased from the beginning of the century. The history of reading instruction can best be seen as a continuing debate about the relative efficacy of these two approaches — decoding individual sounds and words, or relating to the meaning of larger units of text from the outset — with debate sharpened at times when national development is seen to be dependent on improved educational standards.

The role that storying has played for a long time in early learning can be seen exemplified in the life and work of the radical, William Godwin, author of *Enquiry Concerning Political Justice* (1793) and husband of the early feminist Mary Wollstencroft. Godwin concerned himself with both writing and selling children's books. He deplored his contemporaries' tendency to write stories for children which had palpable designs on their moral education, containing characters who are 'so rational that no genuine interest can be felt for them' and which 'stop at every turn to moralise in language which no child's understanding can comprehend, and no child's temper will relish' (quoted in St Clair, 1989, p. 169). To such didactic, emotionally sterile offerings, Godwin opposed works to stimulate the imagination, arguing, in the preface to his first collection of stories, published under the name of William Scolfield,

Imagination is the characteristic of man. The dexterities of logic or of mathematical deduction belong rather to a well-regulated machine; they do not contain in them the living principle of our nature. It is the heart which most deserves to be cultivated: not the rules which may serve us in the nature of a compass to steer through the difficulties of life; but the pulses which beat with sympathy, and qualify us for habits of charity, reverence and attachment. (quoted in St Clair, 1989, p. 170)

He produced a range of little books, including rewritings of Aesop's Fables, Bible stories, English histories and the Greek myths; he further commissioned work from Charles and Mary Lamb and published the first English edition of *The Swiss Family Robinson* (1810). In the continuing popularity of this story, and the works of the successive generations of writers for children who followed, we have strong evidence that 'profit from delight' by the means of story is an important and recurrent theme in the teaching of reading. The major influence on the way in which children perceive the reading task is better understood by the tendency of schools to want to formalize their instruction. In this way, 'reading with real books' is given a professional label which baffles ordinary parents and just like reading schemes suggests this is a 'specialist' school-based activity rather than a continuation of the learning achieved in the home.

Methods of Teaching Writing

If education has become synonymous in some minds with literacy, then literacy itself is often seen as the ability to consume rather than to produce texts. In the early stages of the establishment of state education, writing was taught in a far more limited way than was the case for reading. Founder of Sunday schools for working-class children, commenting in the 1790s, clearly associated writing with dissidence: 'I allow of no writing for the poor. My object is not to make them fanatics, but to train up the lower classes in habits of industry and piety.' Her fears must have been confirmed by the activities of the Chartists in the 1830s, who made good use of their hard-won literacy to produce local periodicals, political dramas, ballads and satirical poetry attacking the government (quoted in Willinsky, 1993, pp. 58–63).

The Revised Code of 1862 demanded little more for pupils to succeed than the ability to copy the words of others with speed and accuracy and in obedience to the authority of the text rather than with any ability to express ideas, let alone reflect on them creatively. Writing as composition was the preserve of those who moved on to secondary education, whilst a fair hand to copy out legal documents, in mean offices in the manner of Dickens' clerks Snagsby and Cratchit, was the limited goal of universal elementary school teaching at its highest level of achievement. The legacy of this approach could still be traced as late as 1937 (BoE) in the emphasis placed on handwriting and letter formation in Board of Education's *Handbook of Suggestions for Teachers*.

Before they leave the Infant School the children should be expected to write at a reasonable speed, and to spell reasonably words they have often seen. Through their work in drawing and making patterns they should acquire the manual control in making curves that will help them later, when the time comes for cursive writing. Written composition as such does not belong to the Infant School, but some children enjoy putting their ideas on paper and should be allowed to do so. (BoE, 1937, p. 43)

The passage clearly recommends that writing should be only of secondary concern for primary teachers. Further, another clear implication of these recommendations is that only a small number of children was expected to take advantage of an opportunity for written self-expression. English in this form is still represented as the learning and practice of skills. As the Newsom Report (Central Advisory Council for Education (England) 1963) reflected later, it was the demand of subjects other than English that first increased the need for written work in school:

English is distinctive in the curriculum in that it is all-pervasive and yet has relatively little subject matter of its own. In the greater part of the pupils' work concerned with communication, with the acquisition of information and with the recording and evaluation of experience, English performs a service function to other subjects: It is the other subjects which supply the content, and the occasion for strengthening the pupils' resources in language. (p. 159)

Most of the work subjects other than English depended not on composition but on copying from the board or transcribing from dictation. This is a situation that current research has shown is not much changed in the modern curriculum, although worksheets have largely displaced dictation (Webster, Berridge and Reed, 1996). Successive generations of English educators and teachers from Matthew Arnold onwards have reacted against this under-estimation and consequent stultification of the child's mind by arguing that learners acquire knowledge not through rote memory and copied information but heuristically, through shaping personal experience at its point of utterance. It was not, however, until the growth of comprehensive education in the 1960s, which abandoned the old certainties about selection and the different curricula appropriate to grammar and secondary modern schools, that all children were acknowledged as having powers to express themselves or given the freedom and guidance to do so.

By the 1970s, a group of post-war teachers, by then engaged in research at the London Institute, had begun to question radically the content of the English curriculum. The group included Barnes, Martin, Wilkinson and Rosen, and at a later date Meek, but it was Britton's work on *Language and Learning* (1970) that was most taken up in the practice of teachers, including English teachers in secondary schools. Britton identified three kinds of writing, which he termed expressive, transactional and poetic. Expressive language — closest to the child, informal in tone, immediate, and carrying feelings and attitudes of the writer — was the mode his work promoted as essential for early learning. This was contrasted with transactional writing — the stuff of reports, plans and explanations. Britton argued that children would develop the ability to manage transactional writing — the 'language to get things done' — 'naturally' as they matured intellectually. More importance was placed on encouraging self-expression with the writer in the role of observer. English lessons began to be overwhelmingly concerned with writing personal accounts, observations and stories with a preference, when marking children's work, for what was both strikingly new and expressive of natural feeling.

Self expression as practised in the English classroom, while instituting an intimate dialogue between pupil and teacher, often, however, ignored a sense of different audiences or purposes. The Bullock Report, *A Language for Life* (DES, 1975), insisted on the importance of variety of the writing task and the audience addressed, stressing that all specialist teachers needed to be aware of the specific reading and writing demands of their subjects. Bullock initiated the debate about the role of language across the curriculum, but the report was never properly implemented, and English teachers were left, after an initial burst of cross-curricular activity, with the full responsibility for all varieties of literacy development. The responsibility continues in the 1990s, as witnessed in the testimony of some of the children, whom I interviewed for *Developing Readers in the Middle Years* (Millard, 1994), when they reported that most of what they were asked to read in subjects other than English consisted of work sheets and that they rarely used text books.

The next major influence on classroom practice developed from Graves' work on the writing process and the importance of audience, ideas which were strongly promoted by LEA English advisers in schools. From an initial premise that all children want to write and have things to say, Graves encouraged practices such as setting up a writers' workshop within the classroom, supported by writing conferences, collaborative writing, and response partnerships (Graves, 1983).

The National Writing Project (NWP), created in 1985 by the School Curriculum Development Committee (later replaced by the National Curriculum Council) which ran until 1989, was also influenced strongly by Graves' work and subsequently helped shape the English Working Party's view on independent writing, drafting and the importance of audience and purpose. Similarly the role of emergent writing, whereby children are allowed to express their own ideas from mark-making to independent writing, was given wider currency through the agency of the NWP, and stress continues to be placed on self expression and creative engagement. Indeed, there is a strong radical strand in English teaching, traceable from the beginnings of educational debate in the nineteenth century from Godwyn to Arnold, which places the work of art and its language at the heart of instruction as a powerful tool for the empowerment of learners (Abbs, 1982; Harrison, 1994).

The Relevance of a Historical Perspective of Early Reading and Writing to this Study

In using particular methods of presenting reading and writing and particular media of instruction, even without necessarily understanding their origins or theoretical underpinning, teachers are not simply developing pupils' technical competence but also sending out very clear signals about the people who might be expected to read or write, and those who are most successful at it. Within the learning process, particular identities are created for the child in school — such as reader, non-reader or creative and non-creative writer — that relate directly to their understanding of themselves as literate individuals. I have argued above that English has come to be seen as essentially a creative and expressive art and that has clear implications for the image of the success-ful learner. There already exists strong evidence to show that girls in general are more ready to see themselves in the role of readers and writers even before the onset of compulsory schooling and that they choose to write more readily for their own pleasure at home (Steedman, 1982; White, 1987; Gorman *et al.*, 1988). There is further evidence that boys are less likely to choose to read stories for themselves and that some prefer factual information from the beginning of learning (Bissex, 1980; Clark, 1976). These are issues that I took up in considering pupils' responses to their own reading, and in enquiring whether the way in which reading is currently taught in the early stages might match the interests of girls rather than those of most boys.

Recent research into early learning has stressed emergent models of lit-eracy that point to the role of parents and carers who act as powerful role models for children when they share activities such as writing letters and cards, reading the newspapers, selecting particular brand names while shopping, as well as sharing picture books and stories (Hall, 1987; Weinberger, Hannon and Nutbrown, 1990). An emphasis in school on basic skills, and reading schemes in particular, often ignores the powerful influence of the home and creates a version of literacy that bears little resemblance to what has been learned through prior experience. Although researchers into early learning now acknowledge the importance of home and school, little evidence has yet been recorded of the relationship in the later years of schooling and so this was a second area I wished to investigate in relation to the 11–12-year-old pupils' views of them-selves as readers and writers.

English in the Secondary School: A Question of Personal Response?

As well as a concern for the ways in which children are taught to read, the debate about what it might be appropriate for them to read is also of long standing. The question of the desirability or undesirability of prescribing lists of set books for children at every Key Stage of the National Curriculum has a history that can be traced back to the beginnings of state education. In a study of the cultural practices that have created our understanding of what constitutes children's literature, Jacqueline Rose (1984) highlights the shift of emphasis in educational policy at the beginning of this century, which created a radical separation of the forms of language to be taught in the different sectors of the state system. She has described how the elementary schools, which were the main educators of workers' children, were instructed by the inspectorate to concern themselves with 'synthetic' language, defined as 'the language of the sights and sounds, the thoughts and feelings of everyday life' (Rose, 1984, p. 119). The method was thought to suit the needs of those children whose adult work would be concrete and manual and depend on understanding and working with objects rather than concepts. This philosophy can be seen in the 1912 recommendations of the Board of Education to its teachers:

> In teaching children, failure to use a direct, simple, unaffected style is doubly harmful: it makes the teaching more difficult for the child to understand and remember and it corrupts his natural taste. (BOE 1912, pp. 31–2, quoted in Rose, 1984, p. 119)

It is also important, therefore, to consider how reading in school has been influenced in the later years by the changing demands of the English curriculum. Secondary schools were not provided with state aid until the 1902 Education Act. At first, they largely mimicked the public school sector, whose curriculum was founded on the classics and gave primacy to the study of literature, where language and literature teaching were seen as a continuum, each dependent on the other.

> The instruction of English in a Secondary School aims at training the mind to appreciate English literature, and at cultivating the power of using the language in speech and writing. These objects are equally important, and each implies the other. Without training in the use of language, literature cannot be fully understood or properly appreciated. Without the study of literature there can be no mastery over language. (BoE, 1910, p. 3, quoted in Rose, 1984, p. 119)

The privileged role accorded to literary studies as the sign of a superior education has left its imprint on debates surrounding the English curriculum at the present time. On the one hand, pressure is exerted for a re-introduction of set texts to include pre-twentieth-century writers and Shakespeare; on the other, there are calls for more skill-based assessments in courses related to professional qualifications, such as the General National Vocational Qualifications (GNVQ). Rose (1984) further describes how, in the earlier part of this century, works of popular fiction, which she calls 'blood and thunder' stories, were roundly condemned in the press:

... they were rubbish, (What Boys Do Read — The Need for Stem-
ming a River of Yellow Rubbish, *The Book Monthly*, September 1910
pp. 883–5) and were leading to a decay of the infantile mind: 'when our
books are bought as rubbish, sold as rubbish and received as rubbish,
it is perhaps natural for anyone to suppose that they are read and
written in the same spirit', *Guardian*, 2 May, 1900. (Quoted in Rose,
1984, p. 108)

Rose's research of these early criticisms provides convincing evidence that
the reading materials many young people choose for themselves has habitu-
ally been treated as undermining, rather than supporting, the development of
school literacy. It is also worth noticing here that in the commentaries quoted
by Rose it is boys' reading that is criticized in particular, just as contemporary
sociology has identified violent elements in boys' preferences in computer
games and videos as a major cause for an anxiety about their influence on
attitude and behaviour.

The Board of Education of 1921 (The Newbolt Report) is commonly held
to mark the beginnings of current English teaching in its promotion of literature as a means of forming the young learner's personality. It was written by
George Sampson, who was also the author of *English for the English* (1921),
in which literature was given the role of embodying the national culture in
suggesting that literary works had the power to re-unite a nation, divided by
the events of the Great War. The report's central argument was that great
writers create for the nation a common cultural heritage, and that the promotion of literature in school would lead to a consensual citizenship embodying
shared values:

All great literature has in it two elements, the contemporary and the
eternal. On the one hand Shakespeare and Pope can tell us what English men were like at the beginning of the 17th and at the beginning
of the 18th centuries. On the other hand, they tell us what men were
like in all countries and at all times. (Quoted in Goodson and Medway,
1990, p. 51)

In arguing that literature was a record of the experience of the greatest
minds, the report was echoing Matthew Arnold's goal of promoting a culture
that would bring to the population the classic attributes of 'sweetness and
light'. It suggested that familiarity with great writing would provide pupils
with guidance both in the acquiring of experience and the basis for a common culture to link 'our language, our literature, our national life'. The intention of the committee was an egalitarian one, embodying a belief in the role
of literature to empower all children to develop their powers of self-expression
coupled with an unshakable faith in individual imagination. However, the division that continued in the education system between elementary and secondary
schooling worked against the early realization of this utopianism.

The 1944 Education Act in fact perpetuated the already well-established class divisions in schooling by prescribing a practical, natural-language based literacy for the secondary modern school and a curriculum based on the study of both grammar and literature for the grammar schools, a division that continued into the 1950s and early 60s and which today is yet resisting change in little pockets of selected education. In 1963 the Central Advisory Council for Education (The Newsom Report), *Half our Future*, described the watered down version of English that existed in many secondary modern schools:

> Much use is made of text books providing endless exercises in comprehension, composition and the like. There are rough books and best books, the former filling up more quickly than the latter with laborious writing, commas are inserted, spelling corrected. Occasionally free composition produces a shapeless mess in which the memory of many televised Westerns often seems to be still riding the range of the pupil's mind. Poetry is done: drama may occur on Friday afternoon and towards Christmas . . . (p. 151)

The reference in the report to 'shapeless' compositions, based on the plots of television westerns, will strike a cord with today's teachers, equally familiar with contemporary versions of boys' narratives that read like storyboard treatments of favourite video and television narratives, all dialogue and no narrative description.

The differences created by a curriculum developed in two parallel systems are still traceable in the dichotomy present in current debates about the English National Curriculum, where an emphasis on prescribing pre-twentieth-century texts and Shakespeare for older pupils is set alongside demands for greater emphasis on correct language and the study of standard English. The latter, it is suggested, will guarantee higher standards and act as a defence against what is characterized in the tabloid press as progressive cultural degeneration and linguistic corruption. The present return to a concern about appropriate set books from an agreed canon of English literature can further be seen as an attempt to reverse trends from the 1970s, where attention to the selection of fiction was focused both on addressing issues of relevance to pupils' interests and on counteracting cultural biases identified in many books offered to children as personal reading.

Analysis of reading schemes, conducted at the beginning of the 1970s, had found that they represented almost exclusively a privileged, white, middle-class reality from which many children were excluded. Similar biases were shown to exist in the subject matter of the fiction chosen for older readers (Baines, 1985). One answer was for schools to diversify and differentiate by promoting individual choice as a way of developing reading habits, the second was to widen the range of books selected for class readers to include representations of a wider spectrum of cultures and ethnicity. The move was already towards a more personal response to literature (Protherough, 1983; 1990), further consolidating a trend that had become a deep-seated element of the practices of English teaching. Reader response is now well established in class-room practice with its attendant emphasis on prior experience, shared under-standing and personal engagement, all of which have contributed to a view of English teaching which the Cox Report (DES, 1989), following the model of Dixon's *Growth through English* (1967), chose to call 'personal growth'.

The Nature of Personal Response

The use of 'personal growth' to describe current orientation to English is rather loosely applied to teaching approaches which place the learner at the centre of the creative process, rather than the text or questions of the structure of the language (DES, 1989). The term evolves from the 1966 Anglo-American Dartmouth seminar, in which delegates from the progressive cutting-edge of English teaching, assembled to face a series of critical problems thrown up in both the United States and the United Kingdom in relation to the perennially recurring question: *What is English?* (Allen, 1980, pp. 27–9). The seminar participants' final adoption of a paradigm of the learning process that posi-tioned the language of the child at the centre of the curriculum, displaced, what for many English teachers was a more important concern, that of the relationship of the learner to culture and, in particular, to literature. Further, its emphasis on the child as the producer of meaning had the effect of stressing the priority of the experience of the learner and relegating literature to servic-ing the pupils' growing emotional needs. Literature was looked on as a key to unlock personal, anecdotal and autobiographical responses in the classroom, rather than as an object of study in its own right, until, perhaps, the final year of compulsory schooling where the imperatives of external examinations rein-forced the importance of the study of set texts.

The intention at Dartmouth in 1966, had been to challenge the idea of 'culture as a given' and to allow the learner to negotiate an individual response in which literature and reading came to be seen as playing an ancillary role. Writing, particularly personal and expressive writing, became a key focus of English teaching. The effect, as Allen (1980) pointed out, was both to create an ethos in which learners were understood to arrive at maturity through their own efforts and further to undermine the confidence of teachers in their role of selecting books for study in terms of questions of quality and value (pp. 36, 49, 66). Work developed in the decade after the Dartmouth seminar frequently drew on thematic approaches to selecting stimulus materials, which in some versions emphasized the relevant content of a piece of writing over the power of its language.

The progressives' prior adherence to an emphasis on literary values was significantly shifted at the Dartmouth seminar by a new focus on the import-ance of common language which had originated in the work of the London Institute, in particular through the influence of Britton, Barnes and Rosen, whose emphasis on personal and anecdotal experience as the starting point for pupils' writing valued the expression of feeling. Critics of the dominance of this perspective have also suggested that it had the effect of promoting a version of English which identified its distinctive role as attending to the world of the child, in particular the inner world of feeling and response rather than that of analysis and evaluation. Medway (1990) has suggested that a bias towards the expressive has overlooked other important concerns, to do with communication and 'generalizing or abstracting' (p. 26). He further suggests that English has concerned itself with 'identity work' which, however, no longer helps the student to identify this 'real self' in 'conformity to institutional values' (p. 32).

Personal growth is widely employed to describe a model of English teaching which stresses 'relationships, directness of feeling and sensory awareness' (Medway, 1990, p. 33). Under the Institute's influence, English teaching for pupils between the ages of 11–16, emphasized the affective aspects of language and the expression of individual experience. It would, however, be quite wrong to suggest, in the manner of Marenbon, that such a 'growth' model constitutes a new orthodoxy in English teaching (1994, pp. 16–24). First, there is nothing new in a proper valuing of the contribution of the child's world when considering education and language development; secondly, many versions of English sit side by side even within individual departments. Cox, in his exploration of the state of English teaching prior to the introduction of the National Curriculum (1989), chose five co-existing ways of conceptualizing English teachers' current practice. In the Cox Report (DES, 1989), these were labelled: personal growth, cultural heritage, adult needs, cultural analysis and cross curricular views. However, English teachers, questioned about these five models of English teaching in recent surveys, identified personal growth as their central concern (Protherough and Atkinson, 1991; Goodwyn, 1992; Peel and Hargreaves, 1995). The Cox Report itself stresses 'the imaginative experience' of children's reading which encourages their development 'emotionally, aesthetically and intellectually' (DES, 1989, p. 16.4). The prevalence of the pleasure principle and personal growth model as an underpinning for English teachers' practice is important because of the version it creates of the most successful readers and writers. The focus on personal subject matter for writing and expressive response in reading exercise a strong influence on the way English, as a subject, is perceived by adolescents. In particular, this influence becomes stronger as pupils begin to distinguish certain kinds of school activity as more appropriate to one sex than the other. It is a tendency that is particularly marked in the response to fiction in the classroom. It is, therefore, important to consider next how a personal growth view of English teaching has influenced the nature of the books chosen for work in English lessons.

The earliest choice of literature for English lessons was adopted by the secondary schools directly from the public school curriculum and consisted of books that make up a canon of the great English writers. These choices were reinforced by the work of the Newbolt Commission, whose intention was to make the best literature available to all. It worked to privilege the writing of male poets and authors, with the honourable exceptions of a few women writers such as Austen, the Brontes and Eliot. It has therefore been the claim of feminist educationalists and critics that the canon represents the values of patriarchy and as such has more relevance for boys than girls. However, looked at from another perspective the secondary schools' choice from amongst even the canonical writers can be seen to favour a particular version of literary production, especially in relation to the novel. Books for sharing in class tend to be chosen to reflect the development of character and to give psychological insight into human motivation. If the English novel has its tap roots in the eighteenth-century writers — Defoe, Sterne, Fielding and Richardson — (Watt, 1966, pp. 308–12), then it is the latter whose influence is more evident in the development of schools' choice of fiction, with its emphasis on authentic realism and on individual problems worked out independently.

The versions of the nineteenth century novel most often chosen for school consumption are largely taken from those that create an interest in the development and psychology of the individual (what the Germans call bildunsroman). It is also my contention that the current form of teenage fiction, which is most often selected in schools, is at the fag end of the variety of authentic realism which examines the nature of human relationships and the individual psyche. Classroom-based discussions of texts are frequently directed to debating the convincing nature of particular characters in relation to the action described. Examination questions in the later stages of Key Stage 4 ask for views on outcomes and character development in terms of the relevance to other texts or to 'real' life. The emphasis is often on reading the stories as ways of making sense of individual experience (knowledge of the human heart), rather than on locating them within historical, cultural or political frameworks.

Moreover, a large proportion of the teenage fiction chosen for sharing in the classroom is written in the first person, from the point of view of the main character, dealing in relationships and the development of character, rather than on a delineation of the physical world through an omniscient narrator. Teachers invite their pupils to become spectators of other people's lives and draw them into speculation concerning motivation and plausibility of their actions. This mode of empathetic response is more frequently associated with women's reading rather than men's, and is reflected in women's choice of popular genres of fiction (romance, family sagas) but also in that of magazines and television programmes (soaps, dramas).

Boys interviewed during the survey, whose views are reported in the following chapters, repeatedly expressed impatience with the books chosen for them by teachers, complaining that nothing of consequence ever happened. A group remarked of one book they were currently reading in class, 'someone goes to the shops, they visit the cinema and they talk a lot — it's dead boring'. Another group of boys suggested that the things they looked for in their narratives were 'death, rape and lots of goals', elements which were generally lacking in the books chosen for them by English teachers. Further, the narratives of popular culture distinguish themselves from what is studied as literature in class by a greater emphasis on plot and action and it is these aspects of narrative that appear to dominate the choices of the boys, while girls welcome breaks in the action which allow them to build up a more complex idea of a character and the relationships involved (Sarland, 1991, p. 54).

I shall not, however, argue that these particular boys' tastes should be met uncritically, as more radical promoters of popular culture such as Sarland, appear to suggest; rather that in current English schemes of work a concentration on a limited range of genres may reproduce inequality and perpetuate differential access to literate practices. Where schools focus on individualized wider reading as the main method of increasing fluency in reading, a personal selection of subject matter works to separate out readers along the lines of conventional gender division, with girls opting for more domestic or romantic tales and boys for adventures, science fiction, and what they generally describe as 'action' (White, 1986, 1990; Roehampton Children's Literature Research Centre, 1993; Benton, 1994). Similarly, the selection of class readers can also be shown to be bound up in a view of English, and reading in particular, that prioritizes a reflection of the real world, relationships and emotions rather than fantasy or fast moving action. The ability to interpret written stories and to learn from them also has its roots in particular forms of socialization (Heath, 1983; Sarland, 1994).

In order to demonstrate the ways in which school literacy perpetuates an inequality of access to early learning, the American linguist, Gee (1993), in his essay 'Post modernism and literacies', has contrasted the linguistic conventions he found in the transcribed oral narratives of an upper-middle-class 5-year-old and a 7-year-old lower socio-economic black girl. By a juxtaposition of the two compositions, he demonstrates that the former child's language is already permeated with the features of the home-based book activities which have introduced her to simple literary devices, whilst the other child relies on rhetorical devices more appropriate to an oral performance to tell her tale. He concludes:

> . . . when the school, in other activities, validates 'literary' practices, it will validate our five-year old's story, thanks to its 'bookishness', and not the black child's, which is rooted in voice, performance and participation. (Gee, 1993, pp. 282–96)

Gee (1993) next relates this to the creation of 'insiders' and 'outsiders' within the social practices of education that, he suggests, have little to do with the intelligence, giftedness, or any ability to work hard on the part of the learner. Heath similarly has drawn educators' attention to the educational disadvantage which ensued in communities where a written traditional story was not part of the bedtime routine (Heath, 1983) and where schools based their curriculum on the written word.

Luke (1993) has also looked at the regulatory role of story in school, examining the ways in which a group of Australian 5–6-year-olds were led by their teacher to an understanding of what 'doing a story' might mean. This involved, amongst other things, the children being presented with 'semantic choices of white, blonde princesses, pink castles and enormous dragons'. He argues that the 'patriarchal discourses of sequestered aristocratic females', and of 'males rescuing females from a threatening nature' act as 'regulative cultural logic' (p. 146). It is important not to take the 'role model' influence of story book characters too literally, but, nevertheless, an understanding of how a prior exposure to story shapes the young readers' expectations of what to expect from school literacy is important. Luke criticizes 'natural' language methods and 'child-centred' pedagogies for masking the way in which the reading subject is constructed, arguing that 'the historic and culture-specific techniques and texts of the social institution of the school constitute the act and practice of narrating' (p. 147). Also of importance is the positioning of the reader by the kind of narratives where traditional and stereotype gender relations are the norm. The consequences of an emphasis on stories as the predominant medium for both early instruction and the extension of reading was a question I addressed in relation to pupils' attitudes to departmental book provision for their age group. In particular, I examined whether the schools' choice of texts was more in keeping with the preferences of the girls or the boys in the survey.

Summary

This brief historical survey of the ways in which the teaching of reading and writing have evolved in schools has of necessity been fragmentary, over-simplifying a complex process of cultural development. What I have sought to accent is the struggle that has always existed between literacy conceptualized as a skill-based activity with the need for disciplined practice and repetition, and literacy as a way of making meaning of the world, where motivation and appropriate reading materials are seen as essential teaching resources.

At certain periods of social change, theorists have sought to emphasize radical differences in teaching methods; yet, in practice, both kinds of teaching have existed side by side. The move to teach skills in a formalized way appears to be a response to political contexts, where a more disciplined youth cohort is the desired outcome. Moral panics about 'yob cultures' or disaffected 'youth' (most often young men) are accompanied by calls for changes in educational practice, usually encapsulated in the phrase 'back to basics'. The main thrust of this view is that children are naturally disinclined to learn and that the sooner they are trained into accepting what is to be taught them the better. Drills and exercises are put forward as a way of concentrating control in the hands of a teacher who decides what constitutes the next step to development. Such an emphasis has re-emerged in popular and political debates about literacy in the 1990s.

However, I have also sought to show that what has had most influence in the development of literacy has been an increasing stress on the individual accompanied by an insistence on a personal response to fictional narrative as a means of early instruction in both reading and writing. Added to this, in the secondary sector, the whole responsibility for developing the processes of reading and writing are often left in the hands of English teachers, who, in turn, frequently see themselves as offering a challenge to a more passive style of learning associated with content heavy subjects.

In my enquiry into the issues surrounding the nature of learning to read and write in a particular culture at a particular time, what has also emerged as a central issue for understanding of pupils' response to reading and writing in school is the relationship of the learner to the dominant modes of thinking. Currently, the role of narrative is central to the way in which teachers conceptualize the acquisition of reading skills and plays a key part in the way that writing tasks are set up in the classroom. The interaction of a stress on personal preference and the social uses of reading fiction are issues I shall explore in detail in the second section of this book which records the result of my enquiry into literacy practices in schools.

Section 2

The Research Evidence

Chapter 3

Pupils' Choice of Narrative Pleasures

> Too big now to cry for old pets, for stopped comics,
> Too small for the evening youth club, the motorbikes,
> Right size for nowhere but the corner on the carpet
> With the scuffed and battered box of records.
> (Katherine Pierpoint, *Winter in August*)

A Questionnaire in Narrative Form

This and the following chapters contain an account of the research process and the data collected, and focus, in particular, on the differences in the kinds of narrative choices reported by the boys and girls in the survey. They are an elaboration of the following research questions:

- What differences do boys and girls report in their reading interests?
- What reading choices are most typical of boys and girls?
- What other sources of narrative pleasures do they find?
- What are the current interests of pupils that may have direct bearing on their literacy development?

The fourth question was further subdivided into the following areas:

- which comics and magazines do they choose?
- what television programmes do they watch?
- what computer games do they play?

The data was collected in three interconnecting ways. First, through direct observation in the classroom, which included recording examples of the books being read both as individual and as class readers; secondly, by a questionnaire survey of the reading habits and interests of 255 pupils in their first year of comprehensive schooling, and; thirdly by semi-structured interviews with a sample of boys, followed up by group interviews in the following year. The questionnaire used, was first piloted in the summer term of 1992 with a group of 11-year-olds in a school not otherwise taking part in the survey. It took approximately 40 minutes to complete, the time of an average lesson in the secondary school. Instead of using a multiple choice questions with a tick box formula as with more conventional questionnaires the respondents were asked to write under headings about their perceptions of themselves as readers.

An open format was chosen to give pupils more scope to provide their answers in the form of a story. This was intended firstly to engage their interest, and secondly to elicit answers as close as possible to the reality of their current experience. There are drawbacks to this variation of a well-tried method of surveying the status of private reading. Most questionnaires confer greater anonymity than was the case in this study; a condition which is generally presumed to achieve greater reliability. A closed question format also facilitates the analysis of data; the limitation of possible answers allows measurement by means of a predetermined scale. I had judged, however, that such closed questions may lead pupils to responses which they assume teachers prefer. Whitehead's survey, for example, identified a high level of interest in the children's classics, books, which in the words of the survey were, 'redolent of the past'. This finding has not proved to hold true in later surveys (Benton, 1995, p. 102) and one possible reason for this is that pupils listed some titles they felt they ought to be reading in order to please. These might include books taken from the lists schools suggested for private reading or those they have recorded in previous reading records. More open questions allowed pupils scope to give their response in a way that would not have been possible on a predetermined scale. Because such questions have less predictable outcomes, a method of coding the responses was used to enter them on a data base. This allowed comparisons to be made between numbers of boys and girls responding in particular ways, and also provided detail to illustrate the individual nature of the responses.

Asking Questions

Given below is an annotated form (the annotation is presented in bold type) of the questionnaire used in the large survey.

Stories of Reading

Stories can be told about all kinds of happenings, especially if they have developed over a period of time.

Write the story of how you learned to read and the reading you do now. It will help your teacher find out about the kinds of books you enjoy reading and the sort of reading you did in your last school. Write as much as you like.

Here are some of the things you might wish to include:

(This introduction was designed to be read out and discussed by the student teacher presenting the questionnaires to the class. Its aim was to act as an invitation to writing.)

I. LEARNING TO READ
Who taught you to read?
Did you find it easy or hard to learn?
Can you remember any of your first books?

II. READING AT HOME
What kinds of books do you enjoy most?
Where and when do you enjoy reading?
Do you like reading to other people? (reading out loud)
Do you share books with anyone else?
Who reads most in your family?

III. READING AT YOUR LAST SCHOOL
What books did you read at your last school?
How were your reading times organized?
What kinds of books did your teacher read to the class?

(Sections I–III request information about the respondent's previous experience of reading and aim to discover how reading is perceived by the pupil at home and at school.)

IV. TV PROGRAMMES
Make a list of your favourite television programmes.
Is there any kind of programme that you particularly enjoy?
Do you have a television in your own room?

V. COMICS AND MAGAZINES
Which do you buy and which do you read?
What do you like about them?

VI. COMPUTER GAMES
What games do you enjoy and how long do you play on your computer each day?

(Sections IV–VI ask for information about leisure activities which compete with reading in the home.)

VII. TIME AND PLACE
Where and when do you read most often?
Do you read most at home or school?

(This question was to discover whether the respondents read from their own choice and independently of school organization of private reading time.)

VIII. COMMENTS
What have people ever said to you about your reading? (parents, teachers, friends)

To finish off how would you complete the following?
I think my reading is. . . . .

**(This final section was to find out whether the respondent had a
positive or negative view of themselves as a reader and how this opinion
had been influenced by others.)**

The questions were used as prompts to the pupils' writing, rather than as set
questions requiring a specific response. Student teachers were used to present
the questionnaires to the pupils. They first read out the questions and allowed
time to discuss appropriate responses. Those who had difficulty in completing the questionnaire on their own were given extra help. Some pupils with
learning difficulties, for example, were allowed to dictate answers to the
student teacher who acted as a scribe to enable all views to be represented in
sufficient detail. I visited several of the classes during the administration of the
questionnaire and found that the pupils showed keen interest in completing
their 'stories' and sharing responses with each other. That they enjoyed taking
stock of a previous stage of their learning this willingness to reflect on their
own experience is reflected in the detailed completion of the questionnaires.
This provided an initial source of rich data and the main findings were then
followed up in a series of semi-structured interviews with a sample of boys
from the respondents. Evidence of this positive engagement with the task are
recorded in this and the following chapter, where I have quoted from the
questionnaires to illustrate a wide range of pupils' views on reading and other
narrative pleasures.

In reporting the findings I have used the coded data from the questionnaire to compare the numbers of boys and girls responding in particular ways
and used quotations from both the written statements in the questionnaires
and the interviews to comment on a range of the attitudes revealed. In quoting
from the findings throughout this section of the book, I have indicated in the
text whether the data was obtained by interview (I); questionnaire (Q); or
group interview (GI). A quantitative analysis has also enabled me to highlight
the differences in the numbers of boys and girls who responded positively or
negatively to each question.

Differences in Narrative Pleasure

The first responses, which I intend to analyse in some detail, concern the
differences in the choices of genre selected freely by boys and girls. These
were significant in both subject matter and in the media each sex chose to
provide narrative pleasures. This was more apparent in the choices made from
popular culture than in the books chosen for individual reading at this stage.
There were, however, clear indications that reading tastes were already beginning to diverge significantly as the Year 8 girls, in particular, moved away from

Table 1: Boys' favourite genres

Choice	No.	%
No named favourites	48	35.8
Adventure/Action	33	24.6
Comedy/Humour (jokes, cartoons)	8	6.0
Science Fiction	7	5.3
Non-fiction	6	4.5
Children's Classics	5	3.7
Fantasy	5	3.7
Mystery/Thriller	5	3.7
Poetry	4	3
Ghost	4	3
Sport	4	3
Point Horror	3	2.2
War	2	1.5
Totals	134	100

choices of adventure, horror and comedy towards what one of the pupils identified as 'books about emoschons' (Q). Each of the nine groups had been working with student teachers in English lessons to identify different story types so they were aware when making a choice of genre of the ways in which books they read could be categorized. The boys' choices looked like this: Boy's preference for 'action' above any other kind of 'subject matter' in their chosen narratives is mirrored later in their choice of television programmes (see Tables 9 and 10, pp. 68–9). The most striking feature of Table 1, however, is the large number of boys who recorded no particular favourite type of reading but saw all genres as equally unappealing. If a check list had been provided for them to mark off the kinds of books they preferred, the results would have been significantly different because many would have recorded the genres they might be persuaded to read. These results show more effectively the extent of many boys' disengagement from reading as a leisure pursuit. Their lack of interest in the topic was borne out by subsequent observations of their habits of choosing books for classroom reading sessions. Boys in the survey whom I observed in set reading times were less likely to have brought a current reading book along with them and would rely on the teacher, or the librarian, to supply a suitable title to keep them occupied. Many more boys than girls were re-reading titles that they had first met in their primary schools, such as Roald Dahl's *Fantastic Mr Fox*, and *James and the Giant Peach*. One interpretation that has been made of the widespread re-reading of favourite books found at this age is that it signifies a continuing interest and commitment to particular kinds of reading. My interview data suggest, however, that this kind of re-reading is more often associated with the requirement by schools that some work of fiction is chosen for set independent reading times and a book that has been read before is a safe option. Respondents who reported that they spent longer periods reading tended to choose books in a particular series or made a collection of the books of a favourite author, rather than returning repeatedly to the same title.

Table 2: Boys' choice of favourite author

Author	Genre
Douglas Adams	Sci-fi, Comedy
Enid Blyton	Adventure
Tom Clancy	Adult Thriller
Roald Dahl	Comedy/Adventure
Nicholas Fiske	Adventure/Sci-fi
James Herbert	Horror
Michael Hardcastle	Adventure/Football
Steve Jackson	Fantasy

The authors named most frequently by the boys reflected the emphasis on action and adventure (see Table 2). I have listed all the authors named by the boys who, apart from Enid Blyton, are all men. They bear little relationship to the titles in the following list which had been selected by teachers for reading with 11–12-year-old pupils in school at the time of the survey.

Titles of Books Used as Class Readers by 11–12-year-olds 1992–93

1	*Boy*	Roald Dahl
2	*Carrie's War*	Nina Bawden
3	*Danny Champion of the World*	Roald Dahl
4	*Dragonslayer*	Rosemary Sutcliffe
5	*Goodnight Mr Tom*	Michelle Magorian
6	*Gowie Corby Plays Chicken*	Gene Kemp
7	*Grinny*	Nicholas Fiske
8	*Hating Alison Ashley*	Robin Klein
9	*I am David*	Ann Holme
10	*Red Sky in the Morning*	Elizabeth Laird
11	*Run for Your Life*	Robert Leeson
12	*The Eighteenth Emergency*	Betsy Byars
13	*The Haunting of Cassie Palmer*	Vivienne Alcock
14	*The Indian in the Cupboard*	Lynne Reid Banks
15	*The Midnight Fox*	Betsy Byars
16	*The Monster Garden*	Vivien Alcock
17	*The Piggy Book*	Anthony Browne
18	*The Silver Sword*	Ian Serrailler
19	*The Turbulent Term of Tyke Tiler*	Gene Kempe
20	*The Hobbit*	J.R.R. Tolkien

Except for the autobiographical work by Dahl these are made up of contemporary works by acknowledged children's writers. It is also worth noting that fourteen of the twenty titles chosen have a central male character. This was seen by the teachers involved in the survey as a way of engaging boys' interest in the story. The girls choice of genre is shown in Table 3.

Table 3: Girls' choice of genre

Genre	No.	%
No named favourites	29	24
Point horror	17	14
Adventure	11	9.1
Funny/Joke	9	7.4
School	8	6.6
Teenage fiction	7	5.8
Children's Classics	7	5.8
Ghost	6	5
Fairy tales	4	3.3
Detective/Crime/Mystery	4	3.3
Poetry	4	3.3
Ballet	2	1.7
Romance	2	1.7
Horses/Saddle Club	1	0.8
War	1	0.8
Other	9	7.4
Total	121	100

Table 4: Girls' choice of favourite author

Author	Genre
Judy Blume	Teenage
Enid Blyton	Adventure
Roald Dahl	Adventure
Daphne du Maurier	Romance
Dick King Smith	Comedy
Lynda Hoy	School/Teenage
Michael Rosen	Poetry/Comedy
Paula Danzinger	Teenage
Catherine Cookson	Historical Romance
Christopher Pike	Horror
Berlie Doherty	Teenage
Natalie Babbitt	Teenage
Jean Estoril	Teenage

More girls than boys in my survey were able to name their favourite book. Girls also chose a wider range of genre. However, a closer inspection of some of the titles that they gave show that whether they were *Point Horror*, School, or Teenage fiction, many of them deal with a similar theme. That is, they commonly usually describe a developing teenage relationship at the centre of the action; a younger version of what Brownstein (1982) called the 'marriage plot', where a boy picks girl from amongst her peers. Girls also included the names of more authors than did the boys and their selection was more evenly divided among the genders with a choice of eight individually named women writers and five men (see Table 4).

The titles and authors chosen by the girls also included more of the kinds

Table 5:   *Boys' and girls' shared genre choices*

Genre	No.	%
No named favourites	77	30.2
Adventure	44	17.3
Horror	20	7.8
Comedy/Joke	17	6.7
Children's Classic	12	4.7
Ghost	10	4
Mystery/Crime/Thriller	9	3.5
Poetry	8	3
War	3	1.2
Choices not shared	55	21.6
Total	255	100

of book that a well-informed teacher might make as suitable for the age group (these are marked with an asterisk in the full list of titles given in Appendix C, see pp. 190–4), whereas boys' choices tended, on the whole, to include more examples of writers from 'popular culture' although they did also include a number of titles recommended to them in school such as *I am David*. However, the girls' growing interest in *Point Horror* stories and writers such as Christopher Pike is beginning to overshadow the popular writers of traditional teenage fiction such as Judy Blume and Paula Danzinger, a trend that becomes even more marked by Year 8. In a comparable study made of the reading interests of Year 8 pupils in Oxfordshire, Peter Benton found that the popularity of *Point Horror* stories out ranked all other varieties of reading named by pupils in his survey. Benton comments, 'the appetite for (fairly mild) horror stories at this age seems to be insatiable and some school librarians have more requests for books of this type than any other' (1995, p. 105). Sarland has also documented the increasing interest of pre-teens in this particular genre (Sarland, 1994a; 1994b).

The boys' and girls' lists converge at the level of the most popular children's authors in the books of Dahl and Blyton, who still head the popularity list in both groups' choices. Incidentally, the dominant position of Dahl was found to be as true for older New Zealand adolescent readers, as it was for the younger age groups in the UK whom I studied (Bardsley, 1991; Millard, 1994). Girls were able to put names to more of the authors they liked, a fact which suggests a greater familiarity with previous searches for particular books and the works of particular writers. Table 5 records the genre favoured by both boys and girls. Table 5 shows that no single genre holds an appeal for anything but a minority of the group. Similarly, the list of book titles recorded reveals few overlapping tastes. Teachers, therefore, require a wide knowledge of all kinds of writing in order to be able to help pupils choose appropriate titles and to judge the suitability of personal choice for reading development. Full lists of the titles supplied by the pupils are included in Appendix C, pp. 190–4).

Table 6: Books chosen by both boys and girls

The overlapping titles in the separate lists are shown below:

(i) *Charlie and the Chocolate Factory; George's Marvellous Medicine; The Twits,*
(ii) *I am David; Stig of the Dump; The Mouse Butcher; The Silver Sword*

They consist of:

(i) Titles that represent a shared interest in the books of Roald Dahl.
(ii) Titles that have been read in school or read to the class by a teacher.

Identifying Shared Interests

Apart from books that are chosen by teachers, at the beginning of secondary school boys and girls choose very different kinds of books for themselves Table 6 shows the areas in which most overlap is to be found. It can be seen that even in the case of Dahl, whose books were frequently chosen by both sexes, boys chose different titles from the ones preferred by girls. The boys' choices included *Fantastic Mr Fox; James and the Giant Peach; Danny, Champion of the World; Charlie and the Great Glass Elevator; Boy*; and *Going Solo*; whilst the girls preferred *Mathilda; BFG*; and *Revolting Rhymes*. On the whole, the girls' favourites have girls as the main character, Mathilda, Sophie, Goldilocks, and represent the more whimsical of Dahl's stories, while many of the boys stated a preference for his two autobiographical pieces, *Boy* and *Going Solo*. It is also still the case that the other titles recorded by both boys and girls in the survey are markedly different. This suggests that any selection of books made for a class by a teacher will be frequently challenged if the rationale for sharing the story is solely as something to be enjoyed. My observation of lessons in the first two years of secondary school in the past five years have shown that a class novel is often allowed to dominate a whole half term of work, with much of the reading being done by the teacher. Dislike of a novel's theme can act as a major disincentive for pupils to become involved and certainly the work does not always involve them in reading for themselves.

Choosing Non-fiction

Several of the boys expressed a preference for non-fiction; Paul, for example, wrote:

> I choose books if they seem interesting. The books I read are often topic books, history and science, those sort of books. I read a bit at night but most of the reading I do is for homework and some at school. (Q)

At one extreme of the spectrum of readers is a group of boys whose interests are dominated by sport, almost to the exclusion of anything else. They buy magazines with names like *Shoot, Match* and *Top Score*, with accounts of teams, players and goals, and supplement these with match programmes and fanzines; they watch every possible football game shown on television; buy videos with titles such as *Goals Galore* and play a computer game based on football tactics called *Football Manager* and, if they have any time left in which to read fiction, choose books by Michael Hardcastle. Five boys mentioned a football option for each kind of leisure activity and a further fourteen boys had football as a content preference for two or more of the media. For this age group football is a key aspect of their social bonding. Mac an Ghaill (1994) has similarly noted the significance of football cultures in the construction of masculine practices and group identity in older teenagers (pp. 58, 108–9) and it is perhaps the last of his three 'Fs' ('fighting, fucking and football') which is used in this way by the younger age group, although 'fighting' particularly in the form of 'fighting fantasy' games and computer 'beat 'em ups' figure prominently in their choices.

James, identified by his teacher as a good reader, explains the ordering of his personal preferences:

> I sometimes read in bed at night for about fifteen minutes. At my last school I used to like reading football books including, *Home and Away* and *In the Net*. Now I usually buy football magazines, especially *Shoot*. I play on my computer for about 2 hours a day. I like playing football games like *Sensible Soccer* and *Goal*. Usually if I have to choose a book, I look at football first, then just look round to see if there are any more interesting ones. I think reading is very good but most of the books we read (in school) are boring. (Q)

He also describes his television viewing as centred round football — naming *Match of the Day*; *Football Italia*; *A Question of Sport* — with only *Red Dwarf* providing any variety.

It is also interesting to note that James' selection of books for personal reading is *hypothetical*; he prefaces his choice with 'if I have to choose books'. Such statements accompanied many of the boys' reports on the books they chose to read, suggesting that they frequently see reading as an imposition from the school, something they ought to do rather than a genuinely personal choice.

The only equivalent of a totally obsessive single interest amongst the girls was found in the fascination with anything to do with horses, shown by one pupil who read *Pony*; *Horse and Rider*; and *Horse and Pony* magazines, chose Saddle Club books for her individual reading and put horse programmes, such as show-jumping and racing, as her main choice of television viewing.

Identifying Light and Heavy Readers

Many more girls than boys described themselves as heavy readers. Hannah used the term 'bookworm' to describe her reading and wrote:

> I read the most in my family. I usually read everyday and by myself. Most of the time I read on my bed and I do recommend good books to my sister and friends. I read twenty-eight Nancy Drew mysteries last year. I think I am a good reader and reading is one of my hobbies, my friends call me a bookworm. (Q)

For Hannah, 'being a bookworm' is a positive attribute, she sees reading as part of her social context. Isabelle also writes enthusiastically about her reading abilities:

> I was taught to read at school but I have always read most at home. At home I read wherever and whenever I can, but especially when there is nobody in the house. I think me and mum read most and mum usually recommends all the books I read because she knows I like Catherine Cookson. Picked at random, some of the books I read last year were, *The Hobbit, The Complete Borrowers* and I particularly like re-reading *Paddington at Large* (all the stories in one). I am a bookworm so I enjoy reading practically anything and I have a long list of books waiting to be read. Reading is the thing I do most. (Q)

Isabelle, poised between childhood and adolescence, uses her re-reading of well-loved books as a form of reassurance; a jumping-off point for her more 'adult' reads with her mother. It is precisely at this stage that sensitive recommendation by the teacher can open up a world of new reading. Several of the girls, however, had already begun to limit their reading almost exclusively to *Point Horror* books and in two of the schools groups of four or five girls in a class regularly collected and exchanged books in this series. It is an extensive series, and one pupil in an inner-city school, which had fewer than average committed readers, reported owning over a dozen titles.

Most significantly, however, out of this sample, 33 per cent of boys and 24 per cent of girls named no favourite book or author, with a further 12 (9 per cent) of the boys, but no girls, stating a positive dislike of reading books. They had recorded 'none' in each space on their story questionnaires left for recording choice in books, magazines and comics; with the exception of two of them who read computer magazines.

Lee had written under the heading: **What books do you read?**

> I read at school, I never used to read at home. The only reading I do is sports pages on the back of papers. My mum and sister read in the

family. I only read when I really have to, for homework and in school. I was a good reader at primary school because my teachers told me.

Of television, he says:

> Sports programmes are my favourite. I watch about 4 hours a night and sometimes I watch tele in my room. I enjoy playing sports managing games and I spend about 2 hours a day on the computer. (Q)

In the growing debate about gender and reading it is easy to polarize this as an attitude typical only of boys for, indeed, more boys overall have reported disliking reading. However, two girls in the survey also expressed a strong distaste for reading in school. Natalie wrote:

> I do not read at all, anywhere, unless I have to at school. The only books I like is *Point Horror* books but otherwise I hate reading. I only ever read in school and I only read for school work. Reading is not very interesting. (Q)

Despite these strong protestations, her admission of an attraction to *Point Horror* titles shows that she could be drawn into a particular community of readers with some effort or compromise by the teacher. Similarly Joanne has also recorded two *Point Horror* titles she has enjoyed reading in the past year, *Emma and I* and *April Fools*, despite writing:

> I'm not really a reader. I actually hate reading but I have a good reading standard. If I read, I read for work. I don't choose books I just read books given to me. I was a very good reader at primary school. (Q)

It is reading in school, rather than reading per se that both girls reject and both provide evidence of continuing engagement outside the classroom.

Just as there were girls who did not choose to read, one or two boys gave accounts of more regular reading habits, though these are different in kind from those of the girl bookworms. Thomas wrote:

> I read in the morning (the newspaper), sometimes when I come in from school on *Ceefax* and at night in the bath. I read at least twice a day. I sometimes read with my little cousin. Everyone in my family reads. My mum recommends the books and my friends. I like science fiction and Roald Dahl. I ask my friends what books are good. (Q)

There is still sufficient cause for real concern about the whole year group's reading, however, when we consider the voluntary reading of continuous prose or narrative as a whole. The lack of interest in naming either a favourite book, or a favourite author, shown by 33 per cent of the boys and 24 per cent of the girls is a significant finding, particularly as a recent study of younger readers' progress has shown that naming favourite books related significantly to their subsequent reading development (Weinberger, 1995).

Boys' Disadvantage in the Reading Curriculum

The confirmation of boys' lesser interest in books is also significant in relation to current findings about boys' relative lack of achievement in English examinations compared with girls at GCSE (Ofsted, 1993). By neglecting fiction many boys in the study appear to put themselves at a greater disadvantage in a subject where the reading and writing of narratives, as I demonstrated in Chapter 3, is essential for success. Further, the individual tastes of those boys who do read regularly for stories which emphasize action over personal relationships, excitement over the unfolding of character and humour most of all, set them at odds with many of the books chosen for study in school. This is a point I will develop more fully in the next chapter, when I consider in more detail how each gender reads (see also Chapter 1, pp. 13–15).

I suspect that in completing the 'story of reading' questionnaires, boys did not always accurately report the amount of reading they actually did. Although the researchers always explained to the class being surveyed that they could include all kinds of reading in their accounts, there is, at this age, a clear sense that 'reading' is an activity they associate with narrative fiction. During follow-up interviews, several of the boys reported reading for a particular purpose, to improve their golf, for example, without recording non-fiction in their reading lists. It is this 'efferent' reading (Rosenblatt, 1978) that is often overlooked by both teacher and pupil. An example of this is provided by Craig, one of the weakest pupils interviewed, who had included no kind of reading on his questionnaire. At the follow-up interview he talked about making visits to the library:

Craig:	I've got a bike, just a kid's trials bike . . .
Interviewer:	That's interesting, do you ever read books about motor bikes? Or do you use magazines?
Craig:	Books.
Interviewer:	Where do you get them from?
Craig:	Library or near my school.
Interviewer:	Do you have any of your own?
Craig:	Yeah. I've got a few books at home.
Interviewer:	What sort of books?
Craig:	Like how to put new things on. 'Cos I've got to put a new chain on it.
Interviewer:	Can you do that, or will your dad help?
Craig:	I'll have to do it, 'cos my dad's working on the cranes today, and I want it done today for tomorrow. (I)

Differently Literate

Craig has an obvious interest in reading to find out about his bike and is sufficiently proficient to follow details of how to complete a repair. However, he does not count this part of his life as involving reading and accepts a view of himself in school as a non-reader.

Reading Comics and Magazines

While there are significant differences in the book reading habits of boys and girls in the first year of secondary school, contrasts in the choice of subject matter are even more marked when we consider the reading of periodicals. By the age of 11, few children continue to read a comic regularly, but in this study those who do are overwhelmingly boys (see Table 7). Just under a third of the boys read a comic regularly, whereas less than a tenth of girls report that they still read one. *Jackie*, the hybrid between the world of comics and older teenage magazines which used to dominate the reading of girls of this age, no longer exists. Instead, apart from the few who read *Beano* and *Dandy*, girls overwhelmingly opt for the wide range of teenage magazines currently on the market which mix information about pop stars, fashion and personal relationships, with picture stories and make-up tips.

Nine boys in the study read nothing but comics (6.7 per cent), and it would be easy to dismiss their continuing interest in the comic format as a question of immaturity, the last vestige of an earlier stage of development. For example, Alex, who is a good reader, describes how he is at the point of moving on from his pleasure in comics to books:

> When I go on a train I just get a *Beano* annual or something like that, because I don't really have time to finish a long book and I always find that a *Beano* suits me. But I think I'll change to a long book because I found that the last time I did that I got a *Beano* annual and I read it basically before the train had even pulled out the station. (I)

Table 7: Comparison of comic reading in boys and girls

	Boys	Girls	Total
No comic	93 (69%)	111 (91%)	204
Any comic	41 (31%)	10 (9%)	51
Total no. of boys and girls responding	**134**	**121**	**255**
Respondents reading only comics	9 (6.7%)	0	9
Breakdown of comics by name			
Beano	24	5	29
Dandy	11	2	13
Judge Dredd	2	0	2
Beavis and Butthead	2	0	2
Other	2	3	5

However, several of the boys interviewed who did still enjoy reading the *Beano* and *Dandy* said that it was because they re-read the old copies they had collected over several years or they read collections of comic strips in old annuals. Alex also mentions his continuing interest in cartoons, one which he shares with his father:

> I'm a real fan of Giles the cartoonist, we've got tons of those, but none of them are mine, they're all my dad's, he collects them, and I nick them and keep them in my bedroom. (I)

Laurence, who reported enjoying *Point Horror* stories, also read the *Beano* because it gave him ideas for writing his own comic production. David, a good reader, both by his own account and in the estimation of his teacher, is a connoisseur of the genre. I interviewed him a month after the questionnaire had been filled in to explore this interest. He told me:

> I usually read them at night, to get me off to sleep like. And then I like, I don't like those little thin ones, that's why I've stopped reading 'em now, I just read the ones I've already got. 'Cos they — they've not got much in 'em now, and they're getting more expensive. The *Beano* and *Dandy* are getting thinner. *Beezer* and *Topper* are like two comics, but they're two really short ones, and it's just a bit bigger than a *Beano*, and the *Beano's* gone up to something like 34 pages. So I have annuals at Christmas. (I)

He went on to explain that he had been collecting comics from 1989 and had some that went back to 1980:

> *David*: I've still got them, 'cos I wanted to see what they're like a bit ago, what the drawings were like, and colour and stuff like that.
>
> *Interviewer*: So is it the drawings in comics you really like, rather than the story?
>
> *David*: No. It's the story that I like. It's just that I like to see how it changes. 'Cos like now I've changed from *Beano* an' all 'cos Dennis the Menace is changed, and he looks like a 5-year-old now. (I)

David had listed adventure as his favourite book genre but it is obvious that he did not choose to read books of this type at home.

> *David*: Books — well I, I read some at school. But — normally at home, if I've got any books I'd read them at night an' all. 'Cos I only read my comics for something to send me to

	sleep, I don't really like 'em now, 'cos I've read 'em over like ten times each.
Interviewer:	So you read — if you've got a book from school you read that at night now.
David:	Yeah.
Interviewer:	You've been reading *The Voyage of the Dawn Trader* and you tell me you like the longer adventure books. Can you tell me something about the books that you chose?
David:	Well — I normally like adventure books, like this one I've got now. But I don't like really short ones, 'cos they're too boring, but I don't like really long ones, like over 200 pages, 'cos they get me bored an' all. 'Cos some are like over 200 pages and it's a rubbish book, and when I've chosen it, I have to read it all, and get totally bored with it. Like this one. This one has got nearly 200 pages.
Interviewer:	Right. Now tell me about a book that fits that category you talked about, that's so good you've read it over and over again. Choose a book that you've read, more than once.
David:	I don't think I've read any book more than once, except for this one. (I)

There is a certain amount of self-contradiction in David's suggestion that he was replacing his comic reading in favour of books, because so far he had read little of his book *The Voyage of the Dawn Trader*. This title had been entered on David's current reading record since the beginning of term and this interview was conducted in the November, six weeks later. David is an example of someone who might read more, if more suitable material that bridged the gap between his interest in comics and his desire for adventure was carefully recommended to him. There are a wide range of sophisticated picture stories by authors such as Raymond Briggs, Anthony Browne and Michael Forman, which might be more motivating than the longer novels his class teacher insists are the only suitable reading for the classroom.

These examples should also serve to make us wary of dismissing comic reading as a 'time-consuming drug' (Whitehead, Capey, Maddren and Wellings, 1977, p. 255) and acknowledge the genuine interest in picture narrative of some pupils. Interestingly, David's description of the change in Dennis the Menace's image to that of a younger boy would suggest that the publishers are aware of the change in the age of their readership and are targeting a younger group.

Judge Dredd and *Beavis and Butthead* represent rather more 'adult' tastes as these comics are addressed at older audiences: the former with a futuristic setting and an emphasis on violent retribution for wrong doing; the second with what passes for 'adult' humour rather than the knock about slapstick of school, bad lads and mischief, represented by more traditional comics and comic strips. Elements from these comics were present in the stories written by several of the boys, who drew on the violent punishments meted out by

Table 8: Comparison of choices in magazines

	Boys	Girls	Total
No magazine	38 (28%)	24 (20%)	62 (24%)
Any magazine	96 (72%)	97 (80%)	193 (76%)
Total no. of boys and girls responding	**134**	**121**	**255**
Respondents reading only magazines	28 (20.8%)	26 (21.4%)	54 (21%)
Breakdown of magazines named as favourite by type			
Teen culture (e.g. pop music, fashion)	4	77 (64%)	81 (32%)
{including *Just Seventeen*}	{0}	{26 (21%)}	{26}
Computer	42	5	47
Football	34	4	38
TV magazines	2	3	
Wrestling	3	2	
Women's magazines	0	3	
White Dwarf	3	0	
Horses	0	3	
Angling	2		
Newspapers	6		

Judge Dredd or *Robocop* as the key actions of their written narratives. These will be discussed in detail in Chapter 8.

Table 8 details the magazines most often read by the group. I have included a percentage figure only for cases where there was a significant proportion of the group naming a specific publication. The most striking feature of magazine reading is that it divides so neatly down gender lines. Girls overwhelmingly choose to read magazines with features about boys and relationships; boys choose to read about football and computers. Whitehead *et al.* (1977) had commented, 'to some extent the slump in comic reading among 14+ boys is no doubt attributable to the fact that no publisher has found a formula to appeal to their interests in comic form' (p. 155). The present range of computer and sports magazines does exactly that. Currently, then, almost as many of the 11-year-old boys read regularly about computers or sport as girls read about relationships and the superstars of the pop world. Matthew, explaining his interest, wrote:

> I buy a lot of magazines and comics. I like them because they are interesting and miles and miles better than books. I like to read humorous bits and something about a killer or like that. (Q)

Publishers of special interest magazines must be gratified by the success of their marketing strategies over the past decade. A large proportion of teenage boys now choose to read a wide range of technical and hobby-related periodicals, while girls have moved upmarket from cheaper comic formats to a glossier range of teenage magazines. Some of the computer magazines favoured by boys now cost almost as much as a paperback book, but their cost is sweetened by free games on CD ROMs and special 'cheats' (tips for completing games) for the latest releases. Boys frequently stated that their main motivation for buying computer magazines was to keep up with new developments in both soft and hardware. They enjoy reading about new technology and fantasize about owning ever more sophisticated equipment.

I will return to a more detailed consideration of the nature of the different choices pupils make and their implications for both reading and writing developments in Chapter 8. It is worth reflecting at this point, however, on how differently the genders defined themselves as readers through their tastes and interests. The boys' choices moved towards action, facts and figures; the girls' to fiction, feelings and relationships. On the one hand, there were girls who stated they did not like reading, but who dutifully chose books for class readers; recorded and remembered their titles; and recommended books which others might like to read. On the other, there were boys who claimed on their questionnaires that they enjoyed reading, but who returned to the same safe class reader again and again and remembered no specific title or author to record as a favourite. The magazine section of the publishing industry accounts for a large proportion of young people's reading outside school and it is important not to dismiss its effect lightly. Instead, the interest should be used to encourage wider reading in school while creating greater debate about the magazines published for this age group.

Further Competition with Reading

Whitehead *et al.* (1977) proposed a leisure displacement theory to explain the decrease in leisure reading of adolescents in the post-war period. They further identified the major competitor for children's attention as television, then accessible only at the time of transmission and with a limited range of programmes specifically aimed at children. Today, not only have the number of television channels multiplied but, in addition, video recording technology makes films and recorded programmes available in many homes for 24 hours a day. Added to this, a much larger proportion of children have a television set in their own room so their personal access to visual entertainment is unlimited. Computer programmes, with sophisticated graphics, offer fictional worlds where quest-like narratives with fantasies of heroic encounters with warriors and monsters can be acted out on the screen. A joystick allows the player to control the progress and outcome of a particular adventure. Nearly all computer games, whatever their origin, are promoted on the strength of their ability to create excitement. For example one home computer club, which provides programmes for a popular computer, typically advertises a new game in the following terms:

> Is your life lacking a bit of excitement? Then why not practice your archery with Robin Hood, control the wrath of the demon, take part in some of the most vivid simulations around, play tennis at professional

level band then put on your suit to do your home accounts. (Quoted
in Millard, 1994, p. 36)

The main attraction of the role of the gamester over that of the reader is
the active nature of the participation offered. Unlike written descriptions of the
actions in a book or magazine, the narrative of computer games is conveyed
in an animated visual form. The youngest players quickly become adept at
predicting outcomes of moves made in the quest structures on which many of
the programmes are based. Many of the boys in the survey reported a preference for adventure stories, and adventure is readily catered for by the computer games market. Moreover, the technology already exists that can transform
children into the physical protagonists of such worlds through 'virtual reality',
giving a whole new dimension to the concept of getting lost in a book. Even
Whitehead's argument for the superiority of the book as a more readily available source of personal gratification is thrown into question by the rapidly
developing technology. The well-named Japanese 'Game Boy' (apt because
owners consist largely of young males between the ages of 8–14) provides a
pocket version of highly sophisticated games. It is exactly the size of a paperback book and has a wide variety of arcade and adventure games available.

Tastes in Television Programmes

I wanted to discover if boys and girls made use of televisual and computer
media to the same extent and for the same purposes. The questionnaire therefore asked pupils to list all the television programmes they enjoyed watching
so that I could compare the kinds of television viewing that boys and girls
reported rather than simply logging the amount of time they spent in front of
a television. As an indicator of the comparative amounts of television watched
I also recorded the number of programmes each respondent reported regularly
to identify heavy and light viewers. These ranged from three boys who watched
no television at all, to a girl who recorded twenty favourite programmes and
included five different soap operas in her selection. A wide variety of programmes were listed as being of interest to the group and in the classes where
I observed pupils completing this question there was a universal buzz of
interest in what was being recorded. They wanted to compare answers and
find out what each other watched, whereas no corresponding enthusiasm was
shown for sharing their answers on books or magazines. A slightly larger
number of boys than girls were found to own a television. This was accounted
for during the follow-up interviews, where boys explained that they used
televisions as monitors for their computers, as well as for watching television
programmes: 70.9 per cent of boys and 63.6 per cent of girls were able to
watch TV in their own room. Only one boy stated that there was no television
at all in his home.

TV ownership correlates positively to the number of programmes watched,

Table 9:   Preferred choice of television genre

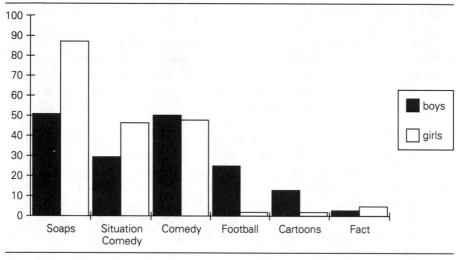

(Expressed as %: n girls = 121, boys = 134, total = 255)

but does not seem significantly to affect reading interests. Carla, who describes herself as a brilliant reader exemplifies the 'heavy' television viewer. She wrote:

> I have my own television in my bedroom and I like he following programmes: *Neighbours, Coronation Street, Byker-Grove, Blossom* and *Happy Days*. I also watch music programmes and funny ones. *Top of the Pops, Cheers* and *Roseanne*. I especially like ones with imagination like *Red Dwarf*, hypnotist shows and crime series. *Casualty* is my favourite. (Q)

On average, girls in the study watched more television than boys and, although there are large areas of common interest, there are significant differences between the sexes, both in the genres chosen and the most popular individual programmes. These are set out in Tables 9 and 10.

The most striking fact to take from Table 9 is that both boys' and girls' television viewing consists largely of varieties of fictional narrative, made up for the most part of soap operas and situation comedies. In keeping with their reading interests, more boys than girls expressed interest in non-fictional television, particularly enjoying the journalistic style of football commentary or the consumer guides to computer games, although narrative still dominated. A handful of girls included games shows, *Top of the Pops* and information programmes such as *Wildlife on One* in their lists, but these made up a small proportion of the total numbers of programmes selected.

In the choice of individual programmes only girls included *Casualty* amongst their favourites, whilst *Red Dwarf* was much more popular with the

Table 10:   Favourite television programmes

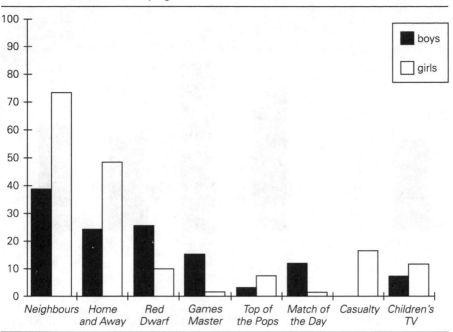

(Expressed as %: n girls = 121, boys = 134, total = 255)

boys. It would be easy to caricature the latter as a slapstick comedy in comparison with the more psychological penetrating drama of *Casualty*, which focuses on relationships and personal dilemmas. In fact, *Red Dwarf* does explore relationships within its comic and futuristic setting, but these are all to do with male bonding, male friendship and personal loyalties with only the most stereotypical presentation of relationships with women. Boys also watch the computer-related magazine programme, *Games Master*, in greater numbers than the girls. Boys' television choices, then, reinforce the difference of their narrative interests and it is girls who watch narratives that are more consistent with the psychological and social realism favoured in school.

If girls of this age are likely to spend more time watching television than the boys, the latter spend a greater proportion of the time available with computer games and the associated media of magazine, television guides featured on Ceefax, and associated programmes.

Table 11 shows that the boys in the study were by far the heaviest users of computer games with over half of them playing on a computer for longer than an hour each day. In contrast, almost half the girls either did not play computer games at all or described themselves as being very infrequent users, giving different reasons for using the technology, such as using it for word processing. Sophie, who describes herself as reading all the time at home, wrote:

Table 11: Time spent on computer games

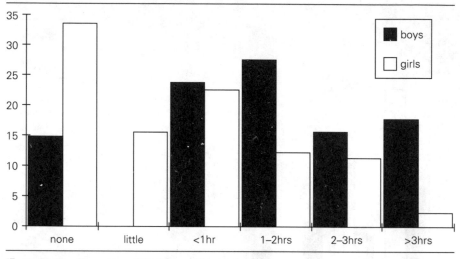

(Expressed as %: n girls = 121, boys = 134, total = 255)

> I don't usually play very much on a computer. But when I do I like to write stories on it. (Q)

and Hannah who has read 'at least twenty-eight Nancy Drew mysteries', writes:

> I like action computer games but I don't play on mine too often, just sometimes at weekends. (Q)

It would have made sense to have asked similar questions about computer ownership to those I had asked about television sets. It does appear from the data that girls have less access to computers and usually gain access to them through other members of the family. The fact that boys use television sets as monitors suggests that they have computers rather than televisions bought for them. At the other extreme from Sophie 'the bookworm' is David who owns several different forms of computer games:

> Well, after school I watch TV programmes, normally. I only watch under an hour 'cos I don't like them right much now, I go and play on the Megadrive, or the Commodore and the Spectrum. That's got puzzle games and adventure games. Me and my dad go on the Spectrum at night, 'cos he absolutely loves these puzzle games and he normally figures out how to complete it. (I)

and Alex who reads no more than an hour a week:

I read more at school than at home and when I do read at home it's usually because I am very bored. I buy PC magazines to keep up to date with new game systems. I play computer games like *Rise of the Robots, Sam and Sid* and *Ali's Incredible Cartoons.* (Q)

Table 12: *Types of computer games*

Category of program	Description
Arcade	Games based on commercial successes found in arcades; usually involve a lot of zapping; frequently enemy space ships. Example: *Street Fighter Three*
Role Play/Adventure	In these games the player selects a character and a starting point for an adventure or quest which points are often built up to exchange for precious objects, keys to rooms or magic weapons; narratives often involve fantasy characters such as warlocks and wizards. Example: *Zelda*
Platform	Games where the player progresses through a castle, dungeon or similar complex environment, moving from place to place to get to a specific point where there is an object to find, or someone to rescue. Examples: *Super Mario; Sonic the Hedgehog*
Sports Simulation	A game based on the rules and strategies of an existing sport such as golf, rugby or football. Examples: *Sensible Soccer; Football Manager*
Beat 'em up	Games in which the player defeats a series of enemies using a range of weapons and battle strategies. Examples: *Street Fighter; Mortal Kombat*
Puzzle	A platform or adventure game where particular problems have to be solved to allow the player on to the next section; used in education to encourage children to solve maths problems. Example: *Monkey Island*
Strategy	Games with more complex problems to solve for example a city to plan or an eco system to establish. Examples: *Sim City; Global Effect*

As well as asking pupils to record how much time they spent each day playing such games they were also asked to record their favourite computer game programs. As was the case with the television programmes, the individual programs were then reclassified into genres. As these are often less familiar to adults than the genres used for categorizing television, it is worth offering a description of the different types of games available (see Table 12). The different types of games played by boys and girls in the survey are shown in Table 13. The most interesting comparison provided by Table 13 is in the difference between the numbers of boys and girls choosing platform or 'beat 'em up' games. Girls prefer the less violent, more quest-based formats of the platform game, in which the goal is usually to get to a particular area of a building to retrieve treasure or rescue a prisoner. Interestingly, the game most frequently named as a favourite by the girls in this survey was *Lemmings* — a game in which the player gains points and moves to higher levels, not by

Table 13: The most popular computer games: Comparison of choice of computer games by boys and girls

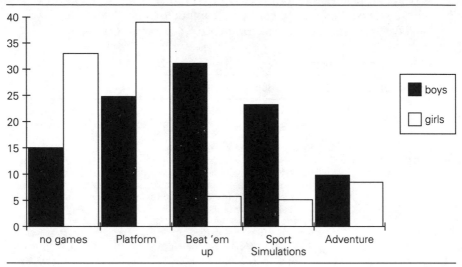

(Expressed as %: n girls = 121, boys = 134, total = 255)

zapping the small mammals but by saving them from destruction. Boys, on the whole, prefer the quicker paced, more violent 'beat 'em ups', with the subset 'shoot 'em ups' being especially popular. Neither of these categories require much in the way of on-line reading, but many boys report secondary reading in magazines in order to progress onto higher levels of particular programs.

In each of the three media under consideration — computer games, television and reading — the narrative satisfactions sought by the sexes appear markedly different. Most popular with boys are computer games and even where there is no computer in the home many boys ensure they make opportunities to play with someone else's. Dwaine, for example, reports:

> I play with my friend at his house. I can play on his computer, go to Anna's, play on the computer. I go to most of them in this class and have a go on theirs. (Q)

Dwaine also says that he buys his own computer magazines and scans them to help him decide which of his friends' games are worth playing.

Girls in general now also read more magazines than books and watch soaps and dramas on television. The narratives they enjoy in each media focus on the development of personal relationships, sometimes spiced with a pinch of horror. There is a continuity in the reading done at home and that required of them in school. Magazines for girls, unlike those aimed at boys, make an assumption that reading is a central part of their lives, as is reflected by the advice given by one of the most read teenage magazines, *Seventeen*, on ways of saving money:

> Want to read more books and newspapers but just can't afford them? Get thee to a library young woman, and if you think your local's a little on the fuddy-duddy side, you can always get the library to order you some cool new titles. (*Just Seventeen* 12 December 1994)

Comparisons with other Related Studies

Because I surveyed the 11–12-year-old pupils at an earlier stage than the youngest secondary group which were surveyed by Whitehead *et al.* (1977), comparisons with that study can only be speculative. It would require a more extensive and widely distributed questionnaire to confirm my findings and make direct comparisons. However, from the data collected it does appear that significant changes have occurred in the reading habits of pupils over the last twenty-five years.

Firstly, far fewer of the kinds of books that used to be the staple of late junior school and early secondary school class libraries are being read voluntarily at home by the whole age group. By this, I mean stories by well-established children's writers who receive literary awards and are recommended frequently by teachers; writers such as Penelope Lively, Alan Garner, Betsy Byars, and Susan Cooper. At ages 10+ and 12+, Whitehead *et al.* reported a strong correlation between the availability of books in school and the score for the number of times a particular book had been read at the time of the survey. The Whitehead team suggested that the predominance of such old favourites as *Black Beauty, Treasure Island* and *Little Women* and the relatively thin representation of more recent writers of books for children was attributable to their availability.

Certainly in one of the schools in my survey, where respondents reported having shared more books with their Year 6 teacher in the previous year, an interest was recorded in titles such as *The Silver Sword, Stig of the Dump* and *I am David*, which seemed to have grown from their teacher's recommendation. Another finding to support the importance of the schools' role in reading is that almost a third of the respondents, and within that group a large number of the boys, chose to read mainly in school (see Table 22, p. 91) so that their reading will be almost entirely shaped by what was made available for them by teachers. What is also evident is that children are moving at an earlier age to more popular forms of teenage fiction, represented by titles in the *Point Horror* series, and literary spin-offs from popular television programmes or films, such as *Red Dwarf* or *Alien*. At 11+ the reading of pupils in all the classes are finely balanced between the childhood tastes of adventure, and slapstick comedy, represented by authors such as Dahl and Blyton, and the fictional teenage world to which they aspire (Sarland, 1994). It is at this stage

73

where the reading of the sexes begins to diverge most significantly with more boys choosing not to read for any significant amount of time and some girls turning to magazines and television for their main narrative satisfactions.

The figures of 33 per cent of boys and 24 per cent of girls who do not choose to read books represents an increase in non-book readers from the numbers recorded by Whitehead *et al.* (1977). The latter survey found 15.8 per cent of non-reading boys at 10+ and 9.4 per cent of girls. My figures record almost twice as many non-reading boys at this state but, even more surprisingly, more than twice as many girls who, at the beginning of the secondary phase, preferred not to read or who choose to read very little. Whitehead *et al.* (1977), however, did record roughly comparable increases in non-readers at 12+, of 33.2 per cent for boys and 23.2 per cent for girls.

One reason for the size of the increase in the proportions of non-readers reported in this study may be caused by a bias in my study towards 11–16 comprehensive schools, located largely in working-class areas. Whitehead *et al.* (1977), however, had included, as part of the national survey with strict sampling, a proportion of selective grammar schools and some independent schools.

A second factor in the difference between these and the 1977 results was occasioned by my decision to ask the respondents to comment on their individual choice of books, rather than requiring them to record the title of the book currently being read. This gave permission to those pupils who had a class reader, which they have been obliged to choose by their teacher but would not read voluntarily, to record no books at all. In previous studies, it is often possible to uncover a relationship between the books most frequently chosen by pupils and those provided for them in their class libraries. This suggests that the books recorded in the surveys are not always chosen as 'voluntarily' as the researchers may have assumed.

A third factor is that the drop in reading occurs most significantly at the beginning of secondary education, and these 11-year-olds were already exhibiting a tendency not to choose works of fiction other than those chosen for them as class readers. Whereas junior schools still tend to provide specific times for independent reading, this is not as often the case in many secondary schools at Key Stage 3 where independent reading is often assumed to be located in the home. The questioning of the Whitehead team's 10+ sample had been conducted in the final year of the primary schools and was therefore strongly influenced by the books provided for their reading by the school. Indeed, in their recommendations, Whitehead's team expressed the opinion that school provision had a powerful influence on pupils' choice (1977, p. 286).

Other recent studies support the evidence for a decline in interest in fiction. Peter Benton conducted a survey of the reading tastes of Year 8 pupils in Oxfordshire comprehensive schools, where he found numbers of boys comparable to mine who chose not to read fiction at all; that is, 30 per cent of his sample reported not having read a book in the four weeks prior to the survey. The list he compiled of the most popular titles of books read by the sample also contains a comparable preponderance of horror series fiction titles, and liberal dashes of Roald Dahl.

A pilot survey of 'Juvenile Reading Habits', conducted by Roehampton Institute (1994), also found that adventure was the most popular genre at Key Stage 2, particularly with boys, while the girls moved towards horror and romance (pp. 20–1). However, it is less easy to make direct comparisons with the Roehampton data because of the research decision to clump together a wide age range by each Key Stage. This is of particular significance at Key Stage 3 when, as other studies have shown, tastes begin to diverge most significantly. The framing of the Roehampton questions, with lists of options to check off, also meant that pupils may have opted for books that they thought they might like to read rather than those they were actually currently reading. This supposition is supported by evidence from a number of boys in my study, whom I have labelled **'hypothetical readers'**, because they wrote about books they 'would choose' rather than particular titles they had recently read.

Whitehead and his team (1977) also noted a movement away from fictional narrative in comics to non-fiction periodicals by boys at 14+ (pp. 156–61). This trend has now moved downwards to a younger age group. The introduction of a wide range of computer-related publishing has meant interest in hobby-related reading has become even more pronounced. Whitehead's 14-year-olds also recorded reading magazines about angling, football, engines and pop music. In my study, the 11+ boys chose mainly to read about computers and football, although specialist interests such as wrestling, guns and ammunition, fishing, motorcycles and classic cars were also represented. From observations of other classes in the schools visited, these specialist magazines become more popular as they mature. Girls' periodical reading consisted almost entirely of teenage magazines, which combine some fictional elements with facts and fantasies about what appears to be young women's main interests, the relationship of the sexes, including explicit advice on sex.

Summary

This chapter has set out in some detail the relationships found to exist between the pupils' choice of reading, their leisure activities and their gender. Significant differences have been shown to exist not only in boys' and girls' choices of books, but also in alternative forms of narrative distraction, such as favourite television programmes, video recordings and computer games. Although a further all round decrease in the amount of time spent reading at this stage has been recorded, it is the boys in the study who are shown to be at a greater disadvantage in the reading curriculum. I have demonstrated above all that not only do they read fewer books, but that their favoured genres are less in harmony with the English curriculum and the choices made for them in class by their teachers. The largest contrast is between boys' interest in action and adventure, and girls' preference for emotion and relationships. It is an issue to which I shall return in Chapter 6, in a discussion of the effects of reading habits in reinforcing stereotypical differences found in pupils' writing. Next, however, I want to concentrate on the act of reading itself, in particular, the manner in which boys and girls are inducted in separate ways into communities of readers, both at home and in school.

Chapter 4

How Do They Read?

The people in Anthony's household, his mother and older sister Paulette, both read and write for their own purpose and pleasure, so it isn't surprising that Anthony shares their delight in stories and wants to gain a mastery over reading and writing for himself. And since his mother and Paulette have both set themselves up to be his teachers, there is a good chance that Anthony's interest in literacy will be carried back and forth between home and school. (Minns, 1990, p. 34)

Overview

This chapter moves away from a comparison of the differences in boys' and girls' favoured content in books, films and computer programs to a consideration of the contexts in which literacy learning occurs and preferences are shaped. It examines some ways in which the social practices of school and those of the wider community work together to create a context in which the separation of the sexes takes place. In Chapter 2, gender differences were shown to have considerable influence on the development of literacy as each new opportunity for learning comes laden with a history of accrued meanings. In this chapter, three spheres of influence are shown to leave a particular mark on the attitudes and expectations that lie behind the scene of reading; these are the family, friendship groups in the local community and the peer group in school. The data from the questionnaires and interviews illustrate how these three influences shape the attitudes of the pupils in the survey. Not only is reading presented generally as an interest more appropriate for adolescent girls than boys by the way in which reading time is structured to include or exclude other members of family or friendship groups but also the school promotes versions of literacy that can be shown to hold more appeal for girls than boys.

The Influence of the Home

The crucial role that families play in the success of emergent literacy is now both acknowledged and well documented (Tizard and Hughes, 1984; Weinberger, Hannon and Nutbrown, 1990; Weinberger, 1994). Parents act as powerful models of literacy users for their children and not only provide them with their first books and materials for writing, but also represent for them what it is to use literacy effectively and how to be literate within particular social contexts. Frank Smith (1984) has argued influentially that adults have the responsibility of welcoming newcomers into a literacy club, demonstrating to young initiates all the advantages of club membership:

> Children learn to use and to understand spoken language by being admitted into the club of spoken language users. Experienced members of the club accept children as apprentices who are expected to become practitioners in due course. The seniors demonstrate all the advantages of the club to the newcomers and collaborate in helping them to participate in all the activities. Children become literate by joining a similar club on similar terms. (p. 40)

Elsewhere Smith (1983) has recommended that the uses of print, like the reasons for using speech, should be introduced in such a way as to make the processes of learning to read and write as meaningful as possible, pointing out that tasks that seem to have no purpose will deter children from wanting to read:

> The insight — that differences on a printed page have a function, that they are meaningful — must be the basis of learning written language. As long as children see print as purposeless or nonsensical, they will find attention to print aversive and be bored. (p. 40)

It was to the identification of the kind of reading that has no personal relevance and which is therefore aversive to the reader that the previous chapter was addressed. I shall consider now how meaningful the context in which they were taught to read appeared to the pupils in the survey.

Facility in Learning to Read

In order to form some picture of how the pupils had been introduced to reading and how natural they had found the process, the questionnaire requested information about what could be remembered of learning to read; it specifically asked respondents to consider whether they had found the early stages of learning easy or hard. The general responses are set out in Table 14.

About a third of the group — rather more boys than girls — could remember little about this stage of their learning, or responded by simply listing the kinds of books they were given, or the reading methods used in the early years. Of those who recorded remembering the learning process, significantly more girls reported finding learning to read easy than did boys, which was confirmed in their descriptive accounts of the process. Laura, for example, typifies those girls who were positive about every aspect of their reading:

Table 14: *Boys' and girls' attitudes to learning to read*

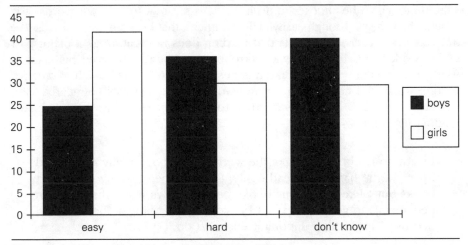

(Expressed as %: n girls = 121, boys = 134, total = 255)

I learned to read using word tubs and colour-coded books in school. Teachers, my parents and myself all taught me. I found it very easy. *The Worst Witch* is the first book I remember reading by myself. I read anywhere and anything I can get my hands on. I think my reading is brilliant for my age. (Q)

Hannah also writes with confidence about her abilities:

I learned to read from my mum from a *Billy Blue Hat* book. It was fairly easy because there were no hard words in the book. At home I read in bed. I spend a long time reading, about 2 hours. I share books with my friends but I am not allowed to read my parents' books. I choose mainly books by Judy Blume. I can read very fast. (Q)

Ben's account represents the opinions of the more enthusiastic of the boys, but it is neither as positive as Laura's nor Hannah's:

I learned to read at home and at school. I think I learned more at home. My mum and dad both used to read to me. I think it was very easy. The first books I remember were *Postman Pat*, *Nasty Rhymes* and *Fireman Sam*. At my last school I read *Point Horror* or sporting books. Now I read most often at school. We have an hour at the most on Thursdays. We also sometimes read *The Midnight Fox* in class. I know I'm a good reader because I got through all the early stages easily. (Q)

He locates his current reading firmly at school and suggests reading is not something which he chooses to do in his leisure time. In his own words, it is a 'stage he has got through easily'. His comment, that he 'sometimes' reads *The Midnight Fox* in class, suggests that reading does not feature as a major part of his work in English. This was corroborated when I observed his class at work. They were set group work on issues arising out of the book and creative writing which did not require any re-reading of the text itself. Similarly, Tim, who also describes himself as learning to read very easily, no longer makes reading his priority:

> I learnt to read by looking at the words in my book really slowly and I just got the hang of it dead easily. I can't remember any of my first books but I like mysterious books best. I always read when I am in bed, mainly to get to sleep, but I never read anything at the weekend because I have other important things to do. (I)

There was also a larger proportion of boys than girls who described learning to read as hard, and whose accounts of their learning process suggest that reading practice had been experienced as something of an imposition. Jamie is typical of these pupils:

> I was taught by my mum. I had to read to her for half an hour each night. I thought it was really hard. My first book was called *Tiddlers*, a book about fish. I used to read for half an hour but its down to 15 minutes now. I read football magazines. I buy *Match*, *Shoot* and *90 Minutes*. I read mostly on a Wednesday at home. (Q)

The book Jamie records is a factual one and his current reading interests all centre on football. Like Ben, he gives the impression that reading is something that is being phased out of his current interests.

Of the girls who reported that they found the early stages of learning to read a difficult undertaking, many now present a more positive picture of their current ability. For example, Lindsay, a pupil at the same school as Jamie, wrote this:

> I learned to read by listening to my mum reading to my sisters. When she read to me she explained about the words. My mum and dad taught me and sometimes my sisters. I thought it was quite hard because words didn't look like they sounded. Now I usually read at night when I am in bed. I read for about an hour. Sometimes I recommend books to my friends and sometimes swap. I read different kinds of books. Quite a few of them are about adventures. I choose books with exciting titles. (Q)

It is also significant that more boys than girls found it impossible to recall very much about their learning process and their accounts of current reading suggested it was something that no longer held their attention. They frequently used the subjunctive mood or conditional tense in their accounts, writing 'If I did read at home . . .' or, 'If anyone wanted to share my books . . .', treating the whole issue as a **hypothetical proposition**, rather than something that directly concerned them. It is important, however, not to assume a simple dichotomy between boys' and girls' attitudes and to make sweeping generalizations about the gender differences emerging from the data. There were also examples of boys, like Ben, who read with facility and take pleasure in books, and there were also a significant number of girls who find reading a chore and do not choose to read for themselves. But, as discussed in the previous chapter, girls who describe themselves as disliking reading often settle down in school to the task of reading a book more willingly than boys with similar views.

The next area of interest in the responses they made in the questionnaire was their identification of support for the learning process and what this might imply about their identification of themselves as a member of a reading community.

Who Provides Support for Learning?

The next questions asked them to name the person or persons they thought had been most helpful in teaching them to read. Many pupils had already mentioned their mothers as the key influence in the early stages of their learning, and where fathers had featured in the accounts it was usually as part of the parental team, rarely alone. As in the case of Anthony, described by Minns in the quotation which heads this chapter (Minns, 1990, p. 4), it is often mothers who play a key role in their children's early acquisition of literacy, and organize the events that involve their children's access to books before and beyond the reach of the school. Table 15 shows the extent of the mothers' influence at this stage.

A rapid scan of Table 15 may suggest that teachers are still the main influence on young readers. However, when the number of times mothers appear as significant figures in the learning process are added together — that is as equal partners with teachers, as part of the parental team and as the sole teacher — we can see that, for the pupils in the survey, mothers play at least as influential a part as the school. When the figures are reorganized in order to compare the roles of home and school, it becomes clear that for both boys and girls there is as strong an influence in the early stage of learning from the home as from the school (see Table 16).

The current attention being given to the partnership of parents and teachers in the learning process is therefore a key one. Equally important, however, is the continuing ethos surrounding reading in the home that identifies different kinds of reading as appropriate to different members of the family.

Table 15:   Boys' and girls' perceptions of who taught them to read

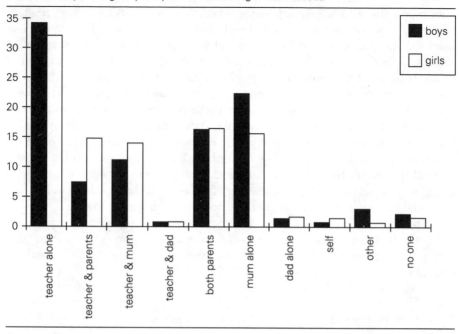

(Expressed as a %: n girls = 121, boys = 134, total = 225)

Table 16:   Boys' and girls' perception of where they learned to read

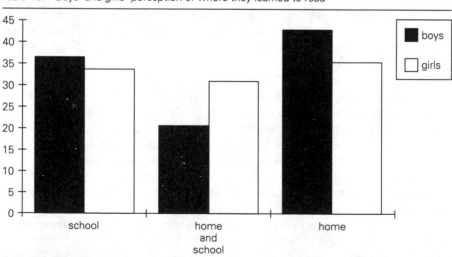

(Expressed as a %: n girls = 121, boys = 134, total = 255)

Table 17:   *Boys' and girls' perceptions of who reads most in their family*

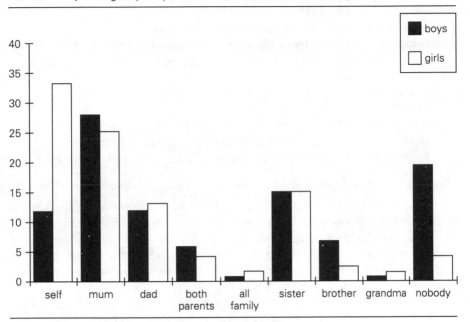

(Expressed as a %: n girls = 121, boys = 134, total = 225)

Who Reads Most in the Family?

It is important to consider next how the roles of reading and readers in the home are manifested to children. Table 17 shows pupils' responses to a question about whom they perceived to be the heaviest readers in their own family. As in Table 15, it is the female members of the family who are most often mentioned by both boys and girls.

When asked to decide who read most at home, boys cited their mothers most frequently and the girls placed mothers second only to themselves as the heaviest readers. Sisters were mentioned more frequently than fathers or brothers by both sexes, and grandmas, but not granddads, were also mentioned. The image of reading in the home then, through the eyes of both sexes, is of an activity associated closely with the women members of the family.

In the follow-up interviews, many of the boys mentioned their mothers as sharing reading with them at some stage in learning to read. They named other kinds of textually based activities which they shared with their fathers, one of which was reading to find out about computer games. When a father was reported as the main reader in the family, the model given was often that of reading for a particular purpose, rather than as a leisure pursuit or a simple sharing of stories. This is true of Craig, who is led by the interviewer to identify a role for his father's reading:

Interviewer:	Who in your family do you think reads most?
Craig:	My dad.
Interviewer:	What sort of things does he read?
Craig:	Newspapers 'bout horses and, er, what time they're running and everything. So he can go and bet on them, before they run.
Interviewer:	Do you ever read those with him?
Craig:	No.
Interviewer:	You don't read them then. Does he read anything else?
Craig:	Oh yeah! He reads football results on telly.
Interviewer:	He reads that on the telly. OK. Does your mum read?
Craig:	No.

Craig is a weak reader and is given a reading task to do several times a week as homework. He does this with his mother, not his father whose reading is of a different kind from the stories he is sent home with from school by his support teacher. There are other activities he shares with his dad, some of which may involve reading for information, however Craig does not immediately recognize such activity as reading:

Craig:	I don't read to him 'cos normally he's either upstairs or at work.
Interviewer:	What does he do upstairs?
Craig:	Plays on the computers.
Interviewer:	He plays on the computers. Do you play on the computers with your dad?
Craig:	Yes.
Interviewer:	Do you and your dad read anything to help you understand the computer better?
Craig:	Not really.
Interviewer:	You don't do those cheats or anything in the magazines?
Craig:	Oh yes, we look for cheats.
Interviewer:	Where?
Craig:	In *Sega Power* books. (I)

Reading with mum is not necessarily creating a positive experience:

Interviewer:	Do you ever read to anybody at home?
Craig:	Just my mum. We have to do it for homework.
Interviewer:	Do you think she likes listening to you read?
Craig:	Don't know . . . but she always gets annoyed when I don't say words right.
Interviewer:	What does she say?
Craig:	She says that you're supposed to say that word right not wrong.

Robert, described by his teacher as a far better reader, experiences similar divisions between male and female readers at home. He identifies his mum's boyfriend, Geoff, as the person who reads most in the home, but Geoff reads the paper. Again, it is the female members of the household whom he has observed becoming absorbed in stories.

Interviewer: OK, and you said these books are full of horror stories?
Robert: Yeah, and my mum and my nan like love stories and that sort of stuff an' all.
Interviewer: What about you?
Robert: Oh me, I buy magazines like *Beano* and *Turtles* and that, and read some of that, and I get football magazines every week. I've got quite a lot of magazines, I've got about eighty to a hundred, something like that, between eighty and a hundred.

It should not be surprising, therefore, that when asked to name those with whom they are most likely to share books or who would recommend new books to them, boys as well as girls named their mothers, although sisters and grandmas are also sometimes mentioned. Weaker readers report relying on mothers or grandmas to help with their continuing reading practice, while those already hooked on books often describe their mother as the person on whom they rely to recommend books or buy them for them. Several girls were reading books in school that they said their mothers had enjoyed and recommended to them. These included *Jane Eyre*, *Little Women* and several novels by Catherine Cookson. The one boy who remarked on getting books from his father was reading his collection of Giles cartoons.

Sharing Books with Others

Table 18 shows the numbers of pupils who reported sharing books regularly with their friends or members of the family, thus creating a reading community in which books could not only be circulated but be discussed.

The large difference in the numbers of boys and girls who report regularly sharing books with others, adds to the growing weight of evidence that reading fiction is perceived in many social settings as a female preferred activity. Over 70 per cent of the boys say they never share books with others, while over half the girls share books with either their friends or female members of their family. Sharing an interest in reading at home and with friends is therefore largely divided on gendered lines. Girls' reading is more likely to involve changing books with friends and recommending favourite reads. The majority of boys do not talk much about sharing books either with their parents or their peer group although they do exchange magazines, particularly football and computer-related publications. For many girls it is an established part of their

Table 18: *Boys' and girls' reporting of book sharing*

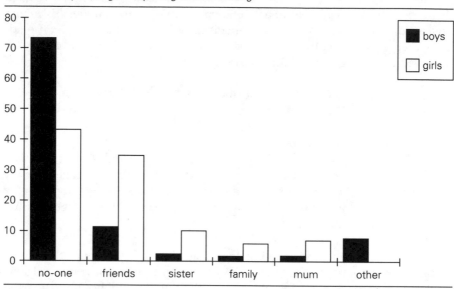

social scene and the habit is reinforced by other aspects of their shared interests. For example, *Just Seventeen*, which came out of this questionnaire as the most widely read magazine for girls in this age group, recommends the pooling of books as a money saving device:

> Set up a 'cool reads' pool with your best chums and get to read each others' favourite books for nothing via your own private library. (*Just Seventeen*, 'Advice on Saving Money', 12 December 1994)

The very existence of such networks draws other girls into reading, as Charlotte explains in response to her friend Claire's suggestion that reading becomes less important as a leisure activity in the secondary school:

> *Claire*: I used to read a lot more in my last school but now I don't really read as much 'cos I don't have as much time.
>
> *Charlotte*: It used to be the opposite for me. I used never to read, did I? and I was always pretending to read in class when you lot were reading. But these days I read more and more, and I read on my own at home as well. (GI)

She adds that she now shares Catherine Cookson books with her mother as well as the *Point Horror* books she is currently sharing with her friends. Boys, on the other hand, are less likely to share reading either with friends or family, unless it is for a specific purpose such as finding out how to complete a new

Table 19: Boys' and girls' estimations of their reading ability

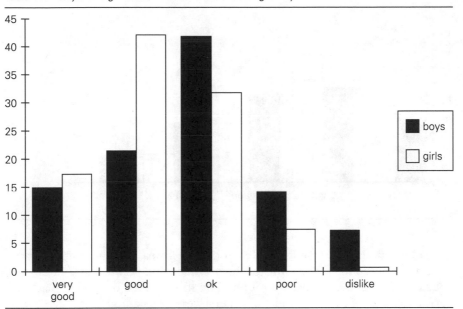

(Expressed as a %: n girls = 121, boys = 134, total = 255)

computer game or updating themselves on football teams, transfer fees and international matches.

Self-assessment of Reading Ability

When I turned my attention from the reading pupils did at home to the reading required of them by school, the trend towards seeing the activity as more appropriate to the girls in the class continued. Significantly, as well as citing themselves more frequently as the person in the family who reads the most, more girls also expressed positive attitudes both to themselves as readers and to the books they were currently reading in school. Their more positive view of themselves as readers is clearly shown in Table 19.

Although the numbers of boys and girls who expressed the most positive opinions — variously describing themselves as 'brilliant', 'excellent' or 'very good' readers — were not very different, in total, far more girls than boys saw themselves as doing well at reading. The boys' comments were far less enthusiastic and often fairly dismissive of their abilities, and included comments like 'not bad' and 'all right'. Ten of the boys expressed a positive dislike of any form of reading and wrote negatively about their experiences at home and in school.

In order to make some comparison between their opinion of themselves

Table 20: *Researcher's estimate of respondents' ability in written English*

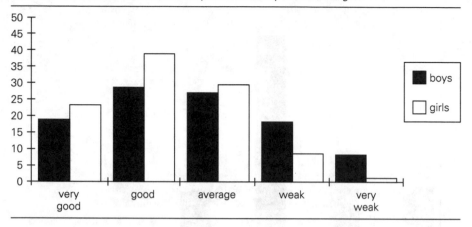

as readers and how they might perform overall in reading and writing, I analysed the questionnaires in terms of the accuracy and complexity of the presentation of their ideas. I used a rough scale to moderate the work, placing it
into five levels of ability: excellent writers were considered to be those who
made no more than two errors of either spelling or punctuation and who
developed a clear line of argument in their writing; the very weak were considered to be respondents who did not write in full sentences and required the
student teacher's support to complete the questions. The results are shown in
Table 20.

The method of assessment I used provided only a crude score, but it
helped to focus on one key issue for further study. Although still showing girls
out-performing boys, the table shows quite a regular pattern of ability, which
indicates that boys who write and express themselves well may be dismissive
about their reading because it holds less interest for them. Twenty-one boys
fell into the category of boys whose writing was assessed as above average,
but who described their reading as nothing more than OK. Their attitude is
well represented by Paul, who wrote:

> I read at home for about a couple of hours a week. Nobody reads
> with me or recommends books. I don't share books with anyone. At
> my old school I read a variety of Roald Dahl books. Now I read foot-
> ball magazines. I buy them to get an update on football. I read them
> mainly on Saturday. My mum reads the most in our family.

A further six boys, whose writing I had judged to be good, had expressed a
strong dislike of reading. Chris wrote:

> Sometimes I read in bed but I usually don't choose to read. My mum
> is about the only one who ever reads in our family. I usually only read

at school in reading lessons I HATE reading. I just don't choose to read. (Q)

David is also representative of those who write hypothetically about the reading they might be persuaded to do:

I don't read much but if I did I would read in bed. I can read a chapter a night. If I found a good book I would recommend it to my friends if they asked. At my primary school we didn't have much time to read because you had to finish your work. I don't think I'm a good reader because I dislike reading. (Q)

Follow-up interviews with groups of boys and girls in Year 8 further confirmed the impression I had formed from reading the questionnaires: that girls saw the reading curriculum as something in which they performed better than the boys in the same class. When asked to identify the best readers in a class they always named girls, only adding, when prompted, the names of boys whom they thought read out loud in class well, but only if they made a positive effort.

Vicki: The boys can be good when we're reading plays like *Baron Bolinggrew*. Tim was good, apart from you never knew when he'd come in.

Charlotte: Jon's good at putting feeling into his reading but he never knows when to start and stop. He always gets distracted. (GI)

Boys, for the main part, were content to see themselves as doing OK at reading, although the number of them who expressed a positive dislike for having to read, presumably in class reading sessions, was significant.

Time Spent Reading

Table 21 shows the amount of time the respondents estimated that they spent reading each day. I have grouped them into four main categories: occasional readers, who read only when necessary for a practical purpose; light readers, who record that they read the back of a newspaper or a magazine article regularly; committed readers, who read frequently but for short periods at a time, usually no more than half an hour in a day; and heavy readers, who like to read whenever they get an opportunity at any time in the day.

It is clear that girls in the sample make up the largest proportion of heavy readers and the smallest number of those who choose not to read unless obliged to do so. One girl, who fell into the 'heavy' category, explained, when interviewed, how books absorbed her time:

Table 21:   Comparison of boys' and girls' commitment to reading

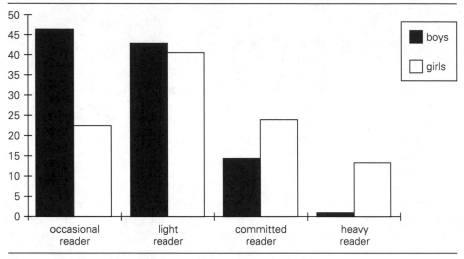

(Expressed as %: n girls = 121, boys = 134, total = 255)

> I read the kind of books I don't want to put down when I've started reading. I like books that happen like to your own life, like a printed version of somebody's diary. I read in bed and if its a book I like I find it quite hard to give up. I used to read to my dad at night and it was good him just being there and laughing at all the bits I found funny. He buys me lots of books and tokens and stuff. (I)

Less than a quarter of the girls, 22 per cent, said they did very little reading, whereas just under a half of the boys who completed the survey, 46 per cent, fell into this category. Further confirmation of boys' lesser interest in reading was provided by the fact that many more of the boys identified school as the place where they did the majority of their reading, as shown in Table 22.

Reasons for selecting 'school' as the main site of reading were influenced by the fact that, in several of the schools I surveyed, sustained private reading had recently been introduced in English lessons, and partly because reading was associated by them with school and work, rather than leisure and personal interest. It became clear when I challenged these attitudes in the group interviews conducted in Year 8, that some boys were using 'reading' to signify school work in general. When confronted with the actual amount of time spent reading books in school, after a student teacher had followed them for a whole week of lessons and found that they spent no more than 15 minutes in any one day actually reading, they made these comments:

> *Matt*:   But in school it feels like you're reading in lots of little things, and I mean, little things always do add up to bigger things. You read in about just everything you do.

Table 22: Boys' and girls' perceptions of where they read most

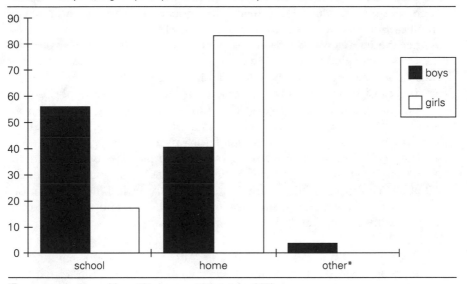

(Expressed as %: n girls = 121, boys = 134, total = 255)

* The other places mentioned by boys for reading were on buses and trains.

Richard: They're always getting you to read stuff off the board.

Kevin: Well you are reading, 'cos when you're writing you think about your reading at the same time.

Richard: I agree. If you're writing you're reading, right? (GI)

The girls, on the other hand, have formed a more realistic picture of the amount of time that they were asked to spend reading in school and felt they were given insufficient time in most lessons to read on their own.

Vicki: Yes, teachers don't let you get on and read stuff. We had a science test today and the teacher kept interrupting to read it out; and say, you were in the middle of it you forgot what you were doing.

Claire: Yes, I don't like writing when we're always filling in them sheets.

Vicki: I don't mind writing, but it's just that if you do too much of it you can't learn as much from writing things out as you can from finding stuff out and reading it in books.

Claire: Yes, I don't mind writing but I don't like copying their (the teachers') stuff out or just writing what the teacher has told you to put. (GI)

It is the boys in this interview who are far more willing to accept a passive learning situation, whether it involved copying from the board or completing worksheets. Contrary to the stereotypes portraying girls as the more passive learners, these girls valued both their independence in learning and any opportunities provided for them to read for themselves.

After the interviews had been completed I made follow-up visits to two of the classes included in the survey in order to observe the groups' behaviour during the set reading period, held for 40 minutes once a week, and to record their choices of fiction. These visits took place at the beginning of the term following the questionnaire surveys. The pupils were accustomed to the routine of independent reading, yet many of the boys still found it much more difficult to find a suitable book to read for any sustained period of time. Richard described how reading among the boys in his class became either a race: 'It's like the first person to win or finish the book and you don't remember it at all. You're just getting through it; you just want to finish it'; or, more usually, how reading time usually broke up in whispers and ultimately confrontation with the teacher:

> People get bored and start talking after about less than 10 minutes. They whisper to each other and it all starts getting into a big uproar. You get bored, you see and your friends all round you are messing about too. (GI)

Vicki agrees with his estimation of the limited nature of the boys' concentration:

> The girls in our class enjoy reading more than the boys do. I think if one of the boys start fidgeting then all the others think they shouldn't read either, but if one of us girl was fidgeting all the rest of the girls wouldn't follow suit. (GI)

This matches exactly the pattern of behaviour in the classrooms where I observed their class reading. Girls who were talking appeared to be sharing bits of their books or swapping them, rather than causing a distraction. Boys frequently got out of their places, allegedly to change their book, but usually to hang round other boys' desks once they thought the teacher had taken their eyes off them. Hannah, part of the small group of girls interviewed together by the student teacher, offered this as an explanation for their behaviour:

> Boys in our class like sport and it takes up all their time and they talk about it all the time. Girls like sport as well, but they manage to share their time more evenly. I think girls think sport in the day time and then read at night, 'cos that's what I do anyway — sport in the day and books in bed. (GI)

Kamaljit also thought a conflict of interests explained the boys' lack of enthusiasm, adding:

> From my point of view, girls are better readers because they tend to
> read more books, whereas the boys in our class do more computer
> games and stuff. (GI)

Many of the boys agreed with Finn when he described the classroom as a
difficult place to read with concentration:

> 'Cos I can't work. I mean, I can't read until I've got something going
> on in the background. I have to have the TV on or the music on. You
> get like nervous when you've got just quiet. (GI)

In the second of the classrooms observed, the boys' private reading was
limited to books brought in to the room by the teacher, which they had to
hand back at the end of the session, whereas a sizeable number of girls
produced their own reading books from home. Most of these were *Point
Horror* titles, which they had begun to share with each other. However, one
girl produced a copy of *Little Women*, which had been her mother's and which
her mother had recommended that she read. The books chosen by several of
the boys were ones they already knew well, such as *Fantastic Mr Fox* and
Harry's Mad, and which they told me they had read or had read to them in
their previous schools. The logic of their repeated choice of these texts was,
as they explained, that when they were asked to write a book report, as they
invariably were at some stage in the term, they could draw on previous knowledge often retained from book reports or reading diaries completed for their
primary school teacher.

One of the commonest reasons given by the boys for the unpopularity of
set reading time in school was the unattractiveness of the books that were
provided for classroom reading. Richard suggested that he would read more
if a wider range of books were provided for him in school:

> In our school like we don't have a lot of reading books. There's just
> a lot of books with facts in. If you haven't got a book for a reading
> lesson she lets you go to the library and choose one. They do have
> quite a lot of them but they don't look very interesting. New editions
> look a lot more interesting because you choose things by the front
> cover. (I)

As many boys report that they read books mainly at school and magazines
and mainly newspapers or annuals at home, it is particularly unfortunate that
school libraries are at present badly under-funded and poorly resourced.

Theoretical Perspectives Re-examined

As shown in Chapter 1, there have been other studies that have highlighted
the differences in children's reading tastes and have contrasted the amount of

reading undertaken by boys and girls at different ages. However, few researchers have gone on to enquire about the set of social relations involved in the practices that surround the habits of reading they have uncovered. The data I have used to contrast boys' and girls' attitudes to reading are derived from the pupils' own story questionnaires of how they learned to read, which included questions about the people who influenced their development and their own opinions of their abilities. These opinions may not necessarily be the same as their teachers' judgments; for example, less able pupils who had recent successes in improving their reading through one school's reading intervention scheme, often described themselves as 'brilliant' readers. In some of their answers pupils suggested they had taught themselves to read, forgetting the structure, usually involving a reading scheme, and continued practice provided by the school. What I have drawn on are pupils' perceptions of what occurred, rather than records of actual events, and, as such, they have the power to illuminate differences in attitude and motivation between the sexes.

In this final section I shall return to current theories of reading difference to locate these findings within a particular perspective of gendered difference. Recent studies of the gender differences in reading have focused on the contrasts in the content of pupils' reading and the likely influence of the range of images they encounter of male and female characters (Barrs and Pidgeon, 1993; Minns, 1993; Swann, 1992). The most common approach has been to concentrate on the cultural content and gender bias of the books and schemes provided for reading in and out of school. Where a cultural analysis of adolescents' reading has been undertaken, it is often girls' reading habits that have drawn most criticism.

A current strand of research into the nature of girls' reading has concentrated on the effect of the powerful pull of romance. In Christian-Smith's (1993) international collection of essays about girls' reading, *Texts of Desire: Essays on Fiction Femininity and Schooling*, feminists have largely criticized the **content** of the teen series fiction, popular with large numbers of young women in English-speaking cultures. Luke (1994), who has written the introduction to this collection, has argued elsewhere that such reading is 'a key strategy in the maintenance of patriarchal power, educational exclusion, and the suppression of difference and divergence in literate practice' (p. 361).

In a similar vein, a particular strand of feminist literary criticism, grounded in theories of authentic realism, has set out to promote women's texts, which are considered to represent a more accurate picture of women than those portrayed by men:

> Thus, authentic realist critics share a notion of what women are really like, and representations are measured against this . . . Male writers have portrayed women as stereotypes or as mythical figures in the past, and authentic realist critics demand a change to figures which are closer to the way women are in real life. (Mills, Millard, Pearce and Spawl, 1989, p. 58)

This argument is aligned to the kind of concerns that have directed English teachers' attention to the search for more **positive female characters** in the fiction they choose to share in class, where novels, read in a frame of authentic realism, are assumed to provide powerful role models for the young reader (NATE Language and Gender Committee, 1985). The model characterizes girls' reading as domestic, private and individualistic; boys' reading — whose preferred genres reflect their interests in computers, football and other hobbies — as efferent, transactional and above all public. Boys are portrayed as the dominant group in the division of reading labour and their reading interests are identified as more sympathetic to the core subjects of the secondary school curriculum. In his introduction as series editor to *Texts of Desire*, Luke (1994) describes the dichotomy thus:

> Educational and scientific taxonomies of literacy invariably affiliate 'male' genres, registers and texts with cognitive and economic power. The gendered construction and distribution of literacy in schools is Cartesian in design, extending the binary opposition which Huyssen noted is so central to modernity and patriarchy: assigning bodily, romantic, affective private genres to women, and cognate, disciplinary, intellectual texts to men. (p. 375)

He concludes that there is a pressing need for a feminist reconception of 'reading' as a gendered practice in the school curriculum (p. 377). Arguments of girls' disadvantage in language also form a consistent strand in the work of the APU (Assessment of Performance Unit). Janet White has argued from the data she collected in relation to girls' greater preference for English activities, particularly that of narrative writing, that they channel their efforts into this subject at the expense of other disciplines without achieving real gains from their greater language facility (Coward, 1984; White, 1990). This line of argument suggests that boys and men are managing to succeed in the current system, and, yet again, it is girls who need to adapt their reading behaviour.

In fact, by choosing to read willingly, a larger proportion of girls than boys locate themselves more successfully within the dominant literacy of schooling and gain fluency in the modes of reading and writing that bring them success in academic work and examinations. Britton (1977) argued forcefully that the habit of reading is most successfully nourished on a history of 'past satisfactions' which may then gradually evolve into an appreciation of more 'literary' values:

> Our sense of literary form increases as we find satisfaction in works which, by their complexity or the subtlety of their distinctions, make greater and greater demands upon us. Our sense of form increases as our frame of reference of reality grows with experience, primary and secondary of the world we live in. A sense of literary form must grow

> thus from within; it is the legacy of past satisfactions. (Britton, 1977, p. 108)

In giving accounts of their reading, more girls communicate a personal sense of past satisfactions and some, in their choices of literature, show that they are already engaging with the more complex forms of fiction approved of by English teachers. The fact that many boys position themselves outside the increasingly female friendship exchange economy of shared reading, works very much to their disadvantage in the school curriculum, particularly in those disciplines that are language based and require sustained reading and interpretation. In the earlier stages of school, the majority of boys describe having been included in the wider reading community, mainly through the agency of their mothers who took them to libraries on the way home from school, heard them read at home from the books chosen for them by their largely female teachers, and bought them their books and comics on weekly trips to the newsagents. It is with the onset of adolescence and the pervasive influence of youth culture that these maternal ties become loosened and boys, in particular, begin to choose other forms of narrative gratification, mainly in the shape of computer games and video movies.

Rather than contrast the content of what each gendered group reads, it is essential to consider first of all why reading becomes so heavily marked as appropriate to one particular gender at this stage of education. One explanation that emerges from the accounts of reading and readers contained in the pupils' own stories is located in the continuing powerful influence of the home, where the consumption of fiction is largely seen to be a concern of mothers, grandmas and sisters. Fathers who read, appear to do so more for instrumental purposes. The following examples taken from the questionnaires make this quite clear:

> My dad reads all the time because he is a farmer. (Richard, I)

> In my family I think my dad reads most as he works as a senior lecturer in the university. (Rebecca, Q)

> My dad reads about the horses: what time they're running and everything, so he can bet on them, before they run. He reads football results on the telly. (Craig, I)

One of the most widely held beliefs of teachers about the nature of reading, and particularly the reading of narrative fiction, is that it is best encouraged through personal choice and individual pleasure. The view is also tied very closely to a personal growth model of language teaching that assumes fiction is the site in which children will come to find a mirror of their place in the world and come to understand it better. Left to their own devices, it is girls who choose the written narrative path to pleasure and self-knowledge more frequently and more consistently than the boys in the same class (Luke, 1994, p. 375).

Summary

It is tempting, when arguing from the kinds of reading undertaken by the majority of pupils, to distribute the subsets of reading genre along gender lines. However, the patterning of reading habits amongst adolescents is far more complex than a simple judgment that most girls are 'good readers' but choose damaging texts, and most boys are 'not good enough' or 'could do better' but somehow gain access to more powerful forms of communication.

The data I have collected do not lend themselves to a simple value judgment of proper and improper literacies. For, although I have found that girls sustain their interest in reading for longer periods of time, the books and magazines they most often choose to read may also be seen as undemanding and repetitive (Millard, 1994). It depends on point of view as to whether this is to their advantage or disadvantage. On the one hand, girls' willingness to read privately and for pleasure has been validated by commentators because the books they choose address aspects of feeling and sensibility that allow them to negotiate questions of agency and control, leading them to oppositional or resistant readings (Moss, 1989). On the other hand, the most popular forms of women's fiction stand accused of confining them to narrow expectations of their gender destiny by tying fantasy and desire to commercialized and slick-packaged images of femininity (Brownstein, 1982; Coward, 1984; Christian-Smith, 1993; Willinsky and Hunniford, 1993). Girls reading romance, as Luke summarizes in the introduction to *Texts of Desire* (1993), 'construct distinct kinds of shared identities and interpretative communities bounded by the experiences, fantasies and desires of popular culture' (p. ix). An analysis of boys' reading, in terms of its cultural underpinning, is much less well developed, but although earlier cultural theorists have focused on comics as a debased and time-wasting form of literacy, current commentators are more likely to present the popular fiction chosen by boys in a more positive light (Sarland, 1991).

For many pupils, boys and girls alike, however, their current reading cannot be described as personal choice in any true sense, but as a chore imposed on them by others, mainly their English teachers. Of the rest, many of those who do read for pleasure choose books which confirm only a narrow, repetitive and stereotyped view of the world and what it is to be either male or female. Their reading is taken from what Barthes has called the 'lisible', that is texts which are no more than predictable re-orderings of what has already been read and which confirm rather than challenge the readers' expectations (Barthes, 1974, pp. 3–11). These 'readerly' texts encourage a passive consumerism which is stale and unprofitable to the reader. *Point Horror* may look to this generation of readers like a brand new 'genre', but, as one girl explains, it is no more than a form of the old romance novel dressed up in new clothes:

The *Point Horror* books tend to be about people who are eighteen or sixteen, 'cos they're all having parties and things like that, and then someone gets murdered and they all try to find it. It's usually like a ghost, an older teenager. Most of them have girls as the main character and they are mainly about girls being rescued by boys. (GI)

In their interviews, many girls claimed not to read romance stories, which they associated with older women's fiction, but the *Point Horror* stories had a very substantial following amongst them. In the next chapters, then, I want to turn from a discussion of the kinds of reading that boys and girls reported, developing outwards from my initial research questions to consider how the content of the pupils' reading influenced their writing. In particular, I shall focus on the differences in language encoded in the organizational structure of the genres chosen, asking how the differences create divergent pathways to literacy for boys and girls. In doing this, I shall move from a description of what boys and girls reported reading to a more theoretical and textually based analysis of the influence of books, magazines and other popular forms of narrative that I found echoed in their writing.

Chapter 5

Reading Beyond the Pleasure Principle

Of no days of our childhood did we live so fully perhaps as those we thought we had left behind without living them, those that we spent with a favourite book. (Marcel Proust, *On Reading*)

They'd quite simply forgotten what makes a book and what books have to offer. They'd forgotten, for example, that the novel, first and foremost, tells a story. They didn't realise that a novel must be read as a novel, to quench, first and foremost, their thirst for narrative. To lessen the pangs of their thirst, they'd long since turned to the small screen, which was doing its assembly-line job, stringing together cartoons, series, soap operas, and thrillers, in an endless chain of interchangeable stereotypes. It would fill their heads in the same way as they'd stuff their bellies, satiating but not sustaining the body. Digestion would be immediate, and they'd feel just as alone. (Daniel Pennac (1994) *Reads like a Novel*)

Overview

In Chapters 3 and 4, I analysed data from the survey to identify differences in the numbers of girls and boys who chose particular kinds of reading. I next discussed differences in the ways in which they organized and shared reading with others. In doing this, I revealed a pattern of developing reading habits strongly marked by gender difference. In this chapter, I intend to widen the discussion to include a consideration of further differences created by teachers' selections of class novels in comparison with those pupils recorded in the questionnaires. Data related to books used as class readers were collected during periods of classroom observation and supported by evidence from the interviews. I shall consider the ways in which pupils might be expected to respond to these books, juxtaposing this with further evidence from the questionnaire survey and follow-up interviews, both of which show the kinds of responses that current reading habits actually encourage.

I have selected three book titles on which to base my discussion of the types of narrative response evoked by different kinds of text. The first, Christopher

Pike's *The Last Vampire*, represents the popular horror genre that is growing in significance as an aspect of teenage reading; the second, Betsy Byars' *The Eighteenth Emergency*, is a book which I found being widely used in the first year of secondary school; and the third, Ursula Le Guin's *The Wizard of Earthsea*, represents a more literary fantasy, suitable for reading in class but less frequently chosen now by teachers for shared reading.

Reading at the Beginning of the Secondary School

The fiction chosen for reading together in class takes on an increased importance in the first years of the secondary school. It is at this stage in education that the processes of learning are reorganized into discrete academic disciplines, and the task of developing reading and writing is most often left firmly with the English teachers. To be 'good at reading' becomes increasingly associated in both pupils' and teachers' minds with choosing to read more demanding and complex fictions. We may marvel at the reading proficiency of politicians such as Kennedy, who was reputed to have a reading speed of 20,000 words a minute applied to large amounts of complex legislative documentation, but there is little emphasis on acquiring these skills within the existing school syllabus.

National Curriculum documents have emphasized the role other subjects should play in developing pupils' information skills in reading and writing, but this remains an area that has largely lagged behind other aspects of implementation. At the time of the survey, a student teacher who was involved in the project undertook a pupil pursuit of one of the groups who had been involved in the survey, which lasted a day and a half. She found that this particular class were asked to read for no more than 15 minutes at any one time and that this longest period was in an English lesson. The total time spent reading, in what amounted to 440 minutes of lesson time, added up to 28 minutes, that is just over 6 per cent of a working day.

She had replicated the findings of the important Lunzer and Gardiner Schools Council Study (1979) in which it was reported that secondary school teachers tended to avoid work that involved extensive reading for their pupils. Writing took up a good deal more of the pupils' time, but much of that writing consisted of copying from boards, filling in worksheets or writing down the teacher's words. In most schools it is, therefore, the fiction and poetry chosen for reading in English lessons, that determine the range and variety of most pupils' experience of reading. Interviews with pupils confirmed that reading was not a frequent activity in other subjects and that they were rarely asked to look for information in books other than those used as class texts. For example, Christine, one of the most accomplished readers who took part in the research gave this explanation for her school's emphasis on a single textbook or worksheets:

We do have class books that are for certain subjects so we don't go down to the school library for information. It's just all in that one book. We have a big history book which we read if we want information. In science we have cards and most of the time we're writing up experiments so we don't read. There are science books but we never read them in our lessons, he tells us a bit about it. In geography sometimes there are passages on the sheets, but it's not very often. We copy the passage and answer questions. (I)

Christine's comments, like those of several other pupils interviewed, reveal a lack of emphasis in school on published materials at this stage of their learning. Finding information in text books is now often seen as the role of the teacher preparing the lesson. Some of the boys interviewed even thought that in subjects other than English too much reading might get in the way of their learning, particularly in science and technology:

Kevin: You don't use texts books every time, 'cos you don't really need to.

Finn: I think if you're reading a text book and you read it for that long, you forget some of the stuff in it.

Matt: Like if you're actually doing it [a science subject] it's better than reading about it for yourself. We do it sometimes if we're doing things with reports on them.

Richard: Well, I don't find that at all interesting. (GI)

If reading is conceptualized as the ability to handle a wide range of different kinds of information in addition to a search for personal satisfactions, there is currently an insufficient base for practising this skill within the school curriculum as a whole. English lessons remain the site where expectations of reading and readers are formed, and what English teachers organize as reading in class determines for most pupils how they construct notions of the good reader.

Reading and the English Curriculum

Since the time of the Newbolt Report (Board of Education, 1921), English teaching has been expected to be the storehouse of the nation's cultural values, and the study of literature has been promoted as central to the education of both the hearts and minds of children. The teaching of narrative is also surrounded by a persuasive mystique about the power of books to change lives and the language used to promote the centrality of imaginative literature in education is perfused by affective values. The first version of English in the National Curriculum produced as the Cox Report, stated:

To foster in pupils a love of literature, to encourage their awareness of its unique relationship to human experience and to promote in them a sense of excitement in the power and potential of language can be one of the greatest joys of the English teacher. (DES, 1989, para. 7.1)

Similar formulations — which emphasize 'the power of story' and its ability to help readers 'to develop as people' and its stimulus 'to seeing through other's eyes' or 'to grow as thinking, caring people' — reoccur in the work of educationalists, writers and critics alike, all of whom place imaginative literature at the heart of the reading process, as is shown in the following examples:

When we read a good story the experience is powerfully creative. The reader or listener is called on to process the text as it unfolds, not only to make sense of the chunks of language as they are read or heard, but also to place the story, and all it consists of, on his/her personal map of experience. (Jack Ouseby, English adviser, 1992, p. 32)

You must read, Alice, before it is too late. You must fill your mind with the invented images of the past: the more the better. Literary images of Beowulf and the Wife of Bath and Falstaff and Sweet Amaryllis in the shade . . . The images apart from anything else will help you put the twos and twos of life together. (Fay Weldon, Writer, *Letters to Alice*)

Aesthetic properties of language are to be found more than anywhere else in literature. Literature is nothing if not language formed in highly deliberate ways. From the earliest pre-school stages of development, children are interested in forms of language . . . Wide reading, and as great an experience as possible of the best imaginative literature, are essential to the development of an ear for language. (Kingman Report, DES, 1988, Chapter 2, para. 21)

[Literature] helps shape the personality, refine the sensibility, sharpen the critical intelligence. In Britain the tradition of literature teaching is one which aims at personal and moral growth. (DES, 1975, p. 125)

At this moment an adolescent girl is immersed in a novel which may take her on a magic carpet ride to the land of romance or, perhaps, into the murky world of the horror story. There she can escape the realities of home and school, fulfil her secret desires and fantasies, ponder the relationships between the sexes and powerfully negotiate her place in the world. (Christian-Smith, educationalist, 1993, p. 1)

As a child gets older, whatever his ability as a reader, one principle remains constant: reading is idiosyncratic. How a child reads reflects his whole person, so that to read at all inevitably involves the stored experiences of the reader and his characteristic way of being and acting. (Benton and Fox, educationalists, 1985, p. 4)

Three strands are woven into in these statements: the first is the potential of literature to represent life and enable readers to make better sense of their experience of the world; the second concerns literature's motivating appeal to the individual through personal pleasure; third, an emphasis on its rich use of the language, which creates a challenge to the reader's understanding. The rhetorical force of these arguments is incontestable. Those who have been influenced by their own pleasurable diet of reading, and who frequently make their living in occupations associated with the printed word, continue to promote its value vigorously. Narrative, it has been argued, is a 'primary act of mind' (Hardy, 1975), through which we give meaning to experience; 'we cannot live, think, act or desire except in narrative' (Eagleton, 1983); the reading of stories makes 'skilful, powerful readers' who come to understand 'not only the meaning but the force of texts', 'it makes writers' (Meek, 1988) and ultimately 'subtly changes the people that we are' (Protherough, 1983, p. 20). These values underpin much of English teaching and remain valuable arguments for the inclusion of literature as a central part of the school curriculum. However, what all of them ignore are the ways in which reading may be conceptualized and approached by those with interests other than narrative ones.

Reading in Practice

It is important, next, to examine how these high principles work out in reality and to enquire specifically what learning experiences or opportunities have been opened up by the choice of reading made by the groups of 11–13-year-old pupils in this survey. To paraphrase Meek's influential work in this area, we need to know what 'private lessons' are made available and to think about how the books pupils read, and those they see being read, teach them what there is to learn about reading (Meek, 1988).

In a previous study of readers in the middle years of school (Millard, 1994) I have suggested that there are contradictions at work in a model of reading that seeks to incorporate notions of personal satisfactions and individual choice with those of cultural enrichment and intellectual growth. The major conflict can be seen in terms of the values implicit in children's own reading set against those that are encouraged by whatever is conceived by their teachers as 'literature'. I shall now examine the three areas of value that I have identified as commonly ascribed to the reading of literature, questioning each in relation to the pupils' recorded response to their own choice of fiction and secondly to those books selected for them by their teachers.

Reading Enables Children to Make Sense of the World

This is an argument frequently put forward when books to be shared in the classroom are chosen in relation to their 'truth to life'. The rationale derives from a concept of literature as mimesis currently interpreted as realistic portrayals of young people and the difficulties they encounter and overcome in their journey to maturity. This is, of course, an over-literal interpretation of the kind of writing best suited to making sense of the world, as books with fantastic settings also create opportunities for an authenticity of emotional response. This is vividly conveyed in the remembered experience of one English teacher when writing about his earliest literary satisfactions. He is describing a first response to the death of Thorin Oakenshield in *The Hobbit*, read to his primary class by the teacher:

> I still vividly remember its impact upon me. I was close to tears and peculiarly numb inside. I felt half-betrayed by the story-line, upstanding heroes did not get killed in the fiction with which I was familiar. Despite this sense of betrayal I was also aware that Thorin's death was somehow true to the story, that dying was part of the nature of things, though I would not have used those words to say what I felt. I was also aware that many of my classmates shared such feelings.

The writer, in the role of his remembered childhood self, seems already to be quite aware that he has entered a fictional world, remarking on not only what he knows about the conventional role of heroes and the logic of the death in terms of the story, but also his understanding taken beyond the individual story that 'dying was part of the nature of things'. It is the kind of lesson from literature that teachers hope to develop in their pupils. Protherough (1983) has also described as an ideal a response that links book to personal experience:

> The presentation of fiction in school is not just an academic exercise if the quality of narrative is intimately related to the quality of life. The ultimate importance of the fiction we read to children or put in their hands lies not in any 'moral' it may convey, but in the fact that through it young people are helping to develop a sense of themselves and of their shifting place in the world as they grow up. (p. 20)

The movement from life to art is one that powerfully concerns English teaching, no matter what strictures are applied by postmodern criticism to a simplistic view of verisimilitude. I thought, therefore, it important to consider the range of books that teachers currently use in school to encourage pupils' understanding of 'their shifting place in the world'. In the first two years of the secondary school, texts selected most frequently for class reading often focus quite literally on representations of pupils' present lives. They represent more or less realistic experiences of children, or young people, at roughly the same stage of development, in similar English-speaking communities, often involving school as well as family and friends.

The list of books reported as being studied by the 11–12-year-olds in the survey contained a large proportion of this kind of narrative and the authors most frequently named by teachers as appropriate for them were the English writer, Gene Kemp, and the American, Betsy Byars, both of whom deal in humorous, irreverent ways with the difficulties of moving from childhood to adolescence and the challenges presented by school. Certainly, these appear to be themes that teachers themselves wish to address in the first year of secondary school when they are introducing their classes to a story. The books are chosen to allow these classes to explore a world with which they are familiar and to discuss in a medium safer than that of personal confession issues of personal interest such as bullying, teenage pregnancy and problems within the family, or to extend their understanding of family issues related to another period, such as World War II.

It is not necessarily the understanding of a school world, however, that the age group is mainly seeking from its narratives. Girls are, on the whole, more sympathetic to the idea of choosing books that reflect the experience of people like themselves. Rosie, for example, looks for books that help her to understand people in real life,

> I like books where you're put in a position like of a child and you know like everything about him or her.

She had just completed her own reading of *The Diary of Ann Frank*:

> I thought it was really, really good. It was so moving to know that she had actually lived, it was deep all the time, whether she was talking about hoping to go back and see her friends, or whatever, like wishing to get out again, it was really special. I cried a lot of the time, it sort of made me cry, even the not very touching bits, but it just sort of made me think about how lucky I am to be able to walk out of my front door. (GI)

Earlier the class had been reading Elisabeth Laird's *Red Sky in the Morning*, which deals with the death of a handicapped child. Rosie describes it as the sort of book she likes and that she would pick to read for herself. She suggests, however, that the boys in her group had not liked the book and when questioned they proved to be particularly scathing about it:

> *Matt*: In the books there's no action or anything, it's just I like some excitement, *Red Sky in the Morning* — all the girls just loved that didn't they?

> *Richard:* Yes it was that, Yuck — let's pop down to the shops today and
> go to the cinema in the evening.
>
> *Kevin:* And Hannah cried in it 'cos Benedict died and all that.
>
> *Finn:* Yeah, that was a girls' book.
>
> *Richard:* Yes, (mumbling) it was like a sad story though a . . .
>
> *Kevin:* And right, next we read, *A Pair of Jesus Boots*, they just said
> 'boys' book', but they failed.
>
> *Richard:* Yes 'cos it was supposed to be about tough guys who hung
> around in gangs, it just gave boys a bad name. (GI)

Perhaps Richard's mumble about the sadness of *Red Sky in the Morning* is
used to cover up the fact that it is not permissible for a boy to respond to the
text openly in class, or in front of his peer group. It may, however, have had
some of the private effect as that of Thorin's death, recorded by the English
teacher (see p. 104).

The main point I want to make here does not concern the book's unsuit-
ability for the boys in the class, but that the main concerns of the realist novel
are more in keeping with the interests of girls, who expect their fictions to
address issues of feeling. The boys' further point about the second book discussed, *A Pair of Jesus Boots*, is also of key importance in drawing attention
to the unhelpful male stereotypes that are perpetuated in some books that are
chosen to appeal specifically to boys in a class. Of *The Machine Gunners*,
Helen remarked:

> It's boring with a load of lads messing about. That's what lads do. A
> girls' book would have more romance in it. (GI)

and Kathryn:

> If there were more women in the story it wouldn't have had much left
> in it. Girls wouldn't go around collecting pieces of planes for a start!
> (GI)

Yet despite their willingness to look closely at psychological problems, a
large proportion of girls were also not particularly interested in books that
focused specifically on childhood issues. Their own reported leisure reading
draws them into the world of an older age group, as the most popular choice
of magazine, *Just Seventeen*, shows. Similarly the reason for the popularity of
the *Point Horror* series with these girls is as much the attractions of the teenage world portrayed as the scary element, a fact found in the comment of a
girl recorded in the previous chapter, which is worth repeating here:

> The *Point Horror* books tend to be about people who are eighteen or
> sixteen, 'cos they're all having parties and things like that, and then
> someone gets murdered and they all try to find it. It's usually like a

ghost of an older teenager. Most of them have girls as the main character and they are mainly about girls being rescued by boys. (GI)

While many boys reject some of the texts chosen for them because they are, in their opinion, appropriate for girls, both sexes dislike any book which smacks of being too young or patronizing. For Alex, who reads Roald Dahl as one of his own choices, together with *Red Dwarf*, Betsy Byars falls firmly into this category:

In English we're doing this book called the *Eighteenth Emergency*. Well, I don't like it. I never have liked Betsy Byars. I once read a book in the Junior School by her called *Cracker Jackson*, and I didn't like that. It's always the same thing, all about bullies and things like baby-sitting jobs. It's about families, not adventure. I've read some silly books about silly families, like *The Twits*. (I)

Alex is voicing opinions of many boys who find the detail of everyday family life tedious and without interest. Betsy Byars' books are humorous but not in the chaotic anarchic manner of Dahl, Douglas Adams, or Grant and Naylor, the co-writers of *Red Dwarf*. Alex's preference for humour and action is also reflected in his recorded television choices, which, like those of many of the boys in the survey, contain far more comedy programmes, particularly those featuring alternative comedians like Rick Mayall and Ben Elton, than do the viewing habits of most girls.

Families Versus Adventures: A Question of Choice

Many girls, on the other hand, actively choose to read books that signal a sense of their arrival at a new stage of maturity. For Christine, an accomplished reader, the books provided in her class library look too undemanding:

Sometimes I wish that I could be with the second year because I like some of the work they do. They read books for their age group and I like reading books above my age group. I don't like reading books like *Moomin Papa*, I don't like those.

Some of the books I want to read it says fourth years only because they think the first years wouldn't want to read them. You have to bring a note from your mother to say that she lets you read those books. I sometimes find that a bit annoying because lots of children in the first year enjoy those kind of books. There was one where robots take over the world, just like a future book. The robots blocked all your minds and they made you forget old times. Maybe it had violent bits where there are people getting punished . . . it wasn't very violent — I'd read it before in primary school, so I don't know why it says 'fourth years only'. (I)

She also chooses to read books from a more adult canon including the *Story of Malcolm X* and *The Godfather* in her school private reading times.

I am not suggesting that authentic realism based on the experience of adolescence is an inappropriate genre for the age group. Current 'problem' stories, particularly the novels of Swindell, Westall and Fine, offer strong challenges to the more complacent images of family life which are a feature of series fiction. They can be an effective way of raising important issues in class: for example, Westall's *Stone Cold* deals powerfully with homelessness and serial killings. What I want to emphasize is the difficulty of arguing for any particular book representing aspects of life that have a relevance or appeal for the age group as an undifferentiated whole.

From the choices of favourite authors discussed in Chapter 5 and the books tabled in Appendix C it can be seen that it is girls who favour a more realistic style of writing. Even so, they usually prefer narratives about people older than themselves and therefore, have less interest in the stories of people their own age, which are often chosen for them by teachers. Boys tend to dismiss the realist genres as lacking action and dealing with the commonplace. A focus almost entirely on this particular vein of authentic realism in school works to confirm in boys an opinion that has already been set up within the home; that reading has more relevance to girls.

In order to draw boys into the reading process, the main character of the fictions chosen by teachers is frequently a boy; such as Gowie Corby, Danny, Champion of the World, or the eponymous David; or failing that a tomboy, or a girl, masquerading as a boy, like Tyke Tiler, an option which leaves the girls without the positive role models that feminist advocates of authentic realist approaches have advocated.

Attempting to balance the books in terms of subject matter and positive role models creates a host of problems. In any case, it is important to consider whether verisimilitude should be the main criteria for teachers who wish to motivate a class through personal interest. It does not feature as a priority in the genres selected by either sex in this survey, nor is it the genre that has been credited with the strongest psychological impact. Chambers, in an interview for the *English Magazine* (Hunt and Plackett, 1986), has suggested that an emphasis in teenage fiction on contemporary issues has a moral rather than an imaginative purpose, and that such works are in fact rhetorical arguments for a point of view more in keeping with journalism. He argues that because stories written specifically for children grew out of a desire to teach them moral values, 'the (moralistic) genes are still in the literature', and he argues forcibly against their 'preachiness':

> In other words, the writer wants the kid to think a certain thing, rather than helping the kid to think. It's a distinction between literature as

giving you images to think with and assisting you as a thinker, and literature as a handbook of what you should think. Now, I'm against the 'what you should think' argument. (Chambers in Hunt and Plackett, 1986, p. 25)

Chambers' analysis suggests that it is important to consider a more imaginative role for literature than the one that has been most prominent in publishing in recent years for this age group. He also contrasts the 'problem novels' for young adolescents unfavourably with the picture books written for younger age groups which have more sophisticated 'layering' in the way 'time is handled, the way space is thought of' (p. 23). Certainly, the adolescent novel compares unfavourably with the vitality of the narrative forms found in picture and comic books, which appeal to real sources of desire and pleasure, not those imposed by curriculum and teaching strategies.

Reader as Hero and Heroine

Appleyard (1991), in his developmental study of the growth of the reader, has labelled the stage of later childhood or pre-teens, 'Reader as Hero and Heroine', suggesting that 'the distinctive role readers take at this stage is to imagine themselves as heroes and heroines of romances that are unconscious analogues of their own lives' (pp. 57–93). In fact, what young teenage readers appear to look for in the texts they endorse are models of the kinds of adult behaviour to which they currently aspire. Moreover, these representations need not be realistic portrayals, but represent embodiments of the qualities they desire for themselves. Many girls willingly choose to read books with central male characters because qualities of resistance found in the heroes of adventure stories are ones that are important to their view of themselves. How many younger girls, for example, have identified with Peter Pan rather than Wendy, despite the allure of the Wendy House? Few boys, however, choose to read books with women or girls at the centre, and this appears to be because female characteristics of empathy and compassion are ones from which they are seeking to distance themselves.

Appleyard further suggests that at this stage both genders' interests can be met in the romance genre, or quest story, where the need for adventure and the working out of relationships are both possible (1991, pp. 92–3). An adventure story, he argues, serves a double function; first to give concrete form to a threatening evil and then to ensure that it is defeated. He relates the genre to the wish-fulfilment dream and turns to a structuralist analysis based on folk stories to rationalize the quest's appeal.

The basic structure of childhood narratives that Todorov and others have described — equilibrium/disequilibrium/equilibrium restored — seems to arise out of the double wish to acknowledge anxiety but to be assured of deliverance from it. (Appleyard, 1991, p. 63)

The kind of psychological satisfactions described for this stage draw upon narratives that may appear formulaic and over-schematic to adults because of the simplicity of the oppositions of good and evil, victim and monster. Such stories, often based on folklore, present a psychological truth rather than a literal one and allowing their readers both to understand and control a world while also allowing the release of 'forbidden impulses' (Lurie, 1990, p. 225). They help, in fact, with the work of creating a yet unformed identity.

It is too easy, however, to think of these more symbolic narratives as an earlier stage of reading and consider the psychological focus of the realist novel with its emphasis on the exploration of 'character' a more mature form of writing. To set against this, we can argue that there is something perhaps as potent as character in the unravelling of a good plot, which partakes of the nature of oral storytelling. Benjamin (1973), writing of the Russian storyteller, Lakov, defines the nature of this power memorably:

> There is nothing that commends a story to memory more effectively than the chaste compactness which precludes psychological analysis. And the more natural the process by which the storyteller forgoes natural shading, the greater becomes the story's claim to a place in the memory of the listener, the more completely is it integrated into his own experience, the greater will be his inclination to relate it to some-one else some-day, sooner or later. (p. 91)

Stories with this powerful effect on memory remain in the culture over time and become added to its mythology, appealing to old and young alike. Modern examples are provided by *The Wizard of Oz* and the *Star Wars* trilogy, both of which have gained added potency by having been translated into films.

Winnicott (1968) designated the period of adolescence as a kind of doldrums in which the young struggle towards a final autonomy, pitching themselves into the same old battles as generations before them. He suggests:

> In this respect the adolescent is repeating an essential phase of infancy. For the infant is an isolate, at least until he or she has repudiated the not-me and has become a separated-off individual, one that can have relationships with objects that are external to the self and outside the area of omnipotent control. Young adolescents are isolates attempting by various means to form an aggregate, through the adoption of an identity of tastes. (p. 132)

One of the means through which this working out of group identity is achieved is through the sharing of images from popular culture which throw into question the easy securities of childhood stories. The formulaic contest between opposites is a recurrent feature of the popular horror genre, whose stories address themes that subconsciously meet adolescent fears of their awakening sexuality and its relationship to questions of personal identity, family conflict and death. The Gothic tale has always had a particular pull for young women in enabling them to indulge in the fear of, and fascination with, male sexuality, in a disguised form. It is a significant element in women's literary novels such as Mary Shelley's *Frankenstein* and Emily Bronte's *Wuthering Heights*, both of which may be read as refinements of more popular examples of the genre. Such interconnections of popular image and literary themes also supports my conclusion that a move from popular fiction to the more literary texts may not appear as discontinuous for the girl reader. This is because their reading for emotional satisfaction and the understanding of relationships chimes more harmoniously with the psychological approaches that mark advanced studies in English in school.

Young men also look to fantasy models of the power and autonomy that both attracts and repels them, whether this is embodied in comic book heroes like superman or in the powerful alien and monster shapes of science fictions. Masculinity is portrayed both as enormously powerful and frighteningly destructive, twin impulses that have importance in boys' negotiation of what it is to be a man. Bettelheim (1976) has argued powerfully for the importance of mythical and fantastical narratives in the growth of security, even expressing the opinion that the denial of the fantastic in childhood can lead to an unhealthy fascination with other aspects of it in later adolescence:

> I have known many examples where, particularly in late adolescence, years of belief in magic are called upon to compensate for the person's having been deprived of it prematurely in childhood . . . many young people who today suddenly seek escape in drug-induced dreams, apprentice themselves to some guru, believe in astrology, engage in practising 'black magic', or who in some other fashion escape from reality into day dreams about magic experiences which are to change their life for the better, were prematurely pressed to view reality in an adult way. (p. 32)

Creators of popular culture understand the power of the fantastic instinctively and the most successful film narratives have a resonance that spills over from childhood into the adult's sense of narrative gratification so, like the best books, they are experienced with pleasure over and over again. I am thinking here of modern films such as *ET* and the *Valley of the Dinosaurs* as well as older productions such as the early Disney versions of *Snow White* and *Bambi*. Yet when teachers select books for study it is most often the sense of authentic representation of real life that holds sway.

How far then is the pleasure principle, both in the form of immediate appeal and latent psychological satisfaction, at work in drawing readers into the texts that their teachers choose for them. Only one or two of the titles selected as class readers for 11–12-year-olds by the teachers in the survey fitted the horror, mystery or fantasy genres that the age group always included as most pleasurable in their own selections. Alcock's *The Monster Garden*, for example, has as its underpinning the Frankenstein story; Cross's *The Demon Headmaster*, draws on fears of alien possession; and *Dragonslayer*, Sutcliffe's version of *Beowulf*, is now sometimes used as an introduction to the influence of Anglo-Saxon on the language. It is perhaps the text which comes closest to the kinds of narrative most favoured in the fantasy reading and computer games of the boys with its gory combat, revenge themes and grotesque mother monster. The difficulty for feminists with such texts is both the violence and the concentration on masculine warrior cultures, but it is more productive to help readers to an understanding of the exercise of power than to ignore its fascination for the age group.

Of further relevance to the understanding of how narrative pleasure is constructed within teenage culture is the fact that television soaps now largely supply the narrative gratification associated with representations of 'real life' for a large section of the age group. Their appeal is clearly shown in Tables 9 and 10, Chapter 4, pp. 68–9. The focus, particularly of the Australian soaps, is on the age group they wish to join and whose lives, therefore, hold many fascinations.

Reading as Individual Choice and Personal Pleasure

> My contention is that these problems (of the impact of class readers) cannot really be solved in terms of the single class-reader, and that . . . the main focus of the teacher's efforts in regards to prose should be shifted away from reading done during lesson-time and on to the voluntary self-initiated reading carried on outside school hours. (Whitehead, 1966, p. 60)

In this quotation from *The Disappearing Dais*, Whitehead establishes a principle that has dominated the provision of fiction for the past three decades and is reflected in the wider reading strand in the National Curriculum. A recent restatement of the position can be found in an advisory teacher's account of her 'book conversations' with a group of 11–12-year-olds, which she conducted by letter.

> I find that in my letters I am often probing to find out more precisely what it is that children have liked or disliked about the books they have chosen and about my correspondence with them has made me think about myself as a reader and what I look for when I want 'a good read'. (J. Smith, 1994, p. 137)

To escape from the limitations of a single class reader in many schools, pupils are encouraged to follow their own tastes when selecting books for wider reading, freeing the teacher to concentrate her efforts on encouraging those who are reluctant to pick up a book at all (Smith, 1994, p. 138). In a later article discussing the importance of quality in reading, Whitehead (1988) quotes Johnson to support an argument for tolerance of any kind of reading that is willingly taken up:

> I would let [a boy] at first read *any* book which happens to engage his attention; because you have done a great deal when you have brought a boy to get entertainment from a book. He'll get better books afterwards. (p. 59)

There is much to support those teachers who desire to whet their pupils' appetite for reading by whatever means is available to them. Sarland (1991) has taken just such a stance in promoting the positive gains to be had from studying the more adult versions of the popular horror genre as represented in the writing of Stephen King and James Herbert as examination texts. The main question to ask, however, is what evidence is there to show that progression from these popular forms will be to more demanding reading without considerable adult intervention? Indeed, the evidence both from my own survey and that conducted more recently by Peter Benton (1995, p. 105) is that the interest in what have been variously described as 'better books' or 'classic' children's fiction, has sharply declined.

In the 1977 list of favourites, *Little Women*, *Black Beauty*, *Treasure Island*, and *The Lion the Witch and the Wardrobe* all featured prominently. My own lists, and those compiled by Benton, were headed by the books of Judy Blume and Roald Dahl, with a range of *Point Horror* titles dominating other choices. Not only had all the nineteenth-century options almost entirely disappeared from personal choices but also most of the more challenging Puffin books by recognized children's authors that had featured in previous selections. Benton believes the size of the discrepancy is the result of children's greater truthfulness in completing their answers for the surveys he conducted. He argues that in his study they recorded the books that they actually had read, rather than those that would meet their teacher's approval. He therefore describes these readers as 'more honest in their responses and less trammelled by what convention expected of them. Although they follow fashion, many individuals appear to be remarkably independent readers' (Benton, 1995, p. 110). However, if wide reading is to do more than confirm stereotypes and provide quick and unchallenging 'easily read' texts, intervention by class teachers is essential and demands more time and expenditure on new and appealing texts than most schools achieve at present.

Narrative Satisfaction and Its Sources

Rolande Barthes, has suggested that the appetite for stories is universal and that narrative is to be found in cultural artefacts as disparate as 'myth, legend, fable, tale, novella, epic, history, tragedy, drama, comedy, mime, stained glass windows, cinema, comics, news items, conversations', because narrative is, 'international, trans-historical, trans-cultural. Simply there like life itself' (Barthes, 1974). Twenty years on from the last national survey of reading behaviour, what we can say with complete certainty is that there are now many more ways of satisfying this particular human need for story than those that are provided by print. In 1977 Whitehead and his team identified television as the major competitor for children's attention in their leisure periods. This was then accessible only at the time of transmission and offered a very limited range of programmes specifically appealing to children.

Today, not only have the number of television channels increased but, in addition, video technology makes films and recorded programmes available in many homes for 24 hours a day. Some children even reported getting up after their parents were in bed in order to make secret use of the family video recorder. Added to this, as I showed in the previous chapter, a large proportion of this age group have a television set in their own bedroom so their personal access to visual entertainment is unlimited. Computer programmes with sophisticated graphics, now entice the operator, more often a boy, into fictional worlds with quest-like narratives which create fantasies of heroic encounters with warriors and monsters. All available research data supports the view that this is the time when readers are confirmed as lifelong addicts of the pleasure and new challenges of literature or the habit can lose its hold on even the most proficient decoder.

Chapter 4 has illustrated that when boys and girls are given freedom to read as they please, they take very different routes to finding their personal narrative satisfactions. Marina Warner, examining popular culture in the 1994 Reith Lectures, identified mythical heroes and monsters as the dominant actants in the kind of narratives found in computer games in which she finds less and less attention being given to women.

> . . . women have pretty much disappeared from the plots altogether. There's the occasional dewy-eyed girl hoodlum or pixie-haired hell-raiser, or 'salacious spider woman' and there are some female street fighters — all active, assertive types and good examples of how positive imaging can backfire. And, as I said, the stock motive of the damsel in distress recurs. But the effect of the almost total absence of women from this all-engulfing imaginary world of boys is to intensify the sense of apartness, of alienation, of the deep oppositeness of the female sex. (pp. 23–4)

In terms of the masculine identities offered by the new mythologies of the computer text, boys are presented with a world in which the life of the emotions has very little significance. An equally stereotyped, if different, view of the relations between the sexes is presented in the popular fictions favoured by girls, which have been described by one commentator as dealing with:

. . . the first meeting, the courting and the final blissful culmination (in a kiss), of a girl's infatuation with a boy. The progress of the infatuation is constructed as the girl's dominant interest in life, often interfering with her school work, her hobbies, her family and with her friendships with other teenagers. All is seen to be sacrificed if the path of the love affair is to run smoothly, and girls in teen romances go to extraordinary ends to achieve their goals. (Gilbert, 1993, p. 61)

Moreover, in the more action-packed *Point Horror* stories, girls or young women are just as much the intended victims of the killers and sexual exploiters as they are of the boys' fighting fantasy and computer quest monsters. It is because of the limiting nature of the narratives of popular culture that attention has been given to altering the balance of what is chosen for reading in school in order to promote a more equal society through the introduction of texts representing a wider social reality. For example, gender was an area singled out for particular comment in the initial Cox Report on the National Curriculum for English for ages 5–16:

It is well known that girls and boys tend to choose different books and indeed that teenage boys tend to drop voluntary reading altogether. If this difference is simply accepted it will only serve to strengthen stereotypes. All teachers should therefore enable and encourage both girls and boys to read a variety of genres by a variety of authors, including those which challenge stereotypes of the roles of the sexes and of different cultural groups. (DES, 1989, para. 11.8)

In practice, most of the books chosen by teachers mirror the lives of a white, fairly comfortably-off social group, usually American or British, and sometimes Australian, and include a central character who is an adolescent and who is taken to represent the interests of the pupil reading. Yet such stories about people of the same age, though raising issues that teachers find important and relevant, such as bullying, family break-up and other trials of growing up, can, paradoxically appear to represent a repetition of the same ('boring') and be thought inappropriate for their age ('babyish'). The decline of interest of this age group in both Enid Blyton's stories and the *Beano*, which were both extremely popular in 1977, can be attributed to market strategies that have redesigned the covers of the former for a younger readership and redrawn Dennis the Menace, hero of the latter, as more childlike. There is a superficial sophistication about the contemporary early teenager, which has been encouraged by exposure to other media. This makes the task of challenging perceptions about role through one or two carefully selected class novels an unlikely proposition. More realistic are strategies that aim to develop critical and analytical approaches to a wide range of narratives and media genres.

Reading as the Enrichment of Language

To return to a consideration of the last of the three criteria identified earlier as used to support the centrality of literature to the English curriculum, the final argument depends on the enrichment of language that 'good' literature provides. How far, then, do the books currently read in and out of school carry the weight of this expectation?

Much of what the pupils in the survey say they choose to read for themselves is a repetition of light, instantly pleasurable reading or simple information, that offers them few fresh challenges or new ways of engagement with ideas or language. Only one girl in the survey wrote of the importance of language in describing the value she placed on the books she read. She was someone who fell into the heaviest reader category and who described herself as a 'bookworm'. She reads 'every night and a lot at weekends' and switches between 'comfy, trashy reads, such as her mum's detective book', to more complex and challenging books, like *Little Women* and *Goodnight Mr Tom*, though she prefers books about women. She represents an ideal reader in the eyes of most teachers:

> I like reading out in class but not silent reading. I do that at home. My reading I think has an effect on how good I am at English, I've always read a lot and I've got a good vocabulary. I think it helps spelling a bit and it helps sort of with creative writing, you get a lot of ideas from books you've read. (I)

(The issue of 'getting a lot of good ideas from books' is one to which I shall return in Chapter 6, where I shall turn my attention from the reading to the writing of narratives.)

In a previous study (Millard, 1994) I have discussed the contradictions that are at work in the determination of what is most important in the choice of texts for reading in school; that is, whether books should be carefully chosen for their increasing complexity and challenge to the reader or whether wide exposure and an emphasis on personal response to books will suffice. Wider reading was the strategy suggested by the Bullock Report as the way of resolving this duality and is widely accepted as a goal for reading in the 1990s. But, as Griffiths (1992), comments:

> It is, I think, defensible to adopt a position of believing that as wide and as varied as possible an exposure to fiction will contribute to an understanding of narrative devices, to intellectual growth and emotional development. It is also possible to adopt another position . . . in which a structured exposure to narrative devices of gradually increasing complexity forms at least one organising principle of the literature curriculum. Bullock appears to marshal a body of evidence for the latter argument, but to be deeply committed to the former one. (p. 61)

It is possible to identify a similar duality at work in the current provision for reading in school. Implicit in an emphasis on reading which stresses personal choice, is a belief that exposure will ensure the development of a more complex understanding. However, the English curriculum in the early years of secondary education begins to expect a more considered and reflective response from the reader, for which most unguided choice leaves many pupils poorly prepared.

Teachers find the identification of criteria to select books for particular classes difficult and are unsure how they might best influence the reading that pupils are asked to do voluntarily. The current emphasis in literary critical theory on the role of the reader as producer of meaning, rather than on the author and her intentions, has made possible readings of popular culture that are more engaging and illuminating than the texts themselves (Barthes, 1974; Moss, 1989; Sarland, 1991). But the critical ability to read texts in this way, that is to tell stories about stories, depends on a developing grasp of narrative conventions based on an increasing sophistication in reading in response to particular kinds of writing. Wide reading, well managed, may very well bring about the kind of exposure to increasingly sophisticated texts that is at the heart of the secondary curriculum, but inexperienced readers respond naively to stories that have been written in a particular cultural context when they are unaware of the genre expectations.

To illustrate the difficulties in balancing language complexity and narrative appeal, I have now chosen to examine in some detail short sections of three books that make very different demands on their readers. The first, which I have selected to represent current popular fiction, is an extract from a Christopher Pike story. His books hold the same fascination for the age group as the *Point Horror* titles, and I have chosen the latest book by this author because it is one that more boys in the survey than usual recorded reading. Pike's stories are more violent than the milder *Point Horror* series. The title is *The Last Vampire* and the book is packaged in a lurid cover that portrays its blonde heroine's naked shoulders swathed in a viper, whose jaws gape to reveal poison fangs. The plot is summarized in the blurb on the back cover:

Alisa and Ray are the last vampires or so they think. But now the evil plague is spreading. A brutal murderer is terrorising Los Angeles. He's hungry for blood and power. Who has created this brutal monster. Has Alisa the power to stop him? or will he destroy her first?

The following passage from the book describes Alisa's encounter with a would-be rapist, one of a gang:

'You don't want to go saying no to me, honey. I don't like that word.'
'Really.'
He glances back at his friends and then nods gravely in my direction.

'You either do it with a smile on your face or you do it screaming. You know what I mean, Alisa?'
I smile, finally, 'Are you going to rape me, Paul?'
He shrugs, 'It's up to you, Honeysuckle.' He draws his piece from his coat. A 45 Smith and Wesson revolver that he probably got for his last birthday. He presses the muzzle beneath my chin. 'And its up to Colleen.'
He nods seriously. 'She's a lady, never lets me down.'
My smile grows. 'Paul you are such a simpleton, you can't rape me. Put it out of your mind if you want to be alive come Christmas day. It's just not going to happen.'
My boldness surprises him, angers him. But he quickly grins because his friends are watching and he has to be cool and in control. He presses the gun deeper into my neck, trying to force my head back. But of course I don't move an inch and this confuses him as much as my casual tone.

The subject matter is sensational and deals with a theme which the age group expect adults to censor. It's dialogue is racy, and mirrors in a reduced way the kind of clever talk that has always fascinated Raymond Chandler's readers and which has had many lesser imitators. The action is swift and the plot moves rapidly from confrontation to struggle, relying on what Barthes (1974) has described in *S/Z* as the Code of Actions (proairetic code), in which sequences are anticipated through the piling up of small detail:

Actions (terms of the proairetic code) can fall into various sequences which should be indicated merely by listing them, since the proairetic sequence is never more than an artifice of reading: whoever reads the text amasses certain data under some generic titles for actions (*stroll, murder, rendezvous*) and this title embodies the sequence, the sequence exists when and because it can be given a name, it unfolds as this process of naming takes place, as a title is sought or confirmed . . . its only logic is that of the 'already done', 'the already read'. (p. 19)

The positive image of a woman presented in this story is subject matter appropriated from feminism. It is, however, an illusory image for it is only as a vampire that Alisa remains independent, as 'woman' itself she will find herself 'in love' with the FBI agent in the story and encoded as part of the scene of romance. The sentences are short with a minimum of subordinate clauses. Focused through Alisa, and narrated in the first person, the text keeps mainly to the simple present, which reinforces the impression of the plot taking place in front of the reader, in the manner of a film. The vocabulary is undemanding but reflects the grown-up world of violent drama. The description is banal, the character's tone is 'casual' he nods 'gravely', later the rapist is described as 'acting like a stud', his buddies are 'hungry panthers'. Every element is drawn from the 'already read' the 'already written'. The whole book is written in a style which offers superficially sophisticated action with little linguistic challenge to its readers. It provides a quick read (the better readers in my survey consume such a book at a single sitting) of the same level of narrative complexity as the works of Enid Blyton, the author who topped the popularity chart in the 1977 survey.

The next extract is from *The Eighteenth Emergency* (1974) by Betsy Byars whose books are frequently chosen as class readers 11–13-year-olds. In contrast with the last passage this offers no false heroics of word or action, except perhaps in the initial decision of Mouse to seek out Mark Hammerman and settle the threat that has hung over him throughout the story. Instead, convincing feelings of inadequacy and dread are conveyed to the reader:

> When Mouse saw them [Hammerman and his friend] his walking suddenly became harder. His shoes seemed to stick to the side-walk, and his legs got heavy. He felt as if he were walking underwater. He pulled down his jacket, smoothed his hair, hitched up his pants, kept his hands busy in order to keep attention from his slow heavy feet. He pulled at his earlobe, wiped his nose, zipped his jacket higher. Foolishly he thought of the hundred and eighteen little people of his father's dreams. He wished they would appear, lift him and carry him away. 'So long, Hammerman,' he would cry as they hurried him to safety. Mouse kept walking, and the three of them met in front of the Rialto. (Byars, 1974, p. 89)

I have selected this extract to be representative of current books that teachers read with younger forms, firstly because it is still widely used and secondly because it provides an alternative to fighting and winning as definitive of masculinity. The passage quoted creates Mouse's feelings through reference to small realistic actions that signal his nervousness. The writing conveys a realistic conflict that ends with honour satisfied, but without heroics, and with something of an anti-climax. The language itself is more honest and carefully chosen, although it is not very much more complex than that of the previous piece, relying on a similar mixture of dialogue and detail of action. If the study of literature is a study of a 'slice of life', then this serves the purpose well, and like all of Betsy Byars' books it is well written and well paced. It does not, however, tap into the deeper imaginative worlds or darker fantasies where more symbolic struggles are enacted. Nor does it employ a specifically literary language to challenge the reader.

It is notoriously difficult to give a definition of literary language as opposed to more functional prose. However, one well-accepted definition of the poetic is that it draws attention to itself in the way that a referential language which concentrates on 'the world' avoids (Hawkes, 1977, pp. 76–87). Both examples I have given so far have aimed at a directness of reference and expression that avoid complex symbolization. I have chosen my next passage to represent a more 'literary text which describes a more symbolic struggle for personal survival'. It is taken from Ursula Le Guin's *Wizard of Earthsea* (1971) and narrates the final encounter of Ged, a young wizard, with the shadow beast that has hounded him since he foolishly summoned its spirit from the dead.

> Still Ged did not stop but went forward, though there were only a few yards left between them now. Then the thing that was between them changed utterly, spreading out to either side as if it opened enormous thin wings and it writhed, and swelled, and shrank again . . . At that Ged lifted up the staff high, and the radiance of it brightened intolerably, burning with so white and great a light that it compelled and harrowed even that ancient darkness. In that light all form of man sloughed off the thing that came towards Ged. It drew together and shrank and blackened, crawling on four short-taloned legs upon the sand. But still it came forward, lifting up to him a blind unformed snout without lips or ears or eyes. As they came right together it became utterly black in the white mage-radiance that burned about it, and it heaved itself upright. In silence man and shadow met face to face and stopped.
>
> Aloud and clearly, breaking the silence, Ged spoke the shadow's name and in the same moment the shadow spoke without lips or tongue, saying the same word, 'Ged'. And the two voices were one voice.
>
> Ged reached out his hand, dropping his staff and took hold of his shadow, of the black self that reached out to him. Light and darkness met and joined and were one. (pp. 197–8)

This is a text which is less frequently used as a class reader, although many schools still have a set for use with 11–13-year-olds. Immediately discernible is a difference in the texture of the writing. Not only is the language heightened from that of the everyday — as in the powerful verbs 'compelled and harrowed' — but the symbolic opposition between light and dark is sustained throughout, culminating in the location of both these aspects in the single character, Ged. The passage is multi-valent or layered, that is, it is capable of being read on many levels, including the psychological, in which the adolescent, Ged, confronts those aspects of self which threaten his ontological security and emerges victorious. Of course I do not suggest that this is the level of discussion appropriate to the younger reader, but that the story works at a deeper level of understanding than the realism of the struggle described in *The Eighteenth Emergency*.

The mystical aspects of the text also link the work to other mythical and legendary quest-based stories while containing elements that are more intense renderings of the themes of their most popular horror series. This type of writing serves to heighten the differences between spoken and written language, helping develop in the reader a sense of what is appropriate for particular genres in terms of tone and register and also enriching expression by introducing a less familiar, but powerful, vocabulary. This is an important lesson for the developing writer as I shall be examining in the next chapter (Chapter 6) in which I shall examine the effects of reading on writing. Such writing as that of the *Wizard of Earthsea* demands more sustained attention from the reader in its insertion of passages of description between those of action and dialogue. It is not a text that classes would find an easy read, and one which teachers would need patience in presenting to mixed ability groups. It is a text, however, that is rich in the kinds of lessons about language that have been attributed to the study of literature, one to which Barthes (1974) might grudgingly afforded the label 'writerly'.

As Meek (1988) has suggested:

> The problem for teachers in secondary school is to give students enough experience of different kinds of text while exploring the secrets and lessons of only some of them. (p. 38)

My analysis of three very different kinds of texts has been to illustrate the complexity of the range of lessons to be learned from reading. I wish to argue further that it is an important role of the texts chosen for close study in class that they should challenge the young reader by offering alternative forms of narrative understanding not made available in the individual books they select for more instant pleasures.

Summary

In order to develop the strand of my argument that questions the **value** of current patterns of young people's reading, as identified in the survey, I have developed a more theoretically based perspective located in textual analysis. I have used this to illustrate that individual pleasure in reading, as it is currently promoted in schools, offers limited opportunities for the full expansion of the many aspects of reading prescribed for the English curriculum. English teachers are much less ready than were the Whitehead team of 1977 to divide children's books according to 'quality' and 'non-quality' categories, seeing this as an assumption which disregards both the value to the individual of a particular book (Moss, 1977, pp. 140–2) and the genuine complexities of some popular fantasy fiction, the writing of Terry Prachett, for example. Yet most English teachers would want to argue that some books have more merit or make more demands on their readers than others and would wish to sharpen their pupils' discrimination as well as pleasure in their reading.

It is also clear that few of the books that are popular with the age group when the selection is left to individual taste, make demands either on the language, or the interpretative skills of young readers. *Point Horror* fiction, for instance, offers repetitive dangers with easy solutions and stock characters.

When personal pleasure or topical relevance is the main criteria for choice, much of the resulting private reading is stereotyped and limited in range. In addition, the teachers' efforts to select class-readers according to their appeal to pupils' interests or current experience may also work to limit the genres made available for study in school and, by extension, the range of creative language.

A repetitive choice of authentic realist texts may concentrate on relevant content at the expense of ensuring exposure and detailed discussion of a range of styles and language. Central, too, is the divisive nature that an emphasis on individual narrative choice has on the 'engendering' of readers and the models of literacy opened up to them. I shall develop this argument further by turning in the next chapter to an analysis of the kinds of written narrative fictions that boys and girls produce in school, arguing that in their encoding of experience in story form, each sex once again patterns out their difference in narrative preference, with boys opting for action at the expense of character, and girls focusing on relationships.

A concentration in school reading on realism, as I have demonstrated, works in the interests of the girls, for whom this is a favourite mode, and whose responses to feelings and relationships are better developed. A focus on individual choice and the pleasure principle in fiction also risks more boys opting out of reading altogether (arguing in effect that it does not give them pleasure), while encouraging them to consider English in particular, and language activities in general, as activities more appropriate for the girls in their classes.

Chapter 6

Reading into Writing

If we want to see what lessons have been learned from the texts children read, we have to look for them in what they write. Of course they draw on the whole of their culture if we let them. We have to be alert what comes from books as well as from life. (Meek, 1988, p. 3)

The Influence of Film on Narrative Understanding

In the previous chapter I looked at the range of print narratives available to young readers in the middle years of school. In this chapter, the discussion is extended to encompass a wider range of narrative forms that can be shown to shape pupils' perception of how stories are told and written and use this to analyse their versions of written narratives, tracing these influences and their effects. First, I want to look in more detail at particularly potent forms of narration.

Fiction takes two major forms in our culture: that conveyed in the visual medium of film, television and, to a lesser extent, in computer games, and that of the more traditional kind, found in the continuous prose of books and magazines. The conventions of prose narrative differ from those of film quite markedly.

Film is based on a flickering of light, which creates the illusion of movement, hence the popular name 'movies'. Since the introduction of cinemas in the 1930s, and the growth of its popular audience, they have established themselves as the rival to novels and short stories as the major source of narrative fiction (Benjamin, 1973; Montgomery, Durant, Fabb, Furniss and Mills, 1992, pp. 145–56).

Conventional prose narratives are constructed to create a smooth development of sequences which aim at both continuity of action and detailed explanation of cause and effect, resulting in an ultimate closure whereby all the actions set in motion by the plot are tied into a satisfying ending. The narration works not only through external description but also by moves inside the thoughts of successive characters to clarify their motivation and elaborate their psychology.

Film, on the other hand, relies less on continuity of detail but more on the rapid juxtaposition of images, using a range of shots that make clear who is at the centre of a particular action. Emotions in films are either registered in facial expressions or through dialogue. The juxtaposition of images occurs both quickly and dramatically, usually without explanation, although sometimes a voice-over will record the passage of time or create a sense of place, particularly in the epic, where the setting is less familiar to a general audience. *Gone with the Wind*, for example, begins with a voice narrating the events which occurred in the Southern States of America prior to the action. In general, however, film images are left to 'speak' for themselves. To give an extreme example of pictorial collage, in Eisenstein's *The Battleship Potemkin*, the opening sequence consists of an image of a woman wearing *pince-nez* glasses, the second shot is of the same woman but with her glasses shattered and her eye bleeding. This juxtaposition of images suggests the action of a bullet being fired and hitting the eye but the intermediary stages are left to be assumed by the audience rather than each action unfolded in front of it.

There have been a hundred years of cinema, and its conventions of fictional narration are now well established (Benjamin, 1973, pp. 238–9) and immediately familiar to the majority of adolescents who will have absorbed far more visual narratives than written ones by the time they reach secondary school. Even very young children are accustomed to making meaning from different media versions of well-loved stories (Mackey, 1994). Their understanding encompasses both the complexities of genre and an understanding of the provisionality of the text. When pupils, who are already sophisticated consumers of visual narrative, write a story, they often use methods absorbed from these media to convey the action. This gives their writing a filmic quality that may seem jerky and undeveloped in contrast to the writing of those which make use of more literary conventions (Millard 1994, pp. 81–3).

Writing Tasks in School

Prose narrative has been accorded an important place in the secondary school curriculum and when last audited by research was shown to make up almost half of the kind of writing undertaken in English lessons (Medway, 1986, p. 32). The degree of this imbalance has been changed in the wake of the National Curriculum with its influence on range of purpose and audience for writing. However, narrative is located at the very heart of the culture, implicated not only in reflecting but also constructing social meanings through its structures and conventions. In a very real sense, subjectivities are shaped by the stories we tell ourselves and those that we watch and read. In assessing the work of older pupils, English teachers, whether consciously or unconsciously, search for a resemblance to the kind of literary narratives that they have internalized as the model for writing, without always making this explicit for the pupils who have been set the task (Sheeran and Barnes, 1991, p. 98). The result is often that girls, with their greater familiarity with a continuous prose style — that is not only the staple of their book reading, but which also permeates the style of the magazines they prefer (Millard, 1994, pp. 103–5) — write narratives that fulfil teachers' implicit criteria of competence more readily. As Margaret Meek cautioned in the epigraph used to head this chapter, stories that are written down are only one element of the influences on writing and, as I have argued previously, it is no easy matter to disentangle the different threads that weave together in the stories pupils produce. It is, however, the intention of this chapter to attempt to do this by looking in more detail at a number of stories written by a proportion of pupils in the survey in order to pinpoint some of the possible sources for their individual compositions.

The stories were collected from three of the classes of Year 7 pupils, who had been working with the student teachers involved on the nature of narrative. They therefore represented approximately a third of the initial participating schools. These pupils were asked to spend one 40 minute lesson writing the beginning of a story suitable for someone of their own age. The method of analysis which drew on the semiotics of narrative was adapted from Roland Barthes' *S/Z* (1974).

Barthes' Method of Narrative Analysis

The theorist who has most successfully systematized the method of decomposing the constituents of narrative is the French post-structuralist, Barthes, whose clearest demonstration of this way of working is the dazzling *S/Z* (1974). In this analytical study, Barthes employs a step-by-step method to 'decompose' the elements of Balzac's classic realist text, *Sarrasine* and by slowing down the reading process and subdividing the full narrative into textual fragments of meaning, which he has called 'lexia', has demonstrated how the fictional world described is made up of a network of overlapping, culturally determined codes. He characterizes the five codes, which he identified like this:

> . . . each code is one of the forces that can take over the text (of which the text is the network), one of the voices out of which the text is woven. Alongside each utterance, one might say that off-stage voices can be heard: they are the codes: in the interweaving, these voices (whose origin is 'lost' in the vast perspective of the *already-written*) de-originate the utterance: the convergence of voices becomes *writing*, a stereographic space where the five codes, the five voices intersect. (Barthes, 1974, p. 21)

I have adapted Barthes' method of semiotic analysis in order to highlight important differences in the pupils' construction of stories. It is the notion of 'voices off stage', which implies that the writer brings to the text voices and influences other than those most immediately obvious to the reader, that I have found most useful in Barthes' methodology. The voices in the pupils' writing examined have made themselves heard from media other than the stories and poems encountered at home and school. The starting point for my analysis of the pupils' writing will then be the five codes that Barthes identified in his reading of Balzac's *Sarrasine* and it is therefore necessary to outline them below. I have also adapted their function to identify literary, media and cultural sources as the origins of particular lexia which appear in the children's texts.

Applying a Semic Analysis to Children's Stories

Proairetic or narrative code: The code of actions which, Barthes explains, are organized into sequences created by the artifice of reading: '*whoever reads the text amasses certain data under some generic titles for action (**stroll, murder, rendezvous**), and this title embodies the sequence*' (Barthes, 1974, p. 19). Readers have well-established expectations of such narrative sequences, Barthes gives as his examples the 'declaration of love', 'the seduction', and 'the murder', all taken from the nineteenth-century novel, describing them as a part of '*the already-read*'.

In the analysis I shall be naming the actions initiated by the pupils' stories to identify their cultural origins, as for example, those commonly found in comics, cartoons and horror stories.

Semic code: This is the code by which a character is brought to life. Authors describe certain attributes and these descriptors are linked as connotations to '*a character (or place or an object)*' and are grouped to make meaning. Barthes describes them as '*flickers of meaning*' dispersed throughout the text. A proper name acts as a magnet for these 'semes' (units of meaning) and creates in the mind of the reader certain cultural stereotypes. Barthes gives the example of Sarrasine's ugliness which, in the conventions of the classic Romance, always conveys genius (1974, p. 103).

In the analysis I shall be looking for the use of stock character and the use of names and descriptions of places from popular culture, as well as those from other more literary sources.

Hermeneutic code: This code operates around the formulation and ultimate disclosure of an enigma or mystery. It is constructed in relation to the readers' sense of coherence of particular kinds of narrative. The hermeneutic code operates by creating a mystery which the plot will resolve.

In the analysis I shall be using this code to identify plot structure and the creation of suspense. It will point to the young writer's sense of what structure they assume to be appropriate to particular kinds of narrative.

Cultural code: This is the code of knowledge, or wisdom, on which the text calls to support its ideas. The knowledge can be 'physical, physiological, medical, psychological, literary, historical' (Barthes, 1974, p. 20). It is the chief area of the '*already-written*' (p. 21). Late in *S/Z*, Barthes devotes one of his '*divagations*' (micro-essays) to describing how this body of knowledge constructs a particular world picture. It is drawn from the 'Book of Life', an anonymous text which resembles a school manual, composed of a series of topics.

In the analysis I shall be using this code to identify areas of knowledge or ideas about the worlds they choose to create, which the young writers have culled from their reading.

Symbolic code: Barthes associates this code with antithesis, the substitution of one thing for another and the play of opposites such as 'young and old', 'life and death', 'male and female'.

In the analysis I shall use this code to identify the writer's sense of the literariness of the story. It is 'par excellence' the code associated with imagery and therefore of more literary production.

Applying a Semic Analysis to Pupils' Writing

Without attempting to imitate Barthes' wide-ranging critical method in detail, I have used the idea of a 'step-by-step' criticism, adapting it to uncover some of the elements common to the writing of the pupils in the survey and using the data collected together to draw out differences in the encoding processes of the girls and boys in the group. Then, as well as individual analysis, I have used the codes to quantify aspects of the whole sample's structuration of their stories. Because Barthes' full method is a slow and time-consuming one I have limited the fuller analysis, with commentary, to five contrasting texts. However, I have also used the coding given to the other stories to facilitate some comparison of the general differences in boys' and girls' writing without adding an extended commentary on them. In order to code the stories, the first step was to divide them into lexia, or units of reading. This process, as in Barthes' model, is a fairly arbitrary one, where a lexia is identified as carrying a particular strand of meaning. It can vary from a single word, usually a name of a person or place, to an extended piece of description.

The pupils who provided the stories analysed in this selection were given the following instructions: *Write the opening of a story. Choose the genre which would appeal to someone like your self. Introduce the main character and give some hint of what will happen next.* All three of the first year of secondary classes involved had been studying genre as part of their regular work in English lessons that term so they had discussed the range of possible plots, characters and settings appropriate to different kinds of narrative. They

Table 23: *Pupils' choice of written story genres*

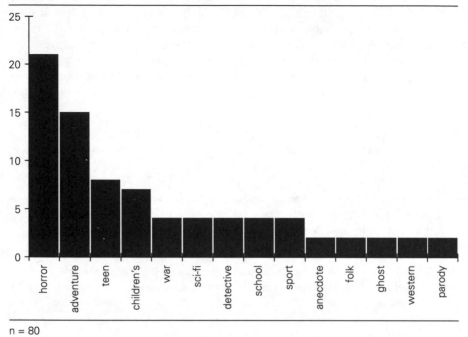

n = 80

were given a single lesson of approximately 40 minutes to complete their story. I analysed eighty stories in total, forty written by girls and forty by boys.

My first responses to the stories that I collected from the sample was one of disappointment. Few of them showed the narrative flair and understanding of different genre that I had initially expected to find. The options open to me were to repeat the research with different groups of children from the survey after more detailed task setting or to make use of the texts as they had been presented. I chose the latter course, arguing that the additional instructions given to the classes might be very different in each case. Further, I had wanted to find out what the 11 year olds knew already about narrative structure from their early experiences of reading at home and in school. The major themes selected by the pupils centred round those of adventure or horror, although the plotting in many of the stories held few of the dramatic changes that might be expected from these genres.

Pupils' Choice of Genre for Writing Stories

The full range of the genres chosen are shown in Table 23. Horror and adventures were by far the most imitated genres — repeating the evidence I had recorded earlier when analysing their reading — followed by a group I have categorized as 'teenage' stories. In this latter category I have included all the

Table 24: Comparison of the genres chosen for writing stories

Genre	Boys' choice	Girls' choice
Horror	7	14
Adventure	9	6
Teen Fiction	0	8
Children's Story	2	5
War	4	0
Sci-fi	3	0
Detective	3	1
Sport	4	0
Anecdote/Recount	2	0
School	2	2
Folk	0	2
Ghost	0	2
Western	2	0
Parody	2	0
Totals	40	40

pupils' stories that raised social issues or dealt with the kinds of school-based problems most frequently found in the books chosen by teachers for the age group, such as bullying or gang conflict. Although it was the third most popular overall genre, it is one that was selected by none of them as can be seen from the next chart. 'Children's fiction' was used to designate those stories that appeared to be aimed at a younger audience, or which dealt with similar problems to the previous category, but with an animal or fantasy creature as the main character.

Again, this was a genre more popular with the girls than the boys, though some boys chose to write humorously in this genre. One boy wrote about focusing on a monster called 'Spotty', which was clearly derived from the media phenomenon, Mr Blobby, currently popular as a younger children's toy and a motif on toddler accessories. In contrast, a girl's story, based on children's magic narrative, conveyed a very sophisticated sense of narrative technique as if this were a genre with which she was thoroughly familiar. The differences found in the genres chosen by boys and girls are represented in Table 24.

The boys were wider ranging in their choice of subject matter and genre, a fact reflected in the range of reference they imported into their texts such as knowledge of guns, scientific specifications or the rules of football. However, it was also the case that the models for their writing were more often non-literary and drew both action and characterization from film or television models. This is reflected in the choice of named characters, such as *Robocop*, *Alien* and *Rocky*, and titles such as *The Loudness of the Sheep*, a parody of a popular film. Their stories, therefore, provide additional support for the theory advanced in the preceding chapter, that boys draw more frequently on a familiarity with visual and oral forms of narrative than on the print-based models which inform the work of the girls.

In an analysis of the developmental stages in children's reading, Appleyard

Table 25: *Comparison of the central characters used in the stories*

Main character	Boys' choice	Girls' choice
Boy	24	2
Girl	1	30
Man	13	2
Woman	0	2
Animal	2	2
Family	0	2
Totals	40	40

(1991) suggests that this age group is most concerned with the development of the subjective self. This involves a search for involvement and identification with the characters in the stories they read. Readers, he argues, look beyond childhood heroes and villains who are caught up in the struggle between good and evil, towards more psychologically complex stories which develop an understanding of how people think and feel (Appleyard, 1991, pp. 89–90). If this is the general case, then it is most often girls who have begun to make the first steps on this developmental path, whereas boys' narratives are still predominantly based on mythical and fantasy figures, such as *Robocop* and *Batman*. Appleyard also comments that gender roles shape the choice of the central character with boys preferring 'stories of male heroes in adventure and mystery and girls stories about female characters in home and school setting' (1991, p. 91).

Pupils' Choice of Characters for Their Stories

The next strand of the analysis which makes use of Barthes' **semic** code, (code of character) supports Appleyard's findings that girls prefer stories about girls and boys about boys. Of the forty stories written by girls, thirty had a girl as the central character, with thirteen of these girls presented in the first person. In comparison, twenty-five of the boys' stories had boys as central characters, with thirteen of them constructed as first person narratives, a further thirteen featured adult males in roles as diverse as a ship's captain or an astronaut. Only two of the girls had written stories that featured an adult female as the main character, one of whom was a witch, the other victim of a murder. (See Table 25.) Table 26 shows that the gender preferences are even more marked in the choice of the secondary characters who were featured in the stories either as a partner or as opponents. Girls' stories that described groups of young people engaged in activities together, divided the groups almost equally into boy and girl companions. Where adults were featured in girls' stories, they were usually included as part of the family — except for four adult males who comprised the threatening figures in four of the stories, for example, a mother's boyfriend, or 'uncle', behaving suspiciously. The boys' stories tended to feature larger groups of males and were often concerned with conflict between groups

Table 26: Comparison of subsidiary characters used in the stories

Secondary character	Boys' choice	Girls' choice
Group of friends of same sex	12	4
Boy	3	9
Girl	1	9
Man	12	4
Monsters	6	1
Mum	3	2
Family	0	4
Animal	1	1
Place	2	3
Other	0	3
Totals	40	40

of boys, for example, between opposing football teams, or aliens against space explorers and even cowboys against Indians. There were few girls or women at all in the boys' stories. The single girl featured as a central character in one boy's story was a parody of a romantic heroine, described as having 'breasts as big as moons' and kissing with an open mouth, but not given a name or any conversation or response. She remained a passive object of the narrator's desire so that the main character, in this instance, was identified as the male narrator. The other group of women who featured in one or two of the boys' stories were their mothers.

The encoding of character and place was, in the majority of both boys' and girls' stories, very sketchy. The choice of a name such as 'Rocky' or 'Antonia' was sufficiently detailed for most of the narrators, with one or two adding description of hair and eye colour, particularly where relationships were being set up between contrasting blond and dark lovers, a classic device of popular romance. Girls chose to give their main characters sophisticated names, familiar from magazine romances, such as Antonia, Natalie, Daniella; boys opted for more down to earth, no-nonsense names, such as Ben, Joe, John and Dave, for their characters. Settings were created by the mention of one or two stereotypical features. For example, one story evoked Cornwall by the mention of cliffs and another used the word 'manor' to suggest a haunted house, the setting for a horror story. Domestic settings were left implicit in the accounts of getting up and having breakfast, which many writers recounted before the main action began.

The Encoding of Actions

A more significant difference between the genders was the tendency of boys' narratives to involve conflict, whether this consisted of fighting monsters or defeating the opposition at football. This I have clearly identified through the analysis of the encoding of actions. Table 27 compares the major actions set in motion by the stories. Where a story involved more than one complete action, each element of note was counted. Propp's *Morphology of the Folktale*

Table 27: Comparison of the main actions in the stories

Main action	Boys' choice	Girls' choice
To journey	12	12
To attack (including make war)	12	1
To be threatened	1	18
To explore	6	4
To get up and go to school	6	6
To meet a member of opposite sex	1	5
To make a discovery	2	8
To win	3	0
To get revenge	0	2
To murder	5	0
To be murdered	0	2
Totals	48	5

(1968) provides a helpful guide in distinguishing actions appropriate to the central character (or hero). His suggestions include stories where the hero:

- is forbidden to do something
- is sent to resolve a lack
- acquires a magic object
- fights the villain
- is injured
- is pursued
- is married and ascends the throne (in modern terms, gains promotion)

In order to encode the stories written by the pupils, I identified actions that were closely related to these, for example 'to be threatened' has a similar narrative function as Propp's 'to be pursued'.

Both boys and girls use the narrative device of being sent on a journey; to propel their characters into another world, to create the setting for a story or the opportunity for a change of circumstances. Girls' stories, however, were more likely to include a threat to their central character — 'is pursued' or 'is injured' — whereas the boys' characters, though placed in danger, were more often involved in 'fighting the villain' or 'resolving a lack' whether the enemy is a dinosaur, alien or gangster-villain. Put simply, boys show their male characters as the perpetrators of violence, girls create their protagonists more often as the sufferers or victims of actions and thus pattern out a classic division that has defined gender difference through their active and passive roles. The girls' stories, however, included a greater number of actions, the result of a greater complexity of some of their plotting.

Comparison of the Plotting Devices Used

Next I analysed the stories in terms of their plot and structures, dividing them into stories which had **simple**, **complex**, or, **confused** plots, with the further

Table 28:   Comparison of the plotting devices in the stories

Plot	Boys' stories	Girls' stories
Simple	25	27
Complex	2	8
Recount	3	3
Confused	10	2
Totals	40	40

addition of a category called 'recount'. I used the term **confused** for plotting where no single action was described effectively and **recount** where the actions were a simple description of everyday events in the first person with no indication of a complication, threat, or mystery, even when constructed in an imaginary setting. 'Recount' is the term most commonly used by genre theorists to designate one of the earliest forms of children's narrative (Martin, 1989). See Table 28 for the comparison.

Some of the boys' texts appeared confused when the writers attempted to involve complex plotting because they opted to use quick moving dialogue instead of true narration. That is, they frequently adopted a mode more appropriate to a tele-visual rather than a textual form of narrative. Girls' complex texts used more literary supporting detail with individualized descriptions of character and place.

Analysis of Five Stories

In order to illustrate these differences more fully I shall now analyse five of the story openings in detail, two written by girls, three written by boys, to identify features that were repeated throughout the sample. (The stories can be found transcribed in full in Appendix B, pp. 186–9.) I have used italics for the pupils' text which I have broken up by my critique set out in conventional print. The codes are designated by the abbreviations used by Barthes:

ACT   code of actions
SEM   code of character and place
SYM   code that sets up symbolic fields e.g., antithesis
HER   code of mystery — the plot
REF   cultural codes, source of references

Story One: The Rainbow Man

HER: The title introduces an enigma. Who is the Rainbow Man and what role will he play in the story? It is an enigma common to children's stories and nursery rhyme, where a name is allowed to suggest a mysterious being, such as Captain Hook, Rumplestiltskin, or the Pied Piper.

We were all much younger when this happened, around the age of nine or so
ACT: To remember, to look back in time, and mark the change from childhood to adolescence, to be the narrator.

But something happened which would change our lives forever.
HER: Repetition of the enigma, a sense of something about to happen.

My name's Alicia, my two friends Anastasia and Grainne
SEM: Sophisticated names, the names of girls likely to have adventures. Such generic names are considered by young writers sufficient in detail to establish the characters.

were about to have the adventure of our lives:
HER: Anticipation of something about to happen, marking the structure of the plot complication.
ACT: To have an adventure, the very essence of children's fiction narrative conventions whose apotheosis is found in Enid Blyton's *Famous Five* and *Secret Seven* series.

We lived around the area of Wimblethwaite. Wimblethwaite was a nice quiet area,
SEM: Establishing place, the first syllable 'Wimble' is familiar from the home of tennis and the story book characters the Wombles, who have made it a likely place for adventure.
REF: Thwaite a northern suffix denoting place and establishing the down-to-earth ordinariness of the location.
SYM: An antithesis is being set up between the ordinary and extraordinary, a classic literary device.

that was, before the Rainbow Man came.
HER: Repeats the first enigma; who or what is the Rainbow Man?
REF: Cultural codes suggests origin in children's stories, television and comics for younger children *The Rainbow*.

Rainbow man, the name still makes me shudder with glee.
SEM: Mystery character, creates both anticipation of pleasure, 'glee', and some fear, 'shudder', the semes that build up character are used to create suspense. As Barthes notes of Sarrasine, 'the character and the discourse are each other's accomplices' (1974, p. 178). Here the build up of response to the character creates an expectation of the plot.
SYM: Contrast with ordinariness, connotations of magic which can bring both rewards and disappointment.

I was in the park, it had been an unusual day
SYM: Once more the antithesis (a classic literary device) is being established between the ordinary and extraordinary as a pivot on which the story turns.

I mean its not everyday you get new clothes and a rise in pocket money is it?
SEM: A fortunate girl, the sort of person who will be given extraordinary opportunities and offered magic.

We were walking round the park and there was a warm pleasing air around the usually drab place. It felt like lemonade bubbling on your tongue and flowers in a summer meadow. We went up to our gang hut, the windmill. As we approached the windmill the feeling got nicer and nicer as if the windmill was the source.
SYM: Extraordinary pleasure prepares for pleasant surprise, the symbolic code draws on literary conventions to create atmosphere in the pathetic fallacy that puts nature in harmony with human action — another classic narrative device.

We went inside and crouched in the corner was an old man. There were lights of all colours coming from his fingers and he was clothed in a robe that shone and sparkled with every shade and haze of colour ever.
SEM: Establishing the character, mysterious origins, magic powers that appear benign.
REF: Role of old men as magicians or sages in stories, often more benign than old women who are crones, and witches.

We walked up to him to try to communicate. We said hello and he sort of grunted. Grainne suggested we should try to gain his confidence. So we went everyday and slowly but surely we gained his confidence and he spoke to us. We couldn't find out his name though. So to us he was always Rainbow man.
HER: The mystery of the name. A classic literary device found in folk tales, *Rumplestiltskin,* and in early literature as in *Sir Gawain and the Greene Knight.* A secret name brings suggestions of magic powers from another world. Knowledge of a name confers power over the other.

But one day something strange happened. Wimblethwaite became as drab as it had always been. Something was wrong but only the three of us noticed. We rushed to the windmill.
ACT: A reversal, a problem to be solved, the three rush to the rescue. This marks the classic turning point of a story where a problem is created in order to be solved.
REF: The structure of fairy tales, from the book of fiction.
SYM: Contrast of ordinary and extraordinary worlds, fact and fiction.

The Rainbow Man was curled up and his coat was fading fast, he looked weak and pale. His voice was croaky so we could only just make out what he said, My name, used only once or twice in my whole life, you must find my name . . . Then he was asleep.
SEM: Magic powers that can fade.
ACT: Start of quest, signalled through the appearance of a 'lack' which requires restitution to complete the tale.

REF: The quest, the classic command given to a character in a fairy or folk tale to solve a riddle or find a secret name.

Comment

This story is constructed with a fair degree of narrative complexity, using a flash back technique to establish a happening in the past. The semic code which builds up both the place and the character derives from fairy stories or children's adventure stories with magic elements like those of Nesbitt or Lewis. There is a consistent symbolic web at work, weaving contrasts between the everyday world of Wimblethwaite and the magic powers of the mysterious stranger, which create a symbolic underpinning to the story. A narrative voice has been established and well sustained. The writer of the story has familiarity with conventional methods of creating a written narrative text and, although the story is a simple one, deploys them well.

In the next story, chosen as a contrast, David also creates an alternative world but in a very different manner.

Story Two: The Time Warp

HER: The title suggests a particular kind of science fiction story which will propel its characters into future or past worlds — the question is, what kind of world will this be?

I got up and I felt rubbish. I had my breakfast and got a wash and went to school. When I got to school our teacher had some bad news for us.
ACT: To recount. The story starts as a simple chronological series of every-day events in the first person. Graves (1983) has described stories which begin in this way and end on the narrator going to bed as 'bed to bed' narratives. It is a favourite opening of the younger writer and a characteristic of a 're-count' rather than a true narrative where a chronological series of events is given without necessarily including elements of cause and effect, the *sine qua non* of plotting.

We all had to sit on the carpet and listen. Mrs Carling said, 'I have some very bad news if we don't raise a million pounds in four days our school will be shut down.'
HER: Problem raised: how to find money?
REF: Adventure stories where groups of children save grown-ups or institutions.
ACT: The first stage in creating an adventure — announcement of a lack, something to seek.

Then our teacher sent me and Simon and Nick and Bill
SEM: 'Regular' names establish the characters as 'regular' guys and a group of friends.

to the loft to find some old pictures but then I saw a flashing piece of glass. It was flashing we looked at us. It said, 'come, come, come in the time wars. So I pushed my foot through, it vanished so then we all jumped in. We were in front of a computer.
HER: Mystery, encoded through technological device of a computer, sound and sight create another dimension as in a filmed narrative.
ACT: To travel in time, start of an adventure.

We looked at it all different times came up on the screen. It said, 2022. We pressed the button, then we vanished
ACT: To travel in time, to explore.
REF: Technology, transformation at the push of a button rather than magic.

We were in a big city. We looked in the sky there was cars flying in the air. It was unbelievable. We walked into the information house:
REF: The book of the future, technological advance, the stuff of comics.

It said:

> No cigs
> No sex
> No drugs
> No swearing
> No Alcohol

REF: Future world, repressive regime, the common theme of comic books such as *Judge Dredd* and science fantasy.

We couldn't believe it.
HER: Unknown world.
SEM: Naïve participants; those to whom adventures happen.

Then the police surrounded us with electric truncheons, they zapped them at us and we fainted.
ACT: Violent attack, the hero is injured.
HER: How will they survive, escape, get back to school, find the money, now?

Comment

The story mainly draws its characters and actions from cartoon and comic representations. All the actions occur rapidly with little descriptive detail and it is left on a cliff-hanger, just as a serial cartoon might encode its plot to keep the readers buying or watching. The action is all important and the effect is one of a series of storyboard frames rather than of continuous prose. The young writer's lack of sophistication in creating a written story is embodied in the use of the 'getting up' device as an opening, which again is one of the earliest narrative conventions that appear in pupils' stories.

The next example is a story that deals with teenage problems, created by family relationships. Its plotting is based on the *Point Horror* genre, where a teenage girl is left alone in a disquieting situation. It is a device also frequently employed in horror movies. Amy exploits the genre to explore problems created by changes in the adult partnerships that affect her home life. Sarland (1991, pp. 63–78) has argued strongly that popular fiction provides a source of cultural information relevant to the adolescent age group and that the horror genre in particular is able to deal with aspects of social disquiet unavailable in more mainstream writing. The plots of the *Point Horror* stories, in particular, embody that 'which has been silenced, made invisible, covered over and made absent'. Sarland further suggests that sex and death are the key aspects of this genre. Amy's text deals with sexual tension and the relationship of the adolescent to her parent's introduction of a new partner in just such a covert way, beginning with the title.

Story Three: Brotherly Love

SYM: The title sets up the paradox on which the story is built, that of the uncle, lover. Love and brother act as opposites suggesting a guilty love and incest (classically, for example, in *Hamlet*), though the narrator and the central character seek to conceal this.

As Ellen walked towards the bright red door through which she passed everyday, she was aware of a faint sound. It sounded like screaming and seemed to be coming from the rusting letterbox flapping in the wind.
SYM: Antithesis, a bright door on the outside and rusty box leading inwards. As in most horror tales the outer treat has become located within the home. The device is a literary one using physical description to create atmosphere and mood. It is similar to the use of descriptive detail in the first story (although there the mood created was of harmony and mystery), and such writing appears to be influenced by the writers' reading. Although film uses establishing shots in just this fashion, young writers rarely draw on film's descriptive potential as they do on that of fiction. Film has other means at its disposal, frequently marrying sound and image.

Ellen felt a shiver up her spine.
HER: The heroine's sense of foreboding foreshadows some horror yet to be revealed — a classic gothic narrative device which marks out the heroine.

SEM: Sensitivity, the sign of the heroine, a seme important in the construction of the horror story, parodied, for example, in Austen's Catherine Moreland.
REF: The book of horror — a terrified female victim.

She was a normal girl with soft and flowing blonde hair, piercing blue eyes. Nothing extraordinary ever happened to her.
SYM: A classic romantic heroine (or horror victim) in that her 'normality' encourages the reader to identify with her and gives vicarious pleasure through her blonde-ness. Emphasis on 'ordinariness' creates a bond with the 'girl' reading, facilitating this process of identification, at the same time preparing for extraordinary happening.
SYM: Antithesis of ordinary and extraordinary encodes the irony of a narrator who is preparing her heroine to undergo the unexpected — a classic literary device.

She cast the noise to the back of her mind and proceeded to unlock the door. She would be all alone in the house. Her mum was at work in the social services office and her dad had been murdered a year ago.
ACT: The intended victim ignores warnings of danger, denial of threat. This is a classic move of horror stories both written and filmed, where young women enter deserted houses or stay in on their own when every sign suggests danger.

She missed him very much. He had promised to take her to Legoland, but as in most things he had never had time, and then, it was too late.
SYM: The unreliability of men, even fathers; Ellen has no one to rely on in this world and is therefore in the classic position of heroine/victim.

He had been shot in the head while protecting his sweet shop from armed robbers, or so they said, she never could be sure, but her mum had told her not to dwell on the past so that thought was put away with the screaming noise.
HER: This raises in the readers' mind the question: who is responsible for the father's death? Does the scream serve the same narrative function as the ghost of Hamlet's father, alerting the main character to something 'rotten' in her family's affairs.

Just then the phone rang, she dumped her bags by the stairs and lifted the receiver to her ears.
ACT: The victim is called to the phone — another device familiar from the horror genre.
SYM: The telephone represents the penetration of the outer (threatening) world into the home.

'Hi,' said the voice on the end of the line, 'It's David, is your mum home yet?' he asked. David was Ellen's uncle and also her mum's new boyfriend. Ellen did not think very much of David, he was very mysterious. But he was her

dad's brother and if that's who her mum wanted to go out with, then who was she to complain.
HER: Mysterious character, possible source of threat.
SYM: Disturbed family relationships, the cause of tragic action, in the plot of the family romance.

'No she isn't, sorry,' she replied and slammed the phone down. She picked up her bag and went into the dining room where she covered the dining table with books and paper. She clearly had stacks of homework.
ACT: The heroine (victim) continues with routine tasks, the signal for something threatening to occur as, for example, in Hitchcock's *Psycho* when the heroine (victim) takes a shower, an act which now always carries with it the threat created by this classic film scene.

Comment

The story has all the elements present in the *Point Horror* genre: mysterious deaths, disturbed family relationships and a threat, represented here by the screaming noise. It has been set up in the classic manner of the thriller. The girl has been manoeuvred into a situation where she is alone, without protection, her father is dead and the house is empty. Tension centres on the feelings of uncertainty that surround her attitudes to her uncle, symbolized in the rusty letterbox flap and the unexplained screaming she hears. The writer makes full use of the conventions of the genre and her plot is being developed with a sense of deliberate control. The story is both complex and engaging. Few of the stories written by the boys explored family relationships with this degree of subtlety.

Here, as a contrasting example, is the manner in which the only boy to deal with a serious change in family circumstances narrates a story which involves a boy and his mother.

Story Four: Me and My Street

REF: The title suggests an anecdotal first person account or autobiography.

Rocky thought it was just another day, but it wasn't. A big surprise from his mum was just go to change his way of living. Rocky was in the bathroom getting a wash.
Rocky, come and get your tea
ACT: To start the day, a simple narrative opening.
HER: Encoding of the secret an ordinary day about to be disrupted by the out of the ordinary.

Coming mum
Rocky ran downstairs he couldn't wait for the football match tonight.

Mum: *Rocky*
Rocky: *Yes mum*
mum: *I'm going to tell you something*
Rocky: *Go on*
mum: *I'm going to have a baby*
HER: Secret revealed; the plotting is therefore shifted to the possibility of a comic account of secret being broadcast to others.

Rocky: *a what?*
mum: *a baby*
Rocky: *a baby?*
mum: *yes, a baby and I don't want you to tell anyone about this*
Rocky: *why?*
mum: *because I want it to be a surprise*
ACT: The prohibition, a secret to keep.
HER: Can Rocky keep a secret, or will he succumb like King Midas' barber and others who have revealed the secrets entrusted to them?

Knock Knock the door went it was Carl
Rocky: *Mum it's Carl I'm going*
mum: *Ok have you got your football kit?*
SEM: Rocky is the sort of boy who plays football, i.e., one of the lads.
ACT: Arrival of friend, start of adventure.

Rocky: *yes, bye*
mum: *bye*
Rocky and Carl was walking when Rocky said
ACT: To walk, to progress to another stage of the story.

Rocky: *I want you to know something and don't tell anyone.*
ACT: The secret revealed.

Comment

The writer presents his narrative as scripted dialogue without supplying any description of either the characters or the setting. This is consistent with stories that have absorbed from television or a film rather than a print medium. In this case the most likely influence is that of the soap opera, which is part of the regular viewing of a large number of both boys and girls in the survey. Character and place are both implicit in the dialogue. It is implied that the kind of person who says 'this kind of thing' lives in 'that kind of place' and so the semic elements of the text are very limited. There is little opportunity to build up a symbolic field of antithesis, and the use of hermeneutic code is very simple, in that the plotting does not conceal the secret but reveals it instantly.

The influence of visual narrative with its reliance on metonymy is also obvious in the next example which is presented as a series of connected episodes of dialogue. The characters are taken from a stereotyped 'cops and robbers' scenario and the main character from a science fiction version of this genre.

Story Five: Robocop 4

SEM: The story and its eponymous central character take their identity from a film person, part of the 'already-seen'. In particular the use of the numeral places the writing firmly within the film genre.

This is the News headline and yes, there is another Robocop out but this time it's even better
HER: A problem to be solved — how to deal with Robocop.
REF: News bulletin, a visual rather than written form of news presentation.
SEM: Robocop, character in popular film the name creates character, an implacable opponent, uncrushable enemy.

'Louis I need back up'
'Murphy hold it there he is'
SEM: Criminals denoted by their stereotypical film or comic book names. Murphy, an Irish-American, Louis, a criminal type — from the book of gangsters.

Dead or alive you are coming with me
ACT: Escalation of the conflict signified by capitalization of speech.
SEM: Capital letters used to indicate words of the robot policeman.
REF: The Robocop's words are familiar from westerns, where the sheriff calls out the gunman in single duel and indeed this is the genre most similar to this science fiction 'shoot 'em up'.

Dream on tin head BANG My arm aargghhhh
SEM: 'Tin-head' — the Robocop — the image and language are taken directly from the films of this name.
REF: A comic book response.

'Book him' 'why?' 'He's a cop killer.'
Crime in progress
ACT: Robbery
REF: Change of scene, as created in film narrative, by a direction rather than narration.

Hey what are you doing in there, mister?
Gimme all your money before I blow your brains to bits.
SEM: Criminals, identified by their threatening dialogue.

Comment

The story is more detailed and has more vitality than the action of the previous example, however, the plot is very difficult to follow because of the rapid changes of time and place. It is stories written in this manner that I have categorized as 'confused' to indicate my difficulty as a reader in recreating the intended sequence of the story (see Table 28). I found that ten boys' stories, a quarter of those collected, fitted this category. In marked contrast, none of the girls' stories were of this kind; on the contrary, of the girls' narratives eight of them could be categorized as complex narratives, involving a series of actions not necessarily in simple chronological order, but which had coherence for the reader, as in the case of *Brotherly Love* (story Number Three).

No boy's story met this criterion. *Time Travel*, for example, involves a switch from a school scene to a future world, but this is achieved by simple chronology and change from one scene to the next, in contrast to the structure of *The Rainbow Man*, which signals its flash backs and changes of fortune through the narration. Even when girls wrote much less complex narratives, they often used a narrative tone that showed an awareness of how 'voice' works within the text. Boys' narratives left many details of the story, including the narrator, implicit. It is as if the young male writer is observing a scene passing before his eyes and transcribing on paper only what has been heard, so that the reader is expected to reconstruct the events in the same way.

The greater facility found in some of the girls' writing offers support to the evidence gathered from the questionnaires, which suggests that girls have a greater familiarity with continuous prose narrative style, and this enables them to write with greater facility and in a style that is preferred by their English teachers. Having taken account of these differences, however, it is important also to note that the kinds of narratives the girls use as implicit sources are also in most cases quite limited in their own way and reflect a narrow range of human experience. Girls' fictions often neglect a wider social perspective by focusing on domestic and personal experience, a charge often levelled by those who despise them as the novels of Jane Austen. Boys' stories draw on a larger set of cultural experiences including those located largely outside of literature. It is also worth noting that the differences in performance, although significant, are not enormous; each group would benefit from the experience of and exposure to more challenging readings as a sustaining form for their own writing.

Using More Literary Genres for Writing

The influence of a more conscious 'literary' model than the ones drawn upon in the previous examples, for which pupils had been given a free choice of subject matter, can be seen in the story that follows. This was collected for a previous work, in which I examined the effect of reading on writing (see Millard, 1994, p. 86). The starting point for this story, which was written in the first month of secondary school by a Year 7 boy, was a reading of Ted Hughes' *How the Whale Became* and a discussion of the role of mythological explanations for natural phenomena. The pupils had then been asked to write a story that offered their own mythical explanation of one aspect of the natural world:

Why the Polar Bear is Pure White

When God created the animals he created the polar bear first.

'My first animal shall be the greatest of them all, therefore he shall have the brightest colours,' God said. He placed him carefully on the earth and set him off on his way. Five days later (when all the animals had been made) the polar bear saw how brightly coloured he was, compared to all the others. He stuck his nose up in the air and turned around as he said,

'I am not staying around with all of you lot. You're all too common and short of colours, whereas I'm bright and brilliant!' and with that he walked away. All of the other animals were shocked and annoyed at this, so the lion, the leader of them all decided to have a meeting.

'We are gathered here to discuss what to do about the polar bear,' the lion said.

'He's *so* stuck-up!' squawked the parrot, and all the other animals agreed.

'I suggest,' continued the lion, 'that we play some kind of trick on him for his selfishness, but what shall we do?'

There was a short pause and then the monkey said, 'I've got it, we'll hide behind a rock with sheet over us and then jump out at him, making horrible noises, that should scare him silly' and the animals agreed that was what they'd do. So in the morning, as the polar bear was taking his morning walk admiring himself by the river, they all jumped out at him. The polar bear was so frightened, that he froze in shock and went totally white. God had seen all of this and called out with a boom,

'Polar bear you have been so snobby, selfish, immature and such a show-off, for that reason your punishment will be to be totally white for ever.'

And that is why the polar bear is white to this day.

(Reproduced from Millard, 1994, p. 87)

A far less able boy, who was being given special help with his reading, produced the following version of a creation myth which also reproduces some of the style and tone of the original:

The Elephant

One cold morning God made an elephant and when the weather was hot he called an elephant with big ears. He told the elephants to wave his ears to cool him down. And God was pleased with Himself.

(Reproduced from Millard, 1994, p. 85)

These two stories provide evidence that the young writers' experience of the Ted Hughes' story acts as the sustaining form behind the creation of a new narrative. The writing of the first story achieves its effects so cleverly that it may appear to have been copied. In fact it is the style, rather than the content, that has been imitated and made the writer's own. Hughes' version of the polar bear story has the bear, proud of her white coat, voluntarily banishing herself to the northern snow to avoid the dirt. The Year 7 boy's story reverses the process using 'whiteness' as the animals' punishment for pride, symbolically associating the lack of colour with deprivation, rather than the conventional connotations of purity or racial supremacy. The writer has also firmly understood the role of rhetoric in establishing leadership and managing the masses and incorporated this into the lion's speech. The story has the simple moralizing conclusion appropriate to that of an animal fable and is altogether perfectly realized.

The two stories above have been reproduced to illustrate the manner in which more explicitly literary tasks for pupils help to create better supportive frames for writing. What I am arguing overall is that because imaginative writing is frequently expected from pupils without the 'ground rules' of what is wanted having been sufficiently well explained to them (Sheeran and Barnes, 1991, p. 84), boys are placed at a disadvantage because, as my data reveal, their models for narrative composition are less literary than those of the girls. Not only this, but the range of characters boys use in their writing, though broader than those favoured by girls, are presented with a lack of empathy for the opposite sex and their feelings. Boys' understanding is focused on action and the factual information provided by the texts they read or the narratives they watch. Girls, on the other hand, develop more sophisticated understandings of psychological aspects of character, and employ more literary devices such as antithesis, suspense and descriptive evocation of atmosphere and mood — a facility that has greater relevance to the later stages of the English curriculum and its examinations, whose focus is most often on these aspects of narrative rather than action or factual detail.

In the next chapter I return to a theoretical discussion of the constructed nature of the gender differences that I found in the pupils' attitudes towards both the reading and writing of narrative, in order to relate this to their differential access to literacy. I shall also make suggestions of what the possible outcome of these differences might mean in terms of both individual development and success in school work.

Section 3

Analysis and Recommendations

Chapter 7

Making Connections from Theory to Practice

> We forget that to be literate is a uniquely human experience, a creative process that enables us to deal with ourselves and to better understand one another. (Taylor and Dorsey-Gaines, 1988)

The concluding section of this book brings together the hitherto separate strands of the theoretical enquiries and the fieldwork to draw some conclusions about the effect of children's narrative and other reading interests on their literacy development. It focuses particularly on ways in which the gender differences identified interact with the range of experiences brought from home. The research, reported in Chapters 3, 4, 5 and 6, has provided strong evidence to support a prior perception that boys' and girls' orientation towards work in language — that is their attitudes to reading and writing — becomes increasingly divergent as they enter the secondary phase of education. This chapter relates the data from the surveys, interviews and textual analyses, reported in the second section of the book, to the theoretical issues raised in the first section. These include:

- The historical role of narrative in the teaching of literacy
- The influence of visual literacy
- Literacy and the new technologies
- Boys' disadvantage in the current language curriculum
- The nature of gendered difference and feminist research
- Masculinity and narrative choice
- The teacher's role
- Literature and literacy

The Role of Narrative in the Teaching of Literacy

The role of story in education has powerful advocates. Narrative is now widely accepted both as an academic genre and as an approach to teacher education (Meyer, 1995). In the early years of education, the influence of story has been shown to be even more powerful. Wells' Bristol study (1987) identified the reading of stories by parents to their pre-school children as the key factor in the creation of difference in academic achievement between social groups. Few social class differences were found in the way parents engaged their children in talk, but those children whose parents had regularly read stories to them at home managed the transition to school literacy far more successfully than those whose parents did not (Wells, 1987, pp. 143–5). Wells devotes a whole chapter to arguing the case for 'storying' (1986, pp. 193–213) and it is important in a study that has taken a critical view of primary teachers' preoccupation with narrative to reiterate his findings that the sharing of pleasurable early literacy experiences around books is vitally important in giving children an early start in learning to read.

There are incontrovertible arguments to support the desire for teachers and parents to introduce young children to the richest array of stories we can provide in all stages of reading, and schools should provide book-rich environments where both children and parents have access to the best of both the old and the new in children's fiction. A story shared with an adult is an ideal literacy event because it creates a situation in which learners come into contact with the linguistic structures of written language and are enabled to enter into discussion of disembedded experience. However, we need also to remind ourselves that part of the correlation between stories at home and success at school is, as Heath (1983) has shown, attributable to the school's implicit assumption that story will play the key role in literacy development and that the development of language skills follows from a love of, and familiarity with, books.

It can be argued, on the other hand, that the advantage of the children whose parents read to them and are seen to want to read themselves is not because of the power of narrative per se, but because reading story books to children ensures their early exposure to written language and its most common genres. Other forms of written language can also be shown to be influential in creating the openness to learning that is essential in an age of continuing education and lifelong learning. Reading stories may not be everyone's choice of pleasurable activity but reading itself is deeply embedded in the educational process of all social groups.

Clark's (1976) study of young fluent readers revealed that they were omnivorous in their interest in print, particularly the boys in her study who dipped into bus timetables and articles in the *Financial Times*. More recent studies of children's ability to develop phonological awareness have shown that early exposure to rhymes teaches the sounds and patterning of the language (Goswami and Bryant, 1990). It is important that strategies for developing competence with print in the first stages of learning move beyond storying alone to encompass a wider range of other genres. It is more important that those charged with the development of readers in the later stages of primary school should look to the many other forms of the written language if children are to become competent in 'reading the world', rather than 'decoding texts' and rushing through reading schemes to 'get off them'.

The evidence, therefore, acknowledges the powerful influence that the telling, reading and encoding of stories has at all ages. Narrative is a genre of such power that it has always been chosen as a favoured medium by the most influential teachers and prophets. It was banned from his ideal republic by Plato, in *The Republic*, arguably the most famous philosopher of all, simply because of its seductive pull. Stories carry within them the history of a culture's imagination and feeling and therefore should form an essential element of any language curriculum. But, it is equally important to understand that narrative is currently available in many other media forms, many of which are more easily assimilated than print. Daily soap operas invite young people to be spectators of other people's lives, which appear to them more psychologically true and immediately relevant to their own interests than the experiences of characters in the books that are frequently chosen for them in school. Video-recorded dramas supply the thrill associated with mystery, horror and suspense; video games, with their increasing sophistication of image, sound and interactive control, invite young players in to action-packed adventures, where they may assume the role of charismatic warrior, hero or sage. The value placed on books and written narratives recorded in the comments of writers and educationalists in Chapter 5 reflect a central concern of English teaching. My argument is, rather, that it is important to understand the more limited role that narrative fiction in book form now plays in the everyday lives of many pupils. All forms of media compete for pupils' attention in the home and it is only the most committed readers who spend more than a fleeting half hour with their books or magazines.

The problem is not that the books currently published for the young are no longer worth reading — in fact there exists a wealth of established fiction for the age group that has powerful uses in the classroom — but that teachers can no longer rely on children engaging in independent reading outside school for sufficient periods of time to ensure that they become flexible and intelligent in their responses to texts. The evidence both from previous studies and the data obtained in this survey suggest that reliance on reading in the home, will leave many unmotivated — and this is particularly the case with adolescent boys.

Only one of the boys, whom I interviewed, could be described from his own account as a 'heavy reader', that is, someone who spends a part of each day reading and had encountered a wide range of books, compared with sixteen (13 per cent) of the girls. Similarly sixty-two boys reported reading only occasionally (46.2 per cent) compared with twenty-seven girls (22 per cent). Such findings lead to the conclusion that schools need to be far more proactive in assessing their pupils' reading interests and providing time for reading in school. Previous studies have demonstrated that schools can make a difference to pupils' interest in reading (Whitehead *et al.*, 1977: West, 1986; Ofsted, 1993; Millard, 1994) and this is an issue I shall re-examine in the final chapter, Chapter 8, when discussing the teacher's role in promoting reading.

The influence of school reading policy is not in most cases, however, as great as might be imagined and in any case is not as important as the effect of the home (Bardsley, 1991). This study has also demonstrated the continuing influence of the home in confirming attitudes to reading. It is important that home interests are built upon and that parents are encouraged to promote reading in the home long after the early stages of learning to decode texts. It is insufficient to depend on the delights of reading to hook children on books without adult modelling or informed intervention in which parents and teachers make time to discuss the books their children are reading with them.

The Influence of Visual Literacy on Narrative Preference

The main point to be taken from the identification of the range of children's interests in other media forms, as recorded in the questionnaires, is that pleasure in narrative now has many more outlets than can be enclosed between the covers of a book. For example, it is exactly a hundred years since the invention of cinematography and a whole new language of narrative has evolved from this medium. Cinema has spread to other forms of media its ways of thinking about narrative. Recently on the Radio 4 *Today* programme, 5 and 6-year-olds were interviewed about their responses to the re-showings of children's television programmes that were, popular in the 60s and 70s, such as *Bill and Ben* and *The Magic Roundabout*, which featured animation and puppets. Their universal response was that the programmes were 'boring' because they lacked 'action' in comparison with the cartoon entertainment with which they were more familiar. It was also 'action' that recurred as a *leitmotif* in many boys' descriptions of what most interested them in their choice of books and film narratives. Their understanding of 'action' has been conceptualized through the pervasive influence of a visual medium whose common name, 'movie', acts as its defining term.

Walter Benjamin (1973) best described the powerful dynamism of the medium in his essay, *The Work of Art in the Age of Mechanical Reproduction*, in which he describes film as 'bursting asunder' locked worlds 'by the dynamite of the tenth of a second, so that now in the midst of the ruins and far-flung debris, we calmly and adventurously go travelling' (p. 238). He further suggests that the camera has introduced film audiences to 'unconscious optics' in the way that psychoanalysis revealed our secret impulses (p. 239). Those children who have known visual media from their earliest days are sophisticated consumers of the movement of filmed narrative and 'action' is their favourite term of approval in describing what they enjoy most in their favourite books.

Benjamin's early analysis of the reception of filmed narrative, therefore, can provide a useful way of understanding the positioning of learners in relation to narrative texts. Benjamin describes the watching of film as 'reception in a state of distraction', suggesting it has a profound effect on apperception because no directed attention is demanded of the viewer. To assimilate visual narrative does not require the same focused attention as the reading of a book or responding to other classic art forms (Benjamin, 1973, p. 243). It is this quality in film, and by extension video, that makes the medium a more attractive leisure pursuit than books and why, ultimately, the reliance on independent reading in leisure time as a strategy for creating flexible readers requires a major re-examination.

Contemporary picture books for children, now widely used in the early stages of reading, also make their appeal to the sophistication of the eye and children's early stories play with postmodern narrative form in a way that is not available in most linear realist narratives aimed at the older reader (Hunt and Plackett, 1986; Meek, 1988; Stephens and Watson, 1994). Children in the first stages of secondary school, therefore, who are asked to switch to longer fiction from other forms often find the books provided dull and banal.

Literacy and the New Technologies

The survey also revealed the increasing influence of another competitor for children's narrative pleasures. For, just as the cinema and television transformed fictional narration for our generation, computer technology has brought a shift in literacy as radical in its effect in the latter years of the twentieth century as the invention of the printing press was on that of the Renaissance. However, despite teachers' and parents' fears that computers would afford simply another distraction from the influence of books, the evidence from these interviews suggests that pupils' engagement with computer technology facilitates and motivates literacy rather than displaces reading.

At the beginning of the research my intention in collecting information about the amount of time that pupils spent on personal computers had, as its motivation, the idea that time spent on the computer distracted from the real business of becoming literate. Literacy was a process that I associated only with immersion in books. As the enquiry progressed I changed my opinion of the computer's distracting influence, and even modified my view of the role of computer games, as negative competitors with literacy activities. This was because I found that working with personal computers not only often involved on-screen reading activities, but that it also engaged young players in a secondary reading of complex texts in order to update their hardware or to progress onto higher levels of difficult games.

National surveys have recorded that four out of every ten households own a computer (TES, 1995 'Computers Update', October 20, p. 3). This survey found that computers were made available to an even larger proportion of this particular age group, suggesting that many adults buy computers for children rather than for themselves. Of the girls, 66.2 per cent had access to computers, whereas 85.9 per cent of the boys used them regularly. This is an average of 76 per cent of the total sample; more than seven out of ten pupils. Those who do not have good access to, or regular use of a computer are therefore likely to find themselves at a disadvantage in a world where messages and information are increasingly relayed and accessed electronically. It also points to a widening generation gap in the growth of a new literacy.

Already the interaction of modems and CD ROMs with computers allows more fortunate pupils to download a wide range of text and images to supplement their school work. The technology that makes such access more available to the general public is gradually being provided in parts of the public library system. Cuts to library funding, however, puts this at risk and current research suggests that a minority of children make adequate use of the existing library provision (Roehampton Children's Literature Research Centre, 1994, pp. 53, 60).

The important analogy to draw from Benjamin's (1973) analysis of changes to apperception attendant on cinematography is of the changes that are being created to perception and habits of reading by the increasingly pervasive influence of computer texts. These are accessed differently with different conventions of organization, such as images, icons, windows. They are more fragmentary and less stable; screens change and writing becomes provisional. Computer software means that many kinds of texts such as graphs, images and spreadsheets can be available at any one time (Tweddle, 1992). These characteristics alter both the speed of reading and the attention span of the reader. Computers promote speed but also enable more detailed analysis of units of text. It is an area of learning that requires detailed monitoring as access to computers increases and the gap widens between those who are computer literate and those who are not.

Boys' Disadvantage in the Literacy Curriculum

The main use of the data from the research has been to illustrate boys' comparative disadvantage in the current school literacy curriculum, which is heavily dependent on the reading and writing of fiction. Further, I have shown how boys' reading interests may often go unacknowledged by their teachers; the result is a lack of interest that contributes to their comparative failure in the English examinations at GCSE and beyond. However, it may be argued equally strongly that the modes of literacy in which girls currently out-perform boys are dated ones, or, put less extremely, they provide ways of understanding texts that have fewer practical applications than the kinds of literate practices now more frequently engaged in by boys (Steedman, 1982; White, 1990; Swann, 1992; Tweddle and Moore, 1994).

Success in school English examinations, therefore, may not correlate significantly with continuing success in adult life, although the role of English examinations as a gate-keeping device by both academic institutions and employers means that inequalities in current performance between boys and girls merit the most urgent attention by curriculum planners and educational theorists. The unexamined and repeated cultural practices associated with the use of specific kinds of narrative in the classroom allow too little room for those who have not become 'hooked on books' in the early stages to gain success in reading. Largely ignored in schools are the possibilities for wider learning created by the new realm of 'on-line' literacy.

However, it is also true that children are in touch with the rapid changes attendant on technology in a much more direct way than most of the adults who teach them, or support their learning at home. This brand new version of the generation gap is likely to widen — at least in the near future. It is therefore important that English teaching puts effort into being and staying 'in touch'. This can be done by making use of the new technologies to expand opportunities for talking, reading and writing. This is no simple sop to rebelliousness, nor should it encourage intellectual laziness, as is the common assumption of the attacks on 'media studies' as an examination topic. It involves keeping up what has always been central to English teaching: the ability to make use of the pupils' current social interests by helping them to make connections between their lived experience and other modes of thought and expression. The use of popular culture as media for analysis makes these connections possible, and does not mean that other forms of cultural study, such as works of pre-twentieth century literature, are no longer valued by teachers.

It is important, however, for teachers to acknowledge the plural, and often contradictory, worlds of the home, the community and the classroom in order to ensure equal access for all to the most powerful genres of our culture. It would be easy, therefore, to conclude, as some politicians already have, that the teaching of the English language requires a more skill-based approach. There are stronger counter-arguments. At the secondary level, more than in any other subject, English is the site where pupils are challenged to make their own meanings and develop a critical attitude to their work while encountering issues that are most directly relevant to their lives. A focus on individual response and personal growth has an important function in education and the substitution of a basic or functional literacy would be an impoverishment and narrowing of the range of experiences available. There are still important connections to be made between 'lived experience, the world of the imagination and encounters with the riches of literature' (Harrison, 1994, p. 36). What it is essential to take away from the evidence of current pupils' reading interests is that it is within the classroom that these encounters will largely take place.

The Nature of Gendered Difference and the Contribution of Feminist Research

The data have shown, firstly, that there have been general changes in children's reading habits precipitated by greater independent access to other media, and secondly, that there are marked differences in access to literacy that are directly related to gender. It is a finding that has been noted previously, both in relation to independent reading (Whitehead *et al.*, 1977, APU, 1989), and positive attitudes to writing (APU, 1987b), and has more recently been shown to affect the differential academic achievement of boys and girls (Ofsted, 1993). What has not been examined in any detail before is the manner in which the social positioning of the genders in relationship to their books and their view of themselves as readers may specifically influence this difference. I have sought, therefore, to demonstrate how differences in the construction of the reading subject are related to the development of literacy both at home and in school as well as society at large.

Previous studies of gender have focused attention on the ways in which girls are at a social disadvantage in school, in terms of both their access to the most powerful forms of social discourse, and of their ability to secure a comfortable space in which to operate within institutions. It is not my intention to undermine the important work that has been done by feminist research in highlighting differences in access to teacher time, classroom space or examination subject choice. What I want specifically to challenge from inside the existing framework of gender differences is the habit of thinking in terms of binary oppositions of disadvantaged girls and dominant boys, a misleading direction that has blinded curriculum theorists to disadvantage in educational achievement of large groups of boys.

Schools have always required that pupils read and reproduce certain kinds of texts and although the class implications of the privileging of certain forms of 'cultural capital' (Bourdieu, 1990) have been well discussed, the role of gender has been more frequently related to social organization of groups or to the subject content of books, rather than the positioning of the learner within the practices of literacy in school and the community. The tendency has been for feminists, who initiated the discussion of gendered difference, to emphasize girls' lack of access to the more powerful genres of society, and to draw attention to the absence of women's lives and histories from academic forms of discourse, such as science and history. The main feminist objective of the late 1970s and 1980s in education was to challenge contemporary restrictive sex roles that were identified as hindering women's access to wider occupational and intellectual aspirations. Projects were designed to redress the perceived imbalances. The achievement of this generation of feminists is well summed up by Bordo (1990):

> They cleared a space, described a new territory, which radically altered the male-normative terms of discussion about reality and experience; they forced recognition of the difference gender makes. (p. 137)

Feminists working in education often began with an implicit assumption that if girls could be helped to succeed in areas that were traditionally the preserves of boys and men then the cause of equality was being well served. This has worked well, for example, in the addressing of girls' motivation in mathematics (Walden and Walkerdine, 1985) and in initiatives to get girls and women interested in a wider range of technologically based career options or management roles (Kelly, Whyte and Smail, 1981, 1984; Whyte, 1985).

In the English classroom, teachers informed by feminist debates have often focused their attention on the role of women in society, linking to this a search for literature that might better represent women's experience. For older pupils, writers such as Angela Carter, Margaret Atwood, Alice Walker and Amy Tan have been incorporated into examination reading lists. This has been accompanied by a search for positive female characters in the books recommended to younger readers and a whole rich rewriting of traditional stories has ensued, beginning with Williams' *The Practical Princess* (1979). Feminists, myself included, were specifically interested in the education of girls and women and hoped to transform their female pupils' lives both by promoting women's writing and by the analysis of our own lived experience. Coward (1985) typifies this phase well when, in the collection of essays, *Female Desires*, she explains:

> . . . my fieldwork has been on myself and on my friends and family; whom I have submitted to incessant interrogation about their personal lives, their hopes and dreams. Quite deliberately these essays aim at no more than understanding how the representations directed at women mesh with our actual lives. (p. 15)

Far less attention has been given to the shaping of the discourses of masculinity; the assumption being that because the roles socially assigned to boys convey privilege and status they were to be envied and emulated rather than contested and changed. Indeed, when I raise the question of the neglect of boys' reading tastes with teachers I am often countered by the argument that such tastes offer a damaging representation of masculinity and that boys benefit from 'more sensitive' treatment of relationships in books.

Sex role theory has been a useful tool in staging feminist change when theorists were working to make sense of the problem of the gender inequalities that denied women influence in the political and social management of their culture. It has created a discourse about gender that allows for the exploration of difference and challenges assumptions about 'common human nature'. It has, however, often neglected one important fact, pointed out as long ago as 1946 by the anthropologist, Mead, in the Jacob Gimbel lectures in Sex Psychology at Stanford University:

> Throughout history the more complex activities have been defined and redefined, now as male, now as female, now as neither, sometimes as drawing equally on the gifts of both sexes, sometimes drawing differentially on both . . . Once a complex activity is defined as belonging to one sex, the entrance of the other sex into it is made difficult and compromising. (Mead, 1949, p. 374)

Later she adds, 'No human gift is strong enough to flower fully in a person who is threatened with loss of sex membership.' We do not have to accept her later suggestions under the guise of 'to both their own', which argues for a limitation to women's career aspirations in the interests of child rearing, to acknowledge the importance of creating a double focus on gender issues. The important point made is that socially constructed genders affect and limit both sexes and an imbalance in defining one in terms of the other — the trap of simple binary opposition — creates a blindness to difference that is ultimately self-defeating.

Feminism has been less helpful until quite recently in identifying difference in what has often been taken to be a **hegemonic masculinity**. For, as I discussed in Chapter 1, the use of sex role theory is too static and deterministic to account for ways in which individuals negotiate a sense of self within particular settings. In terms of masculinity, men have often been judged to occupy a single power position, that of the patriarchal oppressor, even in the nursery (Clarricoates, 1978). Yet if one turns attention to earlier ethnographic studies of young men, particularly working-class boys, it is important to identify the processes of demarcation at work in establishing complex differences in the varieties of masculinity which are made available to them in school (Willis, 1977; Connell, 1989; Mac An Ghaill, 1994). The division between boys who constitute themselves as successful in school (Willis' 'ear'oles'; Connell's 'swots' and Mac An Ghaill's 'academic achievers' and 'new enterprisers') and those who set themselves up in opposition to its institutions (Willis' 'the lads'; Connell's 'cool guys'; Mac An Ghaill's 'macho lads', with their 'fighting, football and fucking', p. 56) became less a question of intellectual ability than one of masculinity. Willis found that in working-class communities achieving in schools was seen to be 'effeminate' whereas opposition to authority and poor learning were seen as an induction into a man's world of labour. The patterning of masculine behaviour, described by Willis, has also been described in Connell's Australian studies of schooling and masculinity (1987, 1989), where the 'cool guys' willingly court trouble:

> Up against authority structure, acts of resistance or defiance mean 'getting into trouble' . . . actions are constantly defined in relation to institutional power. Fights with other boys, arguments with teachers, theft, poor learning, conflicts with parents, are all essentially the same. (1988, p. 294)

Connell further shows that rather than this anti-school orientation of the 'cool guys' creating an alliance between the majority of girls and the 'academic' boys — both of whom are motivated to cooperate with teachers — the 'wimpish' boys find it even more important to distinguish themselves as 'not women'. Mac An Ghaill's (1994) recent study of the way in which school constitutes a 'masculizing agency' (pp. 1–14) takes this analysis further by describing the ways in which the young working-class men he studied are in the process of 'appropriating and re-defining conventional female areas of work in supermarkets, video shops and fast food restaurants' (p. 73).

These are moves used to recreate sexual divisions of labour in order to avoid any of the experiences or attitudes that have been socially constructed as feminine. Willis (1977), Connell (1989) and Mac An Ghaill (1994) have described this 'de-feminization' process as a continuing practice of older adolescent male subcultures. It is also important to understand how the rejection of a 'feminine' self in boys can be seen at work much earlier on. Phillips (1993) describes how, when he starts school, a boy is induced to abandon 'all love of beautiful colours and textures if he is to become one of the boys'. She adds:

> One mother told me, rather sadly: 'He loves pretty things but he knows they are not for him. He sublimates his own desire to dress up and takes a great interest in what I wear. The other day I watched him brushing his sister's hair. He clearly enjoyed the feeling as well as the look of it, but for a boy, pretty is what you look at, not what you are.' (p. 58)

She further suggests that it is only little boys who may be treated for psychological problems using behavioural therapy if they are considered to be behaving inappropriately for their gender role.

If there are to be genuine opportunities within society for both boys and girls to express aspects of personality freely, it is the controlling mechanisms of masculinity that require deconstructing, for currently too many paths are barred to young men simply because the option deemed to be effeminate, whereas a girl with an enthusiastic interest in male pursuits may find barriers to overcome but these will not usually include the disabling derision of her own sex.

Masculinity and Narrative Choice

The data from the research which relate to perceptions of reading at home and in the wider community reveal that it is constituted, 'par excellence', as an activity which is managed by, and seen as appropriate to, women. Mothers were identified by the pupils as more often involved in the support of early reading in the home, and mothers and sisters, and occasionally grandmothers, were named as the members of the family who read most. Boys and girls had consistently different tastes in the narrative genres they selected across the full range of media, for example in books, magazines, television and computer games. Further, the kinds of fiction chosen for study in school, by and large, found more favour with girls than boys, even where the main character of the story was male. Differences of taste were shown to exist in their choice of theme and topic for writing, as well as in the choice of fiction. Although it is no longer the practice to divide school or public library fiction for this age range into separate areas demarcated as girls' books and boys' books, there is no doubt that these categories exist in pupils' minds and that the imagined categories shape pupils' orientation to what is offered to them in English lessons.

The Australian theorist, Alan Luke, has named the habitual reinforcement of the differences in reading taste as a 'sexual division of literacy' (1994, pp. 361–81) but, arguing from an adopted 'feminist' perspective, identifies the major problem for education as the exclusion of women from the registers of science and technology and in particular from the 'new' technologies (p. 371). Here, Luke describes girls' entry into literacy as a 'double displacement' as girls not only enter language as a system of masculine representation, but also learn gender-specific ways of reading, talking and making sense of texts.

In the interviews and observations that I made following on from the questionnaire, it was certainly the case that boys and girls not only chose different kinds of fiction but they were oriented to receive the same books in different ways. Boys read with an eye to finding out new information, even from their fiction; girls enjoyed the dissection of relationships. The binary division of gender differences, of course, depends heavily on the perceptions associated with sexual difference and, just as ambiguities in sexual orientation are poorly tolerated in society, so too, gendered differences within the school context begin to polarize rapidly, obliging children to identify with the practices associated with their peer gender group. Current examination results at 16+ suggest that, because of educational initiatives to redress an imbalance, girls have made up differences in the study of mathematics, science and technology; it is the boys who are currently at a disadvantage in school. One of the difficulties is that 'reading' per se is associated with fiction and a literary response, so that other kinds of reading do 'not count' in school towards the process of becoming literate.

Moreover, as certain literacy activities seen at an earlier stage as gender neutral, for example enjoying story, become far less acceptable for boys, it increases the opportunities for differences in attitude and attainment to be consolidated. A focus on the role of girls and women in society — with an accompanying emphasis on positive female representation in literature, the examination of sexism and the more active promotion of women's interests — can be counter-productive in relationship to the needs for changes in masculinity.

One way of promoting more positive attitudes to the reading curriculum would be to shift emphasis in the early stages by encouraging reading beyond fiction towards other applications of literacy, including technological ones. It is an area in which girls currently gain less experience outside school and a medium in which boys obviously delight. Yet at another level of analysis, which takes in to consideration the wider educational process, problems of masculinity can be seen to involve a failure to deal with personal relationships or feelings effectively, just those aspects of education that are interrogated by the current emphasis on literature. If, since the 1970s, girls have more confidently moved into areas of experience commonly seen as the preserve of boys, there has been very little movement in the opposite direction. For some, the ultimate aim of society is a move towards a transcendence of the male/female dualism, whereby the difference of sex should be forgotten (Thorne, 1993, p. 159); and to some extent this has been a theme of aspects of English teaching. It has been done by a denial of those aspects of femininity that have been seen to disadvantage girls: the model of womanhood presented in schools has been directed towards the masculine pole of achievement in science and technology and the world of business. The suppression of difference in gender, as in race, is not what is really at stake. Progress depends rather on an equity of access to all areas of literacy, a position which may require intervention on behalf of marginalized or disadvantaged groups.

Positive action to compensate for the neglected narrative interests of boys and the likely influence of this on their weaker performance in English would mean that teachers would need to make some changes to the fiction chosen for classroom study. This would involve supplementing the choice of predominantly authentic realist texts to include narratives which emphasized action and plot rather than 'knowledge of the human heart'. I am of course arguing for an injection of fantasy and adventure into the texts chosen for class study so that a wider range of genres become identified as appropriate to English lessons. Some space might be afforded to works of popular fiction such as 'blood and thunder' stories, with their powerful images of masculinity that were so roundly condemned as 'rubbish' by previous generations of teachers and which have been described recently as stories 'of and for the boys' (*Observer Review*, 13 August 1995, p. 14).

The point of their inclusion would be to show how masculinity is constructed by the narratives, rather than a simple acceptance of the 'heroic' image. Perhaps publishers have reached the same conclusion, for Oxford University Press have produced a new range of old popular fiction, which includes Zane Grey's *Riders of the Purple Sage* and Edgar Wallace's *The Four Just Men*. The heroes of the powerful myths and legends that have sustained literature and whose fragments litter the narratives of the comics, cartoons, and video games as well as the stories of the great adventurers, are rich sources of images of masculinity, ripe for deconstruction. A model for approaching texts productively is provided by the use of folk and fairy tales by feminists like Angela Carter and Marina Warner (Warner, 1994). A critical reading of these genres will enable a discussion of masculinity and its limitations as it did of the 'feminine mystique' in the 1970s.

In terms of the findings of this research it is important that classes are presented at times with images of masculinity that do not involve being defeated by the bully, as in *The Eighteenth Emergency* (Byars, 1974). The important move is to see that the reading process can also be something other than the satisfaction of deep psychological needs: a way of learning to make meaning through critically deconstructing popular and stereotypical images.

The Teacher's Role

A further implication from the responses to school reading recorded in the survey is that the teaching of literacy needs to widen in scope in the middle years so that the development of critical habits of reading are not left to chance or to a matter of unguided individual choice. If both the reading of fiction and other forms of creative literature are to be properly valued, they require both careful selection and careful presentation to classes. Although much learning is often best served when pupils are allowed to become wholly involved in their own learning, through engagement with their individual interests (Harrison, 1994, p. 32), it is also the case that new doors need to be opened, new ways of interpreting explored. There is a need for informed teacher intervention at all stages of development, but particularly in the middle years of schooling when tastes are beginning to be formed more concretely and prejudices set in.

This survey and other comparable studies (White, 1990; Millard, 1994; Benton, 1995) have revealed the limitations of range provided by a reading curriculum based on pupils' private choice: it produces a limited range of genre that reinforces attitudes, rather than widens experience. Gender adds an important dimension to this concern as, left to their own devices, both sexes reinforce, rather than question, gender role through the reading they choose, although it is also important to take on board the possibility of resistant readings described in analyses of responses to romance stories (Moss, 1991; Brindley, 1994).

Daniel Pennac (1994), French teacher and writer, described his own approach to what he perceived as the lack of motivation in baccalaureate students studying the classics of French literature. He made a useful distinction between giving learners the knowledge whereby they can make sensible choices in their reading and an adult insistence that all pupils should read certain texts and write reports on what they have read. He suggests that teachers should share books they have enjoyed themselves with their classes and through the power of performance draw pupils into understanding their pleasures. In the following quotation he describes such a teacher at work:

> . . . this teacher was not inculcating a knowledge of something, he was offering up what he knew. He was less a teacher than a master troubadour — one of those jugglers with words who used to haunt the hostelries of the road to Compostela, and sang chronicles of heroic exploits to the illiterate pilgrims. His voice, like that of the troubadour, would address itself to *those who didn't know how to read.* He got eyes open, lit lanterns, got his entourage to set off on the literary trail, on a pilgrimage without destination or certainties, the walk of one man towards another. (1994, p. 89)

Pennac also makes the important point that learners must not see themselves as rejected by reading (1994, p. 152). His teacher-as-inspiring-reader is a romantic, some may say impractical, view, but there is need for a specific teacher input on 'pleasure'. Teachers in the later years of primary school now report spending less time on story as they are under pressure from the National Curriculum (Benton, 1995). It is also a more certain process in choosing books that the teacher has enjoyed than to attempt to select books to please a whole class. In promoting their own favourites, however, teachers need to be aware of the gendered nature of their own tastes and seek to balance them by using other readers. More men need to be seen engaged in reading in school from the earliest years to avoid the perpetuation of the perception of reading as a woman's pursuit. Time has to be given to reading and fiercely protected if it is to be valued and not left, as the time-filler in an over-crowded curriculum.

Teachers also need to question their selection of books for class reading, particularly in terms of ensuring progress and the development of more sophisticated responses to the books used. The research uncovered a tendency for similar kinds of books to be chosen repeatedly for class consumption at Key Stages 2 and 3. For example, it was common to find in Year 7 classes, pupils who had read the texts that had been chosen for their first year in the secondary school while at the junior school. Teachers also need to develop an awareness of different ways of approaching texts other than writing studies of the characters and giving accounts of plots which seek to match the stories chosen with concerns of young people's lives. The tendency is to choose what is read as a class text to reflect directly adolescent experience, focusing on issues surrounding friendship and bullying, for example, or discord between children and their parents. This survey has shown, by an analysis of pupils' unrestrained choice, that the books they most commonly choose themselves feature issues related to later stages of development than the one they are currently experiencing. It is therefore essential that all manner of texts are read more critically and opportunities provided for debating taste and understanding differences than searching for an assumed common interest.

Secondly, choice of fiction is important in motivating interest, but this motivation is not served by limiting what is read to mirror the needs of a single interest group or by directly challenging popular taste. This can be shown by the mixed reception of books such as *The Turbulent Term of Tyke Tyler*, promoted as presenting alternative views of femininity (Millard, 1985; Brindley, 1994). The wide range of pupils' personal interests also make it unlikely that any one piece of fiction can engage every single pupil's personal interest. What well-chosen books can do is challenge understanding, stimulate debate and sharpen critical awareness. In order for this to happen, teachers themselves need to be more aware of the full range of literature available, and this is particularly important at the end of the junior school where tastes are beginning to take a final form: there has been a tendency created by the heavy demands of National Curriculum programmes of study in other subjects to select certain books merely because they fit neatly into a theme or topic studied in other areas of the curriculum.

Rather than attempt to choose a single text that is culturally acceptable to all the class, teachers need to be aware of the wider range of narrative that it is possible to study and create opportunities for different kinds of writing to be read critically. It is possible to read even the most intransigent of texts with a new focus. I am thinking, for example, of a group of Year 8 pupils who examined *The Hobbit* as a 'sexist' text; analysing and categorizing the limited roles given to women in the story. These activities were informed by an understanding of what it is to 'read the world' and are neither based on a theory of individual growth, nor a belief in the ability of books 'per se' to change lives — although both positions have contributed much that is good in the teaching of English. Rather it endorses Jameson's (1981) view of narrative as a 'socially symbolic act' whose meaning is produced by the ways it is read. This view emphasizes the importance of collaborative reading of texts to question widely held assumptions and raise differences of opinion.

Literature and Literacy

One argument I have pursued within this theoretical framework has concerned the focus on narrative as a major tool of literacy development. The teaching of literature remains a central issue for English teachers (West, 1994, pp. 129–32) but there needs to be an accompanying understanding in schools that literacy is a broader category than is contained within the literary frame in which we have become accustomed to place it. I have agreed with West (1986) that to a large extent literature can be defined as 'what gets taught in schools and universities', and have sought to demonstrate in the analysis of the curriculum in Chapter 3 the historical processes through which particular versions of literature have come to dominate the reading curriculum. It is important that what is chosen for inclusion in English schemes of work is more authentically inclusive of the interests of the full range of pupils but equally important that they are offered a chance to extend their current reading habits and interests. West's study showed emphatically that teachers and schools make a real difference to the production of readers.

Many of the student teachers I involved in the project suggested that they had come into teaching because they loved literature themselves and had experienced first hand the pleasures of textual engagement. Initially, they took it as given that their pupils would already be readers and would want to continue to read. Their research work helped them to understand more clearly the interests and current reading practices of their pupils, which they could use as more productive starting points for planning schemes of work.

Home Influence and the Modelling of Reading

The data from the questionnaires strongly indicated that girls are provided with more positive roles from family and friends for their self-image as readers.

Boys reported far less interaction with fiction amongst themselves, their family and their friends. The growing body of evidence that has emphasized the importance of home experiences of reading and writing has generally focused on the early years of schooling (Heath, 1983; Wells, 1987; Hannon, 1994).

A large national survey, sponsored by the Ministry of Education in Australia of 5,000 students between the ages of 5–14, has shown, however, that there are still positive gains to be had in the later years. Although the research found that older children did not spend a great deal of time in shared reading experiences involving oral reading, those who engaged in discussion with other members of the family about personal reading exhibited better attitudes to reading and more positive teacher rating of attentiveness in class (Rowe, 1991, pp. 19–35). My data, though based on a small sample, support this Australian evidence and suggests that more information is needed about the literacy events experienced at home in the later years. Girls have described many more opportunities to talk about their reading with others and for their inclusion therefore in an active reading community. On those occasions where boys were shown to want to share reading, as in the exchange of computer or football magazines, they reported being given less positive support from school to build these networks.

Related to the technical focus of some boys' reading, data which showed boys' and girls' different attitudes towards, and uses of computers, also suggest that it has become increasingly important to ask how the acquisition of personal computing systems has further influenced the modelling of literacy in the home. In the final chapter I shall identify aspects of the data that merit more detailed research while suggesting some ways in which teachers have begun to develop their approach to the extension of all pupils' literacy.

Chapter 8

From Research to Practice: A Concluding Summary with Suggestions for the Organization of Work in the Classroom

In the final chapter of this book, I want to consider some practical lessons that can be derived from the evidence provided by the young readers I interviewed. In particular, I intend to suggest that there are two interconnecting frameworks within which to consider the ways in which teachers may work to change the literacy practices of their own classroom. The first of these is shaped by the current structure and classroom practices of the English or language curriculum. I shall suggest ways in which an over-emphasis on narrative, particularly fictional narrative, in the teaching of reading may be restructured to meet the developmental needs of both boys and girls. The second framework is the one constructed by the wider compass of the whole curriculum, which is taken to include an increasing range of educational practices attendant on the spread of the new technologies. The latter, I shall further suggest, make it imperative that schools re-examine current literacy practices in order to ensure greater access to a full range of experiences for all learners.

Redressing Imbalances

The first stage, then, is to consider how boys' and girls' reading interests may be more equally provided for within the current organization of their reading and writing time. Previous initiatives to redress gender imbalances in school subjects have been able to achieve significant changes in pupils' perceptions of themselves as competent learners. I am thinking in particular of the work of Walkerdine and Walden in the 1980s which drew teachers' attention to inequalities inscribed in the practice of mathematics teaching and encouraged the development of 'girl friendly' programmes of study (Walden and Walkerdine, 1985). Current evidence suggests that in most areas of the curriculum, up to the age of 16+, girls are well able to hold their own, if not surpass their male peers. Now the major cause for concern is schools' realization that boys are falling behind, particularly in the language curriculum. One possible reason for this, is that boys are not sufficiently engaged in the reading process, thereby missing out on an essential element of learning. My first suggestions, then, concern ways of adapting the current approach to reading in ways that are more 'boy friendly', without losing sight of practices that have enabled girls to succeed. Most of the following recommendations are aimed at promoting whole classes' range and motivation in reading, on the basis that boys will be prompted to take more interest in a topic that is given a high profile in the curriculum and where success is openly rewarded (West, 1986). There are some specific activities suggested, however, which draw on other kinds of reading identified by the research as of particular interest to large groups of boys. It will be up to the teacher to decide whether these are to be specifically targeted at boys in the class or shared with girls.

The quantitative data collected in this, and other recent larger surveys, indicate that there has been a significant shift in reading habits since the last adequately funded national survey (Whitehead *et al.*, 1975). It is important, therefore, that a detailed survey of children's current literacy practices is undertaken to identify areas for the focus of specific national development. Such a study would also need to take cognizance of the difference between pupils' reading as accessed by means of questionnaires and conventional school reading records, which rely on pupils recording titles of book and magazine, and the actual amount and range of reading uncovered through individual interview or structured classroom observation. There has been some replication of Whitehead's work by a team of researchers at Nottingham University who employed his methodology of focusing of a single month's reading in a large sample of 11–14-year-olds. The resulting interim report concluded that there had been little decline in the amount children read. These results, however, remain inconclusive because the research does not distinguish clearly between the number of titles recorded and the time spent reading them. The evidence from the very much smaller survey I have reported in Chapters 3 and 4 of this book, suggests that pupils do not always discriminate between having read a book and having accessed a narrative by means of another form such as an audio cassette or video recording.

Schools need to recognize that a decline in sustained reading in leisure time is a feature of modern culture, equally applicable to the parents as to their adolescent children. This means that it cannot be assumed that pupils will encounter sufficient experience of continuous prose through reading at home. The Nottingham survey, and the work of Benton (1995), who concentrated his survey on the reading interests of 12–13-year-old pupils, corroborate my own findings, that the range of children's private reading has shrunk, with a concentration in the middle years on popular authors such as Roald Dahl or on series fiction, which make limited demands on understanding. If we continue to argue that stories carry within them the history of a particular culture and create a cross-hatching of cultural reference which depends on sustaining a reading of narrative, then we also need to acknowledge that most children need help in accessing more complex texts. Not only do children's individual preferences ignore large areas of reading, but the disparity between homes where book reading is encouraged and those where it rarely features increases pupils' inequality in access to a schooled literacy. Difference in exposure to reading increases with age, dropping off most heavily between the ages of 11–14. Junior schools, therefore, have a major role to play in ensuring that pupils have been introduced to a wide range of genres and formats as part of the experience of reading in school. Pupils' choice of reading at ages 8–11 requires the most careful monitoring so that secondary teachers are able to build on young readers' prior interests and enthusiasms.

Auditing Individual Pupils' Reading

My first recommendation for schools, then, is that teachers need to be more aware of the reading habits of the individuals who make up their classes. Although an understanding of national trends is helpful in creating a general picture, each child is making a personal construct of what it is to be a good reader. Teachers can form a complex picture of an individual's reading experience through a personal interview, informed by a reading questionnaire that allows respondents to develop a considered answer, or by means of a reading history constructed together by teacher and pupil in an interview session. I have called my questionnaire in narrative form a 'story of reading' and several schools have adapted its framework to fit their own needs. An extended model of good practice in descriptive and analytical record keeping is also provided by the developmental framework of the *Primary Language Record* handbook, developed by teachers at the centre for Language in Primary Education (CLPE). This gives clear examples of ways of structuring conferences with older children and parents (Barrs *et al.*, 1988; Barrs and Thomas, 1991).

In constructing reading histories I am suggesting that a wider range of both reading and alternative narrative interests should be accounted for. Pupils should record, in addition to the books they read, both fiction and information texts, and their interests in film, media and computer simulations and games. These details help to build a more complex picture of the influences on children's literacy development and the range of texts that they are able to draw upon to sustain their own writing.

Improving Book Provision

It is also important to keep reminding ourselves that evidence from surveys and observations have continued to endorse Whitehead's recommendation that 'schools and teachers need to devote more of their energies and resources to the encouragement and development of voluntary book reading in the 10–15 age range' (Whitehead *et al.*, 1977). There is an element of hypocrisy in the actions of the parents and teachers who decry children's lack of commitment to reading, but who then make little effort to develop their own knowledge of the changing nature of contemporary fiction. The book resources for the later years of primary education and the early years of secondary education are in need of urgent attention and few class libraries have sufficiently exciting books to enthuse children. Most departmental and library stocks need to include more of the range of books that capture boys' narrative attention as well as tapping into all pupils' interest in information about hobbies and out of school literacies. As Lankshear (1987) has powerfully demonstrated in his critical analysis of 'proper' and 'improper' literacies, schooled education has often discounted the more popular forms of culture and associated literacy practices. The ultimate result of this is the existence of a 'structured illiteracy' where the disadvantaged are always at a remove not only from the literacy of the educational process, but the knowledge that provides the means of organizing opposition, lobbying representatives and expressing political grievance over their disenfranchisement. It is therefore important to encourage forms of textual engagement in school which develop habits of critical literacy, while simultaneously making the effort to engage all young readers in reading. This cannot be done on out-dated texts which serve a limited range of interests and represent a limited range of genres. Boys, in particular, reported that they found books provided in school unappealing and out-dated.

Working with Parents

In Chapter 4, home was shown to exert a continuing influence on the development of pupils' attitudes to reading. My second point is, therefore, that schools need to secure the continuing support of parents for the promotion of interest in books and activities associated with reading. Book lists with suggestions for suitable birthday and Christmas presents would help parents choose books for their children with more confidence, and would be particularly effective if the pupils were involved in reviewing and recommending new titles. Male members of families should be specifically targeted in school initiatives to promote book buying and an interest in reading. Schools have used 'Book Weeks' to invite a range of people associated with the school to come into the library and read a favourite story. Local sportsmen, the community policeman, traffic wardens and the owner of the local shop from which children buy sweets are all worth targeting. In one initiative, organized for Sheffield's Year of Reading (1996), members of Sheffield United Football Club were invited to select books to recommend for reading in school. The players made a selection which included information texts, poetry and a range of other fictional genre, as well as football stories. These were used to create reading lists to motivate pupils to '*Read a Team*' — that is eleven books from favourite players to be read in a term.

In secondary schools, teachers of subjects other than English need to be drawn into the promotion of wider reading so that fiction can reflect other aspects of the curriculum. It is well worth schools setting aside inservice time for book selection, where possible using professional advice. Support for schools who require help in selecting from the wide range of books now available are provided by the school library. School librarians will recommend titles, draw up reading lists for both poetry and fiction and keep schools posted with details of the latest books. There are also a range of good children's book-shops who keep abreast of children's tastes as well as award winning books and provide a service for schools. Two I have used frequently are *The Children's Bookshop* in Lindley, Huddersfield run by Sonia Benster and Madeleine Lindley's *Acorn Centre* in Oldham. Both offer a postal ordering service as well as a welcome to visiting teachers on requisitioning sprees. Both offer also a wide range of book lists, specialist packs and a wealth of personal experience and expert advice. In addition there are a wide range of sites now on the Internet to direct pupils, parents and teachers to new titles through recommendations and reviews, some of them written by children.

Promoting Enthusiasm for Books

Imaginative ways of promoting reading that have been used by teachers and schools include: 'Readathons' (marathon reading stints), where children obtain sponsorship for long periods of sustained, uninterrupted reading; reading a 'team' of books, that is a selection of eleven books recommended by a local sports team, and; 'new books for old', in which parents are asked to bring in their children's out-grown books, which are then sold to raise money for new purchases. Most existing school libraries need to be ruthlessly culled to re-move out-dated volumes that are no longer relevant or which no-one cares to borrow. It is not surprising that many teachers and librarians are reluctant to throw out books when this results in empty shelves. However, the preservation of books with unappealing, dated formats and irrelevant information, only serves to discourage some pupils from library use. School libraries also need to adapt to the new technologies to encourage engagement with a wider range of literacies by providing access to CD ROMs and Network services, which address pupils' own purposes and interests. Parents of one secondary school in the survey, with a large library area not always well used, suggested the setting up of tables for role play games, surrounded by books that would build on this particular (usually male) interest. Certainly all schools should have a range of newspapers and special interest magazines for quick reference and an area of the library where talk is positively encouraged. Imposed silence was reported as being least acceptable to the boys in the survey who were always the ones to break the tranquillity of a timetabled private reading session.

Shared Reading Activities

A balance of reading that leads pupils to re-evaluate an emergent view of the world is badly served, however, by a concentration on a personal choice of

Table 29: The ten major text types identified by Lunzer and Gardner (1984), and the DARTs activities recommended as most effective for each (from Harrison, 1994)

Text Type	Suggested DARTs activities
Narrative	Underlining, labelling, diagram completion, prediction, sequencing, question generation.
Structure or mechanism	Underlining, completion, diagram completion, flowchart, sequencing.
Process	Segmenting, tabulation, flow diagram, sequencing, prediction, diagram, question generation.
Principle	Tabulation, hierarchical diagrams, completion.
Theory	Tabulation, underlining.
Problem-solution	Segmenting, labelling, completion, prediction, diagram construction.
Historical situation	Underlining, listing, flow diagram, diagram completion, prediction.
Classification	Labelling, tree diagrams, segmenting, ordering, tabulation.
Instructions	Flow diagram, tabulation, sequencing.
Theme	Listing, diagrams.

narrative fiction which goes unchallenged or developed by interaction with a teacher or interested adult. My third point is, therefore, that more attention needs to be paid to the books chosen for reading together in class. There is anecdotal evidence to suggest that in the middle years of school, teachers' choice of books has been over-influenced by the demands of projects and topics and that the secondary school curriculum has begun to be dominated by 'the classics' required by the national curriculum (Benton, 1995, p. 108). The study of a work of fiction for its own merits needs to be better promoted at an earlier stage in the English curriculum so that reflective reading approaches are well established by the end of ages 8–11. This does not mean that all children in a particular class need always to read the same book together, ignoring questions of taste as well as ability; group reading of a selection of interesting stories will serve as well as a forum for the exchange of views and the organization of DARTs activities (Directed Activities Related to Text), such as deducting the opening of a story from its ending, or sequencing a complex narrative that has been cut up to be re-organized. It has been the experience of teachers in the survey that such activities, carefully organized, provide a focus for pupils' reading and are an impetus to boys eager to solve a problem or get an answer quickly.

Working with Non-fiction

Lunzer and Gardner's (1984) DARTs approach to the development of reading, places an emphasis on interrogating non-fiction texts, extracting relevant content and restructuring what has been found for other purposes. Strategies can as easily be devised for the application of learning from non-fiction as for sharing responses to literary texts. Table 29 summarizes the kinds of activities appropriate to particular textual types and subject contents.

171

More recently the works of Littlefair (1991) and Neate (1992) have described practical ways of analysing the structures of non-fiction texts and of using them well with younger classes. Examples of DART-based approaches to non-fiction for this age group are also provided in 'Making Good use of Information' (Millard, 1994, pp. 148–71). Older pupils can also be supported in sharing interests in information by keeping a collection of articles from hobby magazines in plastic pockets, which are regularly up-dated and added to by staff. For example, those boys (and I encountered a good number of them) whose interests are dominated by football might be drawn into reading the more complex accounts of matches, transfers and players found in the Sunday broadsheets and colour magazines if these were made readily available. It is also worth having some activities that promote competition amongst groups as well as collaboration inside them.

Working with Popular Culture

Pupils also benefit from discussing the forms of popular culture that are of topical interest to them in order to understand the features that are common to their production; the romance element in the *Point Horror* series, for example. Teachers can draw pupils' attention to the ways in which different narrative structures such as quests, romance, riddle tests and rescue — the common stock of both popular and classic literature — represent different ways of gaining competence and agency in the world. The difference in boys' and girls' narrative preferences need to be openly discussed and compared so that the contrasting positions offered in their messages about gendered identity can be understood. This has been more often done in relation to images of femininity than in deconstructing images of masculinity, which have sometimes been treated as if they were unproblematic for boys.

In discussing the role of popular culture in shaping boys' views of themselves, Urquhart (1996) has suggested that:

> In classrooms where attention is paid to the equal opportunities for girls these very practices of giving girls a voice may also act as a new and challenging framework in which boys have to think about their assumptions about being a boy becoming a man. (p. 159)

She also suggests that pupils who have been given wider experiences of other fictions will be better able to 'construct multiple identities and meanings against the grain of any one narrative discourse' (p. 159). Urquhart's emphasis on providing opportunities for girls, however, needs enlarging to considering boys' narrative identities in order to allow every pupil to re-examine their prior assumptions. Pupils bring to discussions of media texts an implicit understanding of their form, narrative intention, tone and network of interconnecting meanings. Well-structured analysis of aspects of cultural representation builds upon this knowledge: for example, comics and magazines may be shown to construct a wide range of cultural representations of both old and young characters, which can be categorized and compared. Often pupils have begun to consider such issues for themselves as, for example, David, described in Chapter 3, who gave a detailed account of changes in the image of the *Beano*'s Dennis the Menace. My next suggestion then relates to an introduction of material that has direct relevance to children's interests and which builds on real, rather than imposed, textual pleasures. These help not only to create new connections from home to school literacies, but can lead on to deeper questioning of a reader's subjectivity. Mary Hilton (1996) who has made an analysis of younger children's relationships to the toy and media industry, which she describes as a 'potent' source of gender identification, warns of the dangers she perceives in ignoring their consumer appeal. She writes:

> It is by ring-fencing our children in an idealised, ungendered childish world, ignoring material which might address their growing adult gendered subjectivities, that we allow them to become bored with literacy. Classrooms rich with popular stories, narrative topic work and possibilities for play are classrooms which, through respecting desire in children, can help them both luxuriate in pleasure and eventually transform for themselves the cultural messages embedded in plastic figures. (p. 44)

Interesting ways of investigating the toy industry have been developed by Catherine Pompe and are to be found in *Language and Learning*, June 1993. Similar areas of experience can be opened up by a more eclectic approach to texts in the middle years which enable comparisons between versions of stories of mythical heroes and muscle-bound mutants, fairy princesses and pink plastic Barbies and Cindies. Charts can be made to trace lines of connection from Beowulf and Grendel to Superman and the Incredible Hulk or to compare cartoon and historical versions of Pocahontas or Robin Hood. Disney's use of animals as substitutes for humans in many film cartoon images, for example, could be compared with the roles given to the same creatures in traditional tales and fables. The movement should be from the known to the less familiar, from the popular to the more challenging or more central, cultural text.

A pedagogy which draws on a cultural analysis model, rather than one which relies heavily on notions of literary heritage (Cox, 1989), provides a choice of a wider range of texts to be studied critically in school, including film and video. Work on the latter can be fed back into a study of more literary forms. For example, an analysis of advertising media can encourage interest in literary aspects of language, through a close, detailed and analytical reading of both magazine and television texts. An identification of the effects of alliteration, punning and word play can then be extended to a reading of poetry and more literary texts, moving pupils on from the familiar to the more challenging text. Television and film adaptations may also provide a stimulus for reading more complex narratives and provide a way into books as different as Mary Norton's *The Borrowers*, Jonathan Swift's *Gulliver's Travels* and Jane Austen's *Persuasion*, all of which have been very successfully adapted for the small screen. Evidence from current reading surveys show that there is an upsurge of interest in reading books when they have been translated to the screen. Pupils can be encouraged to examine an episode from the written text in comparison with a media version to identify what has to be added or omitted in the adaptation.

Catering for Boys' Tastes

Initiatives targeted specifically at raising of boys' motivation would also include selecting more whole class activities based on their current interests by changing the balance of texts selected for class or group work to include more action and humour. It is also important to focus on the identification of facts and narrative functions as well as the analysis of feelings and character when working with books, although this area needs to be handled carefully in order to avoid slipping into a stereotyped view of what boys can achieve, or what interests them: it would be a retrograde step to destroy all opportunities for talking about feelings in school when literature offers a safe arena in which difficult issues can be raised. What I am arguing for is a balance that allows for a variety of textual encounters, rather than the dominant emphasis on authentic realist fiction or issue-based narratives often favoured by teachers when selecting for the age group. Most boys clearly had a range of interests that were not included in current school provision and their needs should be of prime importance when new books are ordered.

In 1977, Whitehead *et al.* suggested that the provision of books by the primary school could be shown to play an important part in determining what children read. My work confirms that schools still make a difference to the overall amount of reading undertaken and the motivation of individuals to see themselves positively as readers. It also provides preliminary evidence for the case that book stocks available for readers in the middle years in both junior and secondary schools are badly in need of up-dating. Existing class and school libraries need to be reviewed in terms of their appeal across the range of interests and their connection with pupils' hobbies and interests. Current book stocks have too few titles which make their appeal through plot and humour rather than in-depth character studies (such as for example Paul Jennings, *Quirky Tales* or Anthony Horowitz's *Groosham Grange*), and that works of non-fiction, or journals, are often excluded by teachers from class reading periods. It is important to encourage personal reading as an active process during the stage of transition from primary to secondary schooling. The librarian of one inner-city comprehensive school in the survey organized liaison between the English department and its feeder primary schools so that the children arriving in September had a book waiting in the library which they had ordered on a preliminary visit to the school at age 10–11. This helped to establish an early interest in the school library and its lending system.

Too little is still known about the books that children might choose for themselves given a wider and better informed personal focus. This is because books used in school are most often pre-selected through awards and prizes, and published book lists set by adult readers, who are either critics or themselves teachers. In America, children are involved in reviewing and compiling selections of the best books recommended for reading at home and in school. The initiative is supported by The Children's Book Council Inc. and published as *More Favorite Books for Kids: A Compilation of Children's Choices 1992–94*. The collation of such a publication, with reviews and opinions from the relevant age groups would be invaluable in helping focus reading policies. Currently the NATE publication, *NATE News*, offers some recommendations written by members' pupils or their own children, but these are limited and not widely seen in primary schools. For the more technologically minded, the Internet has sites where an exchange of views on popular fiction, including a wide range of sci-fi and fantasy genres, already takes place and providing access to these may draw others into more adventurous reading.

Teachers as Readers — Matching Readers to Books

Teachers need to be more proactive in promoting books that have recently interested them and which they can therefore present vividly to their classes. This implies that despite all the other demands on their time for assessment and auditing, teachers must take time to read books themselves. There are two requisites for good reading practice in schools: a wide provision of well-chosen resources and teachers who know them well and can match pupils to appropriate texts.

School librarians can contribute to this matching of child to book in the early stages of secondary school if pupils are given curriculum time to make choices and discuss their selections with both teachers and library staff. In one school the librarian had invented a small icon for the spine of fiction books to draw pupils' attention to texts of the same genre — such as a ghost shape for mysteries and a tank for war stories.

Pupils should hear excerpts from books being read to them by a wider variety of people, both on tape and in the flesh. Stories need to be read aloud to bring them to life and to capture the listeners' imagination, an aspect that is often lost in the grind of 'getting through' a class novel chapter by chapter, with an activity tacked on at the end of each. It can be more productive to whet children's appetites with glimpses of narratives which they can later follow up for themselves.

Literacy in the Whole Curriculum

My second major frame within which literacy development can take place is dependent on re-examination of the curriculum in terms of whole school learning. It is not sufficient to keep encouraging pleasure in individual and personal responses to reading to ensure a 'proper' literacy that will meet the needs of all pupils. Teachers need also to reconsider the links between their individual subjects, literacy, reading and the world outside, in order to provide more class-based activities that require active reconstruction of meaning from the written word. Evidence from this research and other projects such as Webster, Berridge and Reed (1996) suggest that too much material is mediated to pupils by teachers through worksheets and blackboard work.

Combining Fact and Fiction

Some of the teachers whose classes took part in the reading surveys described in the preceding chapters have begun to introduce projects which combine a range of fiction and non-fiction texts to allow for readings of stories that focus on questions other than those of relationships and feelings. One such initiative involved working with a collection of books about wolves, including natural history and anthropological studies, as well as myth and fables and a CD ROM, *Microsoft Dangerous Creatures*. There were also works of fiction such as Gillian Cross' *Wolf* and the humorous *There's a Wolf in My Pudding* by Henry Cecil Wilson. Pupils were asked to consider how wolves were represented in a number of works of fiction and to discuss whether these representations had basis in fact. Working from fiction to fact allows for an interest in the information content of stories to take a central role in the reading process, something which is repeatedly reported by boys as a motivation for their interest. Other teachers have turned the process about and worked from fact to fiction, as in one 11–12-year-old group's survey of venomous beasts. Factual information about snakes and poisonous spiders was used to write poetry describing the creatures, and the initial poems were developed further into images of human beings who aroused the same emotions. The development of the pupils' thinking moved from fact to imaginative response which was then further developed into symbolic and metaphoric representation.

The activities described above were planned as part of the English curriculum, however, it is even more important to identify areas where literacy can be developed in other areas of the curriculum, so that the definition of a good read or good reader can be expanded to include other abilities than that of reading large amounts of fiction. Teachers need to recognize the achievement of pupils who read well in subjects other than English and those who read to good purpose outside of school. Too often when I interviewed children about their reading it was apparent that they had formed the view that reading was a school-based activity, rather than something located in their own lives with a practical purpose. This was best exemplified by Craig, who did not recognize his ability to interpret wiring diagrams of motorbikes as reading and who had taken on his teacher's view of himself as a non-reader, struggling in class with elementary picture books. My next suggestion then is for a school audit of what we might think of as the 'products' of learning.

Managing Reading for Learning

During ages 8–14 (the middle years), pupils need more help in managing the complexities of the variety of reading required for learning and to be given more strategies for engaging with print. My observation of classes during the survey, and while managing follow-up small scale studies conducted by student teachers, have shown that the amount of time spent on making meaning from texts in other subjects of the secondary curriculum continues to be very limited, often confined to teacher prepared materials — 'them sheets' as the pupils interviewed on one occasion described them.

The work of Webster, Berridge and Reed (1996), which analysed the place of literacy in the whole curriculum, has once again revealed that children are not required often enough to read by their teachers or to make their own written meanings from the texts presented to them in schools. Too much of the literacy work observed by researchers had meaning only within a school context and was irrelevant to reading as a function of understanding the world. They reported:

> One of our observation categories is specially focused on pupils constructing their own writing, whilst another category focuses on engagement with different text forms, such as personal reading, or reading a . . . text for information . . . In 76 per cent of cases, generating or redrafting of writing was never observed. In 12.5 per cent of the cases when pupils were generating their own writing this was for less than a total of ten minutes out of a 55-minute lesson. Reading engagement was never recorded in 78 per cent of the cases, whilst in only 7.5 per cent of cases were periods of reading for more than ten minutes in total recorded. (p. 113)

These observations echo the earlier study for the Schools Council by Lunzer and Gardiner (1979) and show that provision for language development across a range of subjects is still only a theoretical model. Many primary schools have developed better ways of helping children to make sense of information, while engaging their active learning skills, than can be found in the various subject areas of the early secondary curriculum (Millard, 1994).

Providing for Technological Changes to Literacy

Literacy, as the key learning goal in all subjects particularly during the middle years (ages 8–14), would ensure that curriculum planners gave thought to the wider applications and uses of reading and writing in society, including the importance of visual literacy and electronically generated texts, which require different modes of reading than those appropriate to continuous prose narrative. Computer literacy needs to be better understood and more carefully defined for purposes of curriculum development. Further, it is essential that all schools have full access to information technology to support pupils' learning, and in this I would include teletext services such as *Ceefax* as well as interactive media on the Internet and the World Wide Web. There exists a range of areas on the World Wide Web dedicated to the needs of children, including school based communications. Indeed some children have already constructed their own individual Web sites, but as yet these are the very privileged few, and are often sustained by parental rather than school initiatives.

Information Technology (IT) is a challenging area in that as the gap between those who have easy access to computer technology and those who are denied practice and familiarity from economic disadvantage widens, it creates a whole new area of potential 'structured illiteracy'. A brief surf of family pages on the Web reinforces the view that boys have greater access to the Web than girls and that the families already involved in their own pages have predominantly academic lifestyles. Currently, boys report that they are taking greater interest in the new forms of literacy than their female peers, as shown in the data related to computer use tabled in Chapter 4. On the one hand this means that IT can be a valuable medium for motivating boys, but on the other, that girls may well be falling behind in this new form of literate behaviour unless schools ensure their equal participation at a time when their confidence is greatest. My next emphasis, then, in the literacy curriculum is for schools to be developing access to on-line literacies more rapidly, in order to prevent the exclusion of the less advantaged from a new and powerful communication tool.

One headteacher had ensured that all 10–11-year-old pupils were given access to lap-top computers, which they were able to use regularly both at home and in school. This meant that drafting, or preparing work at home for discussion in class became far more realistic options, as was the storage of new ideas accessed from a wide range of sources outside school. The class teacher reported that children with writing difficulties, more often or not boys, had benefited greatly from the support provided for composition and word checking. A particular focus in this class has been the creation of a regular school newspaper which kept parents and governors informed of major happenings. Further research is needed to find out the extent to which children have access to information technology in their homes and the uses they make of it there: currently, it is too often dismissed as a mere distraction and unproductive consumer of their leisure time. As the influence of the new technology spreads and the importance of accessing information rapidly increases, it is essential to know exactly who has access to what kinds of information and how pupils' developing competency can best be encouraged both in and outside school.

Researching the Classroom

My final recommendations concern the areas of literacy awaiting examination in greater detail by the teacher as researcher. For example, despite the wealth of material that exists to argue for the centrality of children's literature to education, there are few accounts of how older children actually develop as competent readers and how their habits have changed in relation to the new technologies. In particular, there are insufficient longitudinal studies of the habits of reading amongst older age groups. Studies such as J.R. Appleyard's *Becoming a Reader* are based on generalized perceptions about the stages in children's reading of fiction, as heavily influenced by the school reading curriculum as by accounts of individual responses. As in many critical books that discuss reading response, the reader in question is the ideal reader of the writer's own conception, a melange of all the pupils he has encountered while teaching. Current research shows clearly that the reader who responds to works of fiction is more likely to be female. What are most needed now are detailed case studies of how adolescents are shaping their reading in response to new demands on their literacy and in the company of a wide array of technological support and distraction. Teachers who monitor their pupils' progress through portfolios and interviews are well placed to add to our understanding of this area. I have, therefore, signalled aspects of developing literacy practice which I have associated with changes consequent on the new technologies. These require a planned series of further investigation, located both in the classroom and at home. It is, in fact, the influence of computer access that remains least well mapped in relation to uses of literacy beyond the early years, and is the area which has much to offer teachers who wish to understand the roots of engendered differences in the literacy practices of their pupils.

Many of the activities promoting literacy that have been recommended here, stem from current teachers' commitment to narrative fiction as a way of developing fluent reading. Although the teaching of fiction is well justified in English lessons as one way of developing a critical literacy it cannot carry the whole weight of socially significant interaction with texts. Teachers need also to reconsider the links that they enable between, literacy, reading and the whole school curriculum in order to provide more class-based activities that require active reconstruction of meaning from the written word. The evidence from current school examination results suggest girls are achieving well in the system. However, we need to be wary of concluding, therefore, that they are doing well in terms of their future learning opportunities. Too often, girls' interests are narrowly focused on producing the long established cultural forms, such as, for example, long continuous prose narratives that are less appropriate to the development of flexible responses to learning in all subjects. Schools' definitions of a good read or a good reader need to be expanded to include literacy events other than the consumption of fiction and confirm the achievement of those who read well in subjects other than English and to good purpose outside of school. Frequently, as I interviewed older pupils about their leisure interests, I was made aware that they considered reading books as something imposed on them by schools, rather than as an important part of their own lives.

The Education of New Teachers

There are implications for teacher education where knowledge about teaching reading is often confined to methods of instruction in the early years. During the middle years, pupils need to be given specific help to manage the complexities of the variety of reading required of them for learning and to be given more strategies for encouraging their engagement with print. In order to help them do this, new teachers require an understanding of the wide range of genres important to learning as well as the ways of interpreting them, and to be helped to plan schemes of work that challenge pupils to become actively involved in reconstructing meaning in both their reading and writing.

Summary

In this final chapter I have begun to consider literacy as a whole school issue, rather than focusing entirely on the needs of the boys themselves. It may appear, therefore, that I have moved a good distance from the initial findings, which concerned boys' underachievement in the literacy curriculum. In the short term, I believe it is of prime importance that teachers take steps to draw boys in to the classroom community of story book readers and writers in a proactive way, by making provision in their resources for difference in tastes and by planning classroom activities for the difference in their interests. Boys' attitudes claim our attention, not least because the result of their disaffection is being mirrored in a relative lack of progress as measured by the school examination system. However, while considering the reasons for boys' indifference to, and sometimes aversion for, the varieties of reading and writing most often set for them in school it seemed to me to be also symptomatic of a much larger concern. Most boys are less tolerant than most girls of activities and focuses which they consider to be irrelevant to their lives; girls, on the other hand, largely enjoy the 'literacy curriculum' whatever its function, often importing their interest in reading and writing to more practical subjects, as when producing carefully documented projects in technology, for example. There is some ground, then, to consider boys' gradual alienation from current literacy activities in school as an important indicator of the need for a more appropriate and demanding curriculum for all pupils.

If we also consider the range of boys' literacy interests outside of school, and their greater interest in the new technologies it becomes clearer that girls also have a stake in our re-examination of literacy practices in the whole of schooling. Michael Apple (1981) has, through a critique of the institution of schooling, already powerfully drawn attention to the effect of pedagogical practices on perpetuating, and indeed, emphasizing aspects of inequality in 'reproducing a social order that remains strikingly unequal by class, gender and race' (p. 131). Girls currently appear to be doing better than boys in terms of school work, but we need to question further whether their expressed literacy preferences are the best preparation for developments that are redirecting attention away from the page to the screen, from the pen to the mouse, and from a well-structured essay to a well-organized Web site.

The difference in boys' and girls' performance in current language examinations may well be a sign that boys are already staking a claim to the more powerful means of communication by participating more actively in the biggest revolution of literacy practices since the introduction of print. It may therefore follow that, as men, they will continue to control entry to the most influential ways of making meaning through the interrelated media of film, computer and CD-ROM. Certainly, the first access to books in western Europe, after the Guttenberg revolution, was confined for more than three centuries to men in positions of power; it took until the late nineteenth century for mass literacy to become established. Without more carefully planned provision, general access to the newer forms of literacy may be similarly restricted to those in advantaged positions thereby increasing the inequality between those who are information rich and those with no or very limited technological resources. These issues, which I have foregrounded in this final section, should therefore orient us towards identifying ways in which we can encourage all the members of the school community to exercise what Lankshear (1987) has described as a 'proper' literacy. This would be embodied in a range of practices that encourage both sexes to become increasingly critically aware through an equal access to and familiarity with all forms of text and therefore more able to understand and control their own learning.

Appendix A: Examples of Unstructured Stories of Reading Transcribed from Children's Work Collected in the Pilot Study*

My First Books

I first picked up a book when I was about 5 and ready for school. My teacher taught me to read. I thought it was extremely boring and so I hardly ever changed my book. But as I got older I found that if I couldn't read I couldn't do other things so I quickly learned. My favourite writer is Enid Blyton. When I read one of her books it was called *The Secret Seven*. I read a lot of her books. I mainly read now when I have nothing to do. I prefer adventure stories. (Girl, 11yrs, 6mths)

Reading

I started reading my first book when I was 3 years old, called *The Town Mouse and the Country Mouse*. I think that because it was my favourite book and I had it read to me so many times over I got to know the words of it off by heart.

When I started school we did reading in a selection of colours. Red then yellow and then orange and blue. Then at last in Year 5 [age 9–10] I got onto free reading where I could choose my own books instead of having to get the next number and doing them all in order. Now I like reading Roald Dahl books. I have read them all. One summer day I read three whole Dahl's they were, *James and the Giant Peach, Danny Champion of the World* and *George's Marvellous Medicine*. I have lots of books at home and I read all the time. (Boy, 11yrs, 5mths)

---

* The spelling in these stories has been corrected.

Reading

At school we had some boxes and when you put a card in a box the box used to say whatever was on the card, like 'the' or 'and'. We had some little books. The teacher read a sentence and we had to repeat it. It was really good but now it is boring. I like to look at the pictures and guess what it will say. I don't like reading the words. My favourite book is *Star Trek* and my favourite author is Jim Davis. I prefer information books, facts and things like that.

Nobody has ever said anything to me about my reading because I have never read much to anyone at home or at school. (Boy, 11yrs, 3mths)

About My Reading

I first learned to read by picture books what my mum used to buy me. But when I started nursery I started to read words. Then when I was in the infants we used to get little pieces of paper with words on which I used to read to my mum and dad. As I got older I got better. When I first learned to read I liked it because I could understand more things. I mostly liked the books I can read for myself because they are exciting. I don't like the boring books we read in school. I used to share books in my old school with the infants every Wednesday. I like reading funny stories. My favourite is *Charlie and the Chocolate Factory*. My favourite author is Enid Blyton. I also like reading Roald Dahl. My reading is not bad and people say it's got a lot better. (Boy, 11yrs, 5mths)

My Reading

My mum first taught me to read. I can't remember really but I think I found it quite easy. The first books I read were at home when my mum taught me. They were *Peter and Jane*. I read them at school when I first properly learned to read. At my last school I didn't read that many school books and I didn't often read to anyone. At home I read all different books from different authors. Sometimes we had to spend about 10 minutes on reading quietly. My teacher didn't read much to us but we had to go up to the desk and read to her. I didn't like doing that. (Girl, 11yrs, 1mth)

My parents helped me to read as well as school books and teachers did. My teacher gave me school reading books that were easy to read. We were allowed to take them home and let my parents hear me read.

I made quick progress and moved on to harder books. I was glad when I learned to read and so were my parents. My favourite reads are *Sweet Valley Twins*. These books are written by Francine Pascal (a nice name). I like these books because the characters are about my age so I understand the way they act. I share my books with my best friend Verity who lives next door. We go the library together and get books. We read them together and then swap them over. When I settle down with a book my parents say that they like to see me reading. (Girl, 11yrs, 4mths)

Appendix B: Examples of Story Openings Collected in the Second Phase of the Study and Analysed in Chapter 6*

Story One: The Rainbow Man

We were all much younger when this happened, around the age of nine or so. But something happened which would change our lives forever. My name's Alicia, my two friends Anastasia and Grainne were about to have the adventure of our lives: We lived around the area of Wimblethwaite. Wimblethwaite was a nice quiet area, that was, before the Rainbow Man came. Rainbow man, the name still makes me shudder with glee.

I was in the park, it had been an unusual day I mean its not everyday you get new clothes and a rise in pocket money is it? We were walking round the park and there was a warm pleasing air around the usually drab place. It felt like lemonade bubbling on your tongue and flowers in a summer meadow. We went up to our gang hut, the windmill. As we approached the windmill the feeling got nicer and nicer as if the windmill was the source.

We went inside and crouched in the corner was an old man. There were lights of all colours coming from his fingers and he was clothed in a robe that shone and sparkled with every shade and haze of colour ever. We walked up to him to try to communicate. We said hello and he sort of grunted. Grainne suggested we should try to gain his confidence. So we went everyday and slowly but surely we gained his confidence and he spoke to us. We couldn't find out his name though. So to us he was always Rainbow man.

But one day something strange happened. Wimblethwaite became as drab as it had always been. Something was wrong but only the three of us noticed. We rushed to the windmill.

The Rainbow Man was curled up and his coat was fading fast, he looked weak and pale. His voice was croaky so we could only just

---

* The spelling in these stories has been corrected: the grammar remains as written.

make out what he said, My name, used only once or twice in my whole life, you must find my name . . . Then he was asleep.

Story Two: The Time Warp

I got up and I felt rubbish. I had my breakfast and got a wash and went to school. When I got to school our teacher had some bad news for us.

We all had to sit on the carpet and listen. Mrs Carling said, 'I have some very bad news if we don't raise a million pounds in four days our school will be shut down. Then our teacher sent me and Simon and Nick and Bill to the loft to find some old pictures but then I saw a flashing piece of glass. It was flashing we looked at us. It said, 'come, come, come in the time warp. So I pushed my foot through, it vanished so then we all jumped in. We were in front of a computer. We looked at it all different times came up on the screen. It said, 2022. We pressed the button, then we vanished We were in a big city. We looked in the sky there was cars flying in the air. It was unbelievable. We walked into the information house:
It said:

```
No cigs
No sex
No drugs
No swearing
No alcohol
```

We couldn't believe it. Then the police surrounded us with electric truncheons, they zapped them at us and we fainted.

Story Three: Brotherly Love

As Ellen walked towards the bright red door through which she passed everyday, she was aware of a faint sound. It sounded like screaming and seemed to be coming from the rusting letterbox flapping in the wind.

Ellen felt a shiver up her spine. She was a normal girl with soft and flowing blonde hair, piercing blue eyes. Nothing extraordinary ever happened to her.

She cast the noise to the back of her mind and proceeded to unlock the door. She would be all alone in the house. Her mum was at work in the social services office and her dad had been murdered a year ago. She missed him very much. He had promised to take her to Legoland, but as in most things he had never had time, and then, it was too late. He had been shot in the head while protecting his sweet shop from armed robbers, or so they said, she never could be sure, but her mum had told her not to dwell on the past so that thought was put away with the screaming noise.

Just then the phone rang, she dumped her bags by the stairs and lifted the receiver to her ears.

'Hi,' said the voice on the end of the line, 'It's David, is your mum home yet?' he asked. David was Ellen's uncle and also her mum's new boyfriend. Ellen did not think very much of David, he was very mysterious. But he was her dad's brother and if that's who her mum wanted to go out with, then who was she to complain.

'No she isn't, sorry,' she replied and slammed the phone down. She picked up her bag and went into the dining room where she covered the dining table with books and paper. She clearly had stacks of homework.

Story Four: Me and My Street

Rocky thought it was just another day, but it wasn't. A big surprise from his mum was just go to change his way of living. Rocky was in the bathroom getting a wash.

Rocky, come and get your tea
Coming mum

Rocky ran downstairs he couldn't wait for the football match tonight.

mum:	Rocky
Rocky:	yes mum
mum:	I'm going to tell you something
Rocky:	go on
mum:	I'm going to have a baby
Rocky:	a what?
mum:	a baby
Rocky:	a baby?
mum:	yes, a baby and I don't want you to tell anyone about this
Rocky:	why?
mum:	because I want it to be a surprise

Knock Knock the door went it was Carl

Rocky: Mum it's Carl I'm going
mum: OK have you got your football kit?
Rocky: yes, bye
mum: bye

Rocky and Carl was walking when Rocky said

Rocky: I want you to know something and don't tell anyone

Story Five: Robocop 4

This is the News headline and yes, there is another Robocop out but
this time 'Louis I need back up'
'Murphy hold it there he is'
DEAD OR ALIVE YOU ARE COMING WITH ME
Dream on tin head BANG My arm aargghhhh
'Book him' 'why?' 'He's a cop killer.'
Crime in progress
Hey what are you doing in there, mister?
Gimme all your money before I blow your brains to bits.

Appendix C: Titles of Books Recorded in the Questionnaires as Well Liked

Books Listed by Boys as the Most Enjoyable

1. *Adrian Mole Age 13³/₄*   Susan Townsend*
2. *Alien 3*   Alan Dean Foster
3. *Alien Trilogy*   Ridley Scott
4. *Animals of Farthing Wood*   Colin Dann
5. *Biggles*   Captain W.E. Johns
6. *Boy*   Roald Dahl*
7. *Charlie and the Chocolate Factory*   Roald Dahl
8. *Charlie and the Great Glass Elevator*   Roald Dahl
9. *Conan the Barbarian*   Cartoon Books
10. *Count Duckula*   Cartoon
11. *Danny, Champion of the World*   Roald Dahl
12. *Disc World* novels   Terry Pratchett
13. *Dune Trilogy*   Frank Herbert
14. *Fantastic Mr Fox*   Roald Dahl
15. *Free Kick*   Michael Hardcastle
16. *George's Marvellous Medicine*   Roald Dahl
17. *Going Solo*   Roald Dahl*
18. *Goodnight Mr Tom*   Michel Magorian*
19. *Hitch Hiker's Guide to the Galaxy*   Douglas Adams
20. *I am David*   Ann Holm*
21. *In the Net*   Michael Hardcastle
22. *Isaac Campion*   Jenni Howker*
23. *James and the Giant Peach*   Roald Dahl
24. *Jurassic Park*   M. Crichton
25. *Mossflower*   Brian Jacques
26. *Mr Bean's Diary*   (unspecified)
27. *Myths and Legends*   Unspecified Author*
28. *Penalty*   Michael Hardcastle
29. *Placing Red Dwarf*   Grant and Naylor
30. *Red October*   Tom Clancy

---

* Represent books read in class.

31. *Redwall*	Brian Jacques
32. *Second Chance*	Michael Hardcastle
33. *Soccer at Stanford*	Michael Hardcastle
34. *See You Later*	Christopher Pike
35. *Super Fudge*	Judy Blume
36. *The Demon Biker*	Robert Leeson*
37. *The Demon Headmaster*	Gillian Cross*
38. *The Ghost of Thomas Kempe*	Penelope Lively*
39. *The Girlfriend*	R.L. Stine
40. *The Hobbit*	J.R.R. Tolkien*
41. *The Last Vampire*	Christopher Price
42. *The Lion, the Witch and the Wardrobe*	C.S. Lewis*
43. *The Magic Finger*	Roald Dahl
44. *The Silver Sword*	Ian Serrailler*
45. *The Twits*	Roald Dahl
46. *The Weirdstone of Brisangemmon*	Alan Garner*
47. War stories	(unspecified)
48. *The Weathermonger*	Jan Mark*
49. *The Witches*	Roald Dahl
50. *The Wizard of Oz*	L. Frank Baum
51. *Which Witch?*	Eva Ibbotson*

Books Listed by Girls as the Most Enjoyable

1. *Adrian Mole Age 13³/₄*	Susan Townsend*
2. *Anne of Green Gables*	L.M. Montgomery
3. *April Fools*	R.T. Cusick
4. *Are you there God, It's Me Margaret*	Judy Blume
5. *BFG*	Roald Dahl
6. *Carrie's War*	Nina Bawden*
7. *Charlie and the Chocolate Factory*	Roald Dahl
8. *Charlotte's Web*	E.B. White*
9. *Die Softly*	Christopher Pike
10. *Dirty Beasts*	Roald Dahl
11. *Flat Stanley*	Jeff Brown
12. *Forever*	Judy Blume
13. *Friends and Brothers*	Catherine Cookson
14. *George's Marvellous Medicine*	Roald Dahl
15. *Good Wives*	Louisa May Alcott
16. *Gowie Corby Plays Chicken*	Gene Kemp*
17. *Grinny*	Nicholas Fiske*
18. *Hit and Run*	Nigel Hinton*
19. *How Green You Are*	Berlie Docherty*
20. *I am David*	Ann Holme*

21.	*Little Women*	L.M. Alcott
22.	*Matilda*	Roald Dahl
23.	*Mother's Helper*	A. Bates
24.	*My Cousin Rachel*	Daphne du Maurier
25.	*My Naughty Little Sister*	Dorothy Edwards
26.	*Nancy Drew Mysteries*	Various
27.	*Paddington at Large*	Michael Bond
28.	*Please Mrs Butler*	Janet and Alan Ahlberg*
29.	*Rebecca*	Daphne du Maurier
30.	*Revolting Rhymes*	Roald Dahl*
31.	*Sheep Pig*	Dick King Smith
32.	*Stig of the Dump*	Clive King*
33.	*Superfudge*	Judy Blume
34.	*Sweet Valley High*	Francine Pascall
35.	*Tales of a Fourth Grade Nothing*	Judy Blume
36.	*Teacher's Pet*	R.T. Cusick
37.	*The Babysitter*	R.L. Stine
38.	*The Lifeguard*	R.T. Cusick
39.	*The Borrowers Omnibus*	E. Nesbit*
40.	*The Cheer Leader*	C.B. Cooney
41.	*The Faraway Tree*	Enid Blyton
42.	*The Famous Five*	Enid Blyton
43.	*The Fib*	George Layton*
44.	*The Haunting of Cassie Palmer*	Vivien Alcott*
45.	*The Indian in the Cupboard*	Lynne Reid Banks*
46.	*The Iron Man*	Ted Hughes*
47.	*The Last Vampire*	Christopher Price
48.	*The Lifeguard*	C.B. Cooney
49.	*The Secret Garden*	Frances Hodgson Burnett*
50.	*The Silver Sword*	Ian Serrailler*
51.	*The Story of Tracy Beaker*	Jacqueline Wilson*
52.	*The Street Child*	Noel Streatfield*
53.	*The Suitcase Kid*	Jacqueline Wilson*
54.	*The Sweet Valley Twins*	Francine Pascall
55.	*The Turbulent Term of Tyke Tiler*	Gene Kemp*
56.	*The Twits*	Roald Dahl
57.	*The Wizard of Oz*	Frank L. Baum
58.	*Tuck Everlasting*	Natalie Babitt*
59.	*What Katy Did*	Susan Coolidge
60.	*What Katy Did Next*	Susan Coolidge

Titles of Books Used as Year 7 Class Readers 1992–93

1.	*Boy*	Roald Dahl
2.	*Carrie's War*	Nina Bawden

 3. *Danny, Champion of the World* Roald Dahl
 4. *Dragonslayer* Rosemary Sutcliffe
 5. *Goodnight Mr Tom* Michelle Magorian
 6. *Gowie Corby Plays Chicken* Gene Kemp
 7. *Grinny* Nicholas Fiske
 8. *Hating Alison Ashley* Robin Klein
 9. *I am David* Ann Holme
10. *Red Sky in the Morning* Elizabeth Laird
11. *Run for Your Life* Robert Leeson
12. *The Eighteenth Emergency* Betsy Byars
13. *The Haunting of Cassie Palmer* Vivienne Alcock
14. *The Indian in the Cupboard* Lynne Reid Banks
15. *The Midnight Fox* Betsy Byars
16. *The Monster Garden* Vivien Alcock
17. *The Piggy Book* Anthony Browne
18. *The Silver Sword* Ian Serrailler
19. *The Turbulent Term of Tyke Tiler* Gene Kempe
20. *Tuck Everlasting* Natalie Babbitt

References

ABBS, P. (1982) *English Within the Arts*, Sevenoaks, Hodder and Stoughton.

ADAMS, M.J. (1990) *Beginning to Read: Thinking and Learning about Print*, Cambridge, Mass, MIT Press.

ALBSU (1987) *Literacy, Numeracy and Adults: Evidence from the National Child Development Study*, London, Adult Literacy and Basic Skills Unit.

ALLEN, D. (1980) *English Teaching Since 1965. How Much Growth?* London, Heinemann Educational.

APPLE, M. (1981) 'Social structure, ideology and curriculum', in LAWN, M. and BARTON, L. (eds) *Rethinking Curriculum Studies*, London, Croom Helm.

APPLEYARD, J.A. (1991) *Becoming a Reader: The Experience of Fiction From Childhood to Adulthood*, Cambridge, Cambridge University Press.

APU (1987a) *Pupils' Attitudes to Reading: Pupils Age 11 and 15*, London, HMSO.

APU (1987b) *Pupils' Attitudes to Writing at Age 11 and 15*, London, HMSO.

APU (1987c) *Language Performance in Schools: Review of APU Language Monitoring, no. 2*, London, HMSO.

ARNOT, M. and WEINER, G. (eds) (1987) *Gender and the Politics of Schooling*, Milton Keynes, Open University Press.

BAINES, B. (1985) 'Literature and sex-bias in the secondary school English curriculum', in NATE Language and Gender Working Party (eds) *Alice in Genderland*, Sheffield, NATE Publications.

BARDSLEY, D. (1991) *Factors Relating to the Differential Reading Attitudes, Habits and Interests of Adolescents* (Research Affiliateship Report No. 1), New Zealand, Department of Education, Massey University.

BARRS, M., ELLIS, S., HESTER, H. and THOMAS, A. (1988) *The Primary Language Record: Handbook for Teachers*, London, Centre for Language in Primary Education, pp. 14–15.

BARRS, M. and PIDGEON, S. (eds) (1993) *Reading the Difference*, London, Centre for Language in Primary Education.

BARRS, M. and THOMAS, A. (1991) *The Reading Book*, London, Centre for Learning in Primary Education, p. 146.

BARTHES, R. (1974) *S/Z: An Essay*, (R. Miller, trans.) New York, Hill and Wang and London, Fontana Press (original work published 1970).

BENJAMIN, B. (1973) 'The work of art in the age of mechanical reproduction', in ARENDT, H. (ed.) *Illuminations*, (H. Zohn, trans.) Suffolk, Fontana Press (original work published 1955).

BENNETT, A. (1994) *Writing Home*, London, Faber and Faber.

BENTON, P. (1995) 'Recipe fictions: Literary fast food? Reading interests in Y8', *Oxford Review of Education*, **21**, pp. 108–11.

BENTON, M. and Fox, G. (1985) *Teaching Literature: Nine to Fourteen*, Oxford, Oxford University Press.

BERLIN, J. (1993) 'Literacy, pedagogy and English studies: Postmodern connections', in LANKSHEAR, C. and MCLAREN, P.L. (eds) *Critical Literacy: Policy, Praxis and the Postmodern*, Albany, State University of New York Press.

BETTELHEIM, B. (1976) *The Uses of Enchantment: The Meaning and Importance of Fairy Tales*, New York, Knopf.

BISSEX, G.L. (1980) *GYNS at WRK: A Child Learns to Write and Read*, Cambridge, MA, Harvard University Press.

BLUNT, J. (1977) 'Response to reading: How some young readers describe the process', *English in Education*, **1**, 3, pp. 34–47.

BOARD OF EDUCATION (1921) *The Teaching of English in England* (The Newbolt Report), London, HMSO.

BORDO, S. (1990) 'Feminism, postmodernism and gender-scepticism', in NICHOLSON, L. (ed.) *Feminism/Postmodernism*, London, Routledge.

BOURDIEU, P. (1990) *The Logic of Practice*, (R. Nice, trans.) Cambridge, Polity Press (original work published 1980).

BRAIDOTTI, R. (1989) 'The politics of ontological difference', in BRENNAN, T. (ed.) *Between Feminism and Psychoanalysis*, London, Routledge.

BRINDLEY, S. (1994) 'Girls and literature: Promise and reality', in BRINDLEY, S. (ed.) *Teaching English*, London, Routledge.

BRITTON, J. (1970) *Language and Learning*, London, Allyn Lane.

BRITTON, J. (1977) 'The nature of the reader's satisfactions', in MEEK, M., WARLOW, A. and BARTON, G. (eds) *The Cool Web*, London, Bodley Head.

BROPHY, J. (1985) 'Interactions of male and female students with male and female teachers', in WILKINSON, I.C. and MARRETT C.M. (eds) *Gender Influences in Classroom Interaction*, New York, Academic Press.

BROWNSTEIN, R. (1982) *Becoming a Heroine*, Harmondsworth, Penguin Books.

BYARS, B. (1974) *The Eighteenth Emergency*, London, Bodley Head.

CENTRAL ADVISORY COUNCIL FOR EDUCATION (England) (1963) *Half Our Future* (The Newsom Report), London, HMSO.

CHALL, J. (1983) *Stages of Reading Development*, New York, McGraw-Hill.

CHERLAND, M. (1994) *Private Practices: Girls Reading Fiction and Constructing Identity*, London, Taylor and Francis Ltd.

CHODOROW, N. (1978) *The Reproduction of Mothering; Psychoanalysis and the Sociology of Gender*, Berkeley, University of California.

CHRISTIAN-SMITH, L. (1993) *Texts of Desire: Essays on Fiction, Femininity and Schooling*, London, Falmer Press.

CLARK, M. (1976) *Young Fluent Readers*, Oxford, Heinemann Educational.

CLARRICOATES, K. (1978) 'Dinosaurs in the classroom: An examination of some of the aspects of the hidden curriculum in primary schools', *Women's Studies International Quarterly*, **1**, pp. 353–64.

CLAY, M. (1979) *Reading the Patterning of Complex Behaviour* (2nd edn), London, Heinemann Educational.

CONNELL, R.W. (1987) *Gender and Power*, Cambridge, Polity Press.

CONNELL, R.W. (1989) 'Cool guys, swots and wimps: The interplay of masculinity and education', *Oxford Review of Education*, **15**, 2, pp. 291–303.

COWARD, R. (1984) *Female Desires: How They are Bought, Sought and Packaged*, London, Paladin.

D'ARCY, S. (1991) 'Towards a non-sexist primary classroom', in TITCHELL, E. (ed.) *Dolls and Dungarees: Gender Issues in the Primary School Curriculum*, Milton Keynes, Open University.

DAVIES, J. and BREMBER, I. (1993) 'Comics or stories? Differences in the reading attitudes and habits of girls and boys in years 2, 4 and 6', *Gender and Education*, **5**, 3, pp. 305–20.

DE BEAUVIOR, S. (1984) *The Second Sex*, (trans. H.M. Parshley), Harmondsworth, Penguim.

DELAMONT, S. (1990) *Sex Roles and the School* (2nd edn), London, Methuen.

DEPARTMENT OF EDUCATION AND SCIENCE (DES) (1975) *A Language for Life* (Report of the Committee of Inquiry appointed by the Secretary of State for Education and Science under the Chairmanship of Sir Alan Bullock, Committee of Inquiry into Reading and the Use of English), London, HMSO.

DEPARTMENT OF EDUCATION AND SCIENCE (DES) (1988) *Report of the Committee of Inquiry into the Teaching of English Language* (The Kingman Report), London, HMSO.

DEPARTMENT OF EDUCATION AND SCIENCE (DES) (1989) *Report of the English Working Group* (The Cox Report), London, HMSO.

DOWNING, J., MAY, R. and OLLILA, L. (1982) 'Sex differences and cultural expectations in reading', in SHERIDAN, E.M. (ed.) *Sex Stereotypes and Reading: Research Strategies*, Newark, IRA.

EAGLETON, T. (1983) *Literary Theory: An Introduction*, Oxford: Basil Blackwell.

EVANS, E. (1987) 'Quality and non-quality: Some new criteria', *English in Education*, **21**, 3, pp. 36–43.

FIRESTONE, S. (1970) *The Dialectic of Sex*, New York, Bantam.

FISHER, P. and AYERS, G. (1990) 'A comparison of the reading interests of children in England and the United States', *Reading Improvement*, **27**, 2, pp. 111–15.

FOUCAULT, M. (1973) *The Order of Things*, New York, Vintage.

FOUCAULT, M. (1979) *Discipline and Punish: The Birth of the Prison*, (A. Sheridan, trans.) London, Penguin Books (original work published 1972).

FOX, C. (1993) *At the Very Edge of the Forest: The Influence of Literature on Storytelling by Children*, London, Cassell.

FRY, D. (1985) *Children Talk about Books Seeing Themselves as Readers*, Milton Keynes, Open University Press.

GEE, J. (1993) 'Postmodernism and literacies', in LANKSHEAR, C. and MCLAREN, P. (eds) *Critical Literacy: Policy, Praxis and the Postmodern*, Albany, State University of New York Press.

GIDDENS, A. (1991) *Modernity and Self-identity*, Cambridge, Polity Press.

GILBERT, P. (1993) 'Dolly fictions: Teen romance down under', in CHRISTIAN-SMITH, L. (ed.) *Texts of Desire*, London, Falmer Press.

GOFFMAN, I. (1976) 'Gender display', *Studies in the Anthropology of Visual Communication*, **3**, pp. 69–77.

GOODENOUGH, R. (1987) 'Small group culture and the emergence of sexist behaviour: A comparative study of four children's groups', in SPINDLER, G.L. (eds) *Interpretative Ethnography of Education*, Hillsdale, NJ, Lawrence Erlbaum.

GOODWYN, A. (1992) 'English teachers and the Cox models', *English in Education*, **26**, 3, pp. 4–10.

GORMAN, T., WHITE, J. and BROOKS, G. (1987) *Language Performance in Schools 1982: Secondary Survey Report*, London, HMSO.

GORMAN, T., WHITE, J., BROOKS, G., MACLURE, M. and KISPAL, A. (1988) *Language Performance in Schools: Review of APU Language Monitoring 1979–1983*, London, HMSO.

GOSWAMI, U. and BRYANT, P. (1990) *Phonological Skills and Learning to Read*, Hove, Lawrence Erlbaum Associates.

GRAVES, D. (1983) *Writing: Teachers and Children at Work*, Exeter, NH and London, Heinemann.

GREANEY, V. and NEUMANN, S. (1983) 'Young people's views of the functions of reading: A cross cultural perspective', *Reading Teacher*, **37**, 2, pp. 158–63.

GREEN, B. (ed.) (1993) *The Insistence of the Letter*, London, Falmer Press.

GRIFFITHS, P. (1992) *English at the Core*, Buckingham, Open University Press.

HALL, N. (1987) *The Emergence of Literacy*, Sevenoaks, Hodder & Stoughton, in association with the United Kingdom Reading Association.

HANNON, P. (1995) *Literacy, Home and School: Research and Practice in Teaching Literacy with Parents*, London, Falmer Press.

HARDING, D.W. (1977) 'Psychological processes in the reading of the novel', in MEEK, M., WARLOW, A. and BARTON, G. (eds) *The Cool Web*, London, Bodley Head.

HARDY, B. (1975) *Tellers and Listeners: The Narrative Imagination*, Dover, NH and London, Athlone Press.

HARRIS, S., NIXON, J. and RUDDUCK, J. (1993) 'Schoolwork, Homework and Gender', *Gender and Education*, **5**, 1, pp. 3–15.

HARRISON, B.T. (1994) *The Literate Imagination: Renewing the Secondary English Curriculum*, London, David Fulton Publishers.

HARRISON, C. (1994) 'Information skills', in BRINDLEY, S. (ed.) *Teaching English*, London, Routledge.

HAWKES, T. (1977) *Structuralism and Semiotics*, London, Methuen.

HEATH, S.B. (1983) *Ways with Words: Language, Life and Work in Communities and Classrooms*, Cambridge, Cambridge University Press.

HILTON, M. (1996) 'The toy industry', in HILTON, M. (ed.) *Potent Fictions*, London, Routledge.

HOFFMAN, M. (1988) 'Children's reading and social values', in MERCER, N. (ed.) *Language and Literacy From an Educational Perspective: Vol 2, In Schools*, Milton Keynes, Open University Press.

HOGGART, R. (1958) *The Use of Literacy: Aspects of Working-class Life with Special Reference to Publications and Entertainments*, Harmondsworth, Penguin.

HUNT, P. and PLACKETT, E. (1986) 'Book talk: An interview with Aidan Chambers', *The English Magazine: Literature*, 17, Autumn, pp. 22–5.

HUNTER-CARSCH, M. (1995) 'Stance meaning and voluntary reading', in OWEN, P. and PUMFREY, P. (eds) *Emergent and Developing Reading: Messages for Teachers*, London, Falmer Press.

ISER, W. (1978) *The Act of Reading: A Theory of Aesthetic Response*, Baltimore, John Hopkins University Press and London, Routledge and Kegan Paul.

IVANIC, R. and HAMILTON, M. (1990) 'Literacy beyond school', in WRAY, D. (ed.) *Emerging Partnerships: Current Research in Language and Literacy*, Clevedon, Multilingual Matters.

JAMESON, F. (1981) *The Political Unconscious: Narrative as a Socially Symbolic Act*, London, Methuen.

JENKINSON, A.J. (1946) *What Do Boys and Girls Read: An Investigation into Reading Habits with Some Suggestions about the Teaching of Literature in Secondary and Senior Schools*, (2nd Edition), London, Methuen.

JOFFE, L., FOXMAN, D. and JORDAN, E. (1988) *Attitudes and Gender Differences: Mathematics at Age 11 and 15*, London, HMSO.

JOHNSTON, P. (1985) 'Understanding reading disability: A case study approach', *Harvard Educational Review*, **55**, 2, pp. 153–77.

JORDAN, E. (1995) 'Fighting boys and fantasy play: The construction of masculinity in the early years of school', *Gender and Education*, **7**, 1, pp. 68–95.

KELLY, A., WHYTE, J. and SMAIL, B. (1981) *Initial GIST Survey: Results and Implications*, Department of Sociology, University of Manchester.

KELLY, A., WHYTE, J. and SMAIL, B. (1984) *Girls into Science and Technology (The final report)*, GIST, Department of Sociology, University of Manchester.

KELLY, P. (1986) 'The influence of reading content on students' perceptions of the masculinity or femininity of reading', *The Journal of Reading Behaviour*, **XVIII**, 3, pp. 243–56.

KESSLER, S., ASHENDEN, D.J., CONNELL, R.W. and DOWSETT, G.W. (1985) 'Gender relations in secondary schooling', *Sociology of Education*, **58**, 1, pp. 34–48.

KRESS, G. (1989) 'Texture and meaning', in ANDREWS, R. (ed.) *Narrative and Argument*, Milton Keynes, Open University Press.

KRISTEVA, J. (1984) Revolution in Poetic Language, (trans. Margaret Waller), New York, Columbia University Press, (original La Revolution du Langue Poetique (1974), Paris, Sevil).

KRISTEVA, J. (1986) 'Revolution in Poetic Language', in MOI, T. (ed.) *The Kristeva Reader*, Oxford, Blackwell.

LACAN, J. (1977) *Ecrits a Selection*, (trans. Alan Sheridan), London, Tavistock.

LANGERMAN, D. (1990) 'Books and boys: Gender preference and book selection', *The School Library Journal*, March, pp. 132–6.

LANKSHEAR, C. and LAWLER, M. (1987) *Literacy, Schooling and Revolution*, Lewes, Falmer Press.

LANKSHEAR, C. and MCLAREN, P.L. (1993) (eds) *Critical Literacy, Policy, Praxis and the Post-modern*, Albany, State University of New York Press.

LEES, S. (1986) *Losing Out: Sexuality and Adolescent Girls*, London, Hutchinson.

LE GUIN, U. (1971) *The Wizard of Earthsea*, Reading, Puffin, (First published 1968).

LICHT, B.G. and DWECK, C.S. (1983) 'Sex differences in achievement orientations: Consequences for academic choices and attainments', in MARLAND, M. (ed.) *Sex Differentiation and Schooling*, London, Heinemann.

LITTLEFAIR, A. (1991) *Reading All Types of Writing: The Importance of Genre and Register for Reading Development*, Milton Keynes, Open University Press.

LUKE, A. (1993) 'Stories of social regulation: The micropolitics of classroom narrative', in GREEN, B. (ed.) *The Insistence of the Letter: Literacy Studies and Curriculum Theorising*, London, Falmer Press.

LUKE, A. (1994) 'On reading and the sexual division of literacy', *Journal of Curriculum Studies*, **26**, 4, pp. 361–81.

LUNZER, A. and GARDNER, K. (1979) *The Effective Use of Reading*, London, Heinemann Educational.

LUNZER, E. and GARDNER, K. (1984) *Learning from the Written Word*, London, Oliver and Boyd.

LURIE, A. (1990) *Not in Front of the Children*, London, Cardinal.

MAC AN GHAILL, M. (1994) *The Making of Men*, Milton Keynes, Open University Press.

MACKAY, D., THOMPSON, B. and SCHAUB, P. (1970) *Breakthrough to Literacy*, London, Longman.

MACKEY, M. (1994) 'The new basics: Learning to read in a multi-media world', *English in Education*, **28**, 1, pp. 9–20.

MARENBON, J. (1994) 'The new orthodoxy', in BRINDLEY, S. (ed.) *Teaching English*, London, Routledge.

MARLAND, M. (1983) *Sex Differentiation and Schooling*, London, Heinemann.

MEAD, M. (1949) *Male and Female: A Study of the Sexes in a Changing World*, New York, William Morrow and Company.

MEDWAY, P. (1986) 'What gets written about: Selections from real and imaginary worlds in school writing assignments', in WILKINSON, A. (ed.) *The Writing of Writing*, Milton Keynes, Open University Press.

MEDWAY, P. (1990) 'English and English society at a time of change', in GOODSON, I. and MEDWAY, P. (eds) Bringing English to Order, Lewes, Falmer Press.

MEEK, M. (1988) *How Texts Teach What Readers Learn*, Stroud, Thimble Press.

MEEK, M. (1991) *On Being Literate*, London, Bodley Head.

MEYER, R. (1995) 'Stories to teach and teaching to story: The use of narrative in learning to teach', *Language Arts*, **72**, April, pp. 213–76.

MILLARD, E. (1985) 'Stories to grow on', in NATE Language and Gender Working Party (eds) *Alice in Genderland*, Sheffield, NATE Publications.

MILLARD, E. (1987) 'Re-reading D.H. Lawrence', in TALLACK, D. (ed.) *Literary Theory at Work*, London, Batsford.

MILLARD, E. (1989) 'Frames of reference: A study of three women poets', in MURRAY, D. (ed.) *Literary Theory and Poetry*, London, Batsford.

MILLARD, E. (1994) *Developing Readers in the Middle Years*, Buckingham, Open University Press.

MILLARD, E. (1995) 'What Christine knows about reading', in CORCORAN, B., HEYHOE, M. and PRADL, G. (eds) *Knowledge in the Making*, London, Heinemann Educational.

MILLS, S., MILLARD, E., PEARCE, L. and SPAWL, S. (1989) *Feminist Readings — Feminists Reading*, Hemel Hempstead, Harvester Wheatsheaf.

MINNS, H. (1990) *Read it to Me Now! Learning at Home and at School*, London, Virago.

MINNS, H. (1991) *Language, Literacy and Gender*, London, Hodder and Stoughton.

MINNS, H. (1993) 'Three ten year old boys and their reading', in BARRS, M. and PIDGEON, S. (eds) *Reading the Difference*, London, Centre for Language in Primary Education.

MONTGOMERY, M., DURANT, A., FABB, N., FURNISS, T. and MILLS, S. (1992) *Ways of Reading*, London, Routledge.

MORRIS, J. (1972) 'The first "R": Yesterday, today and tomorrow', in MELNIK, A. and MERRIT, J. (eds) *Reading: Today and Tomorrow*, London, Open University.

MORRIS, J. (1979) 'New phonics for old', in THACKRAY, T. (ed.) *Growth in Reading* (Proceedings of the fifteenth annual course and conference of the United Kingdom Reading Association, Nene College, Northampton, 1978), London, Ward Lock.

MOSS, E. (1977) 'The peppermint lesson', in MEEK, M., WARLOW, A. and BARTON, G. (eds) *The Cool Web*, London, Bodley Head.

MOSS, G. (1991) *Un/Popular Fictions*, London, Virago Educational.

NATE, LANGUAGE AND GENDER COMMITTEE (1985) (eds) *Alice in Genderland*, Exeter, NATE.

NATIONAL WRITING PROJECT (1989) *Becoming a Writer*, Walton-on Thames, NFER/Nelson.

NATIONAL LITERACY TRUST (1993) *Research into Adult Literacy*, Consumer Research undertaken by Thomas Allen Associates.

NEATE, B. (1992) *Finding Out About Finding Out: A Practical Guide to Children's Information Books*, Bury St Edmunds, Hodder and Stoughton in association with the United Kingdom Reading Association.

NELSON, C., TREICHLER, P. and GROSSENBERG, L. (1992) (eds) *Cultural Studies*, New York, Routledge.

NICOLLE, R. (1989) 'Boys and the five year void', *School Library Journal*, March, pp. 132–6.

NILAN, P. (1995) 'Making up men', *Gender and Education*, **1**, 2, pp. 174–86.

NOTTINGHAMSHIRE ADVISORY AND INSPECTION SERVICE (1991) *Teaching Reading in Nottinghamshire Primary Schools* (Report No. 18/91), Nottingham, County Council.

OFSTED (1993) *Boys and English*, London, HMSO (Ref. 2/93/NS).

OSMONT, P. (1987) 'Teaching inquiry in the classroom, reading and gender set', *Language Arts*, **64**, 7, pp. 758–61.

OTTO, W. (1992) 'How things are not', *Journal of Reading*, **36**, 3, pp. 234–7.

PALEY, V.G. (1984) *Boys and Girls: Superheroes in the Doll Corner*, Chicago and London, University of Chicago Press.

PATTERSON, A. (1986) 'Leisure reading and the year 11 student', *English in Australia*, **75**, pp. 40–8.

PEEL, R. and HARGREAVES, S. (1995) 'Research into adult literacy', *English in Education*, **29**, 2, pp. 48–65.

PENNAC, D. (1994) *Reads Like a Novel*, (D. Gunn, trans.) London, Quartet (original work published 1992).

PHILLIPS, A. (1993) *The Trouble with Boys*, London, Pandora.

PIDGEON, S. (1993) 'Learning reading and learning gender', in BARRS, M. and PIDGEON, S. (eds) *Reading the Difference*, London, Centre for Language in Primary Education.

PIERPOINT, K. (1995) *Truffle Beds*, London, Faber.

POMPE, C. (1993) 'Toys "R" Texts', *Toys and Media Education, Language and Learning*, June.

POTTER, D. (1986) *The Singing Detective*, London, Faber.

PROPP, V. (1968) *Morphology of the Folktale*, (L. Scott, trans.) Austin, London, University of Texas Press.

PROTHEROUGH, R. (1983) *Developing Response to Fiction*, Milton Keynes, University Press.

PROTHEROUGH, R. (1990) 'Children's recognition of stories', in HAYHOE, M. and PARKER, S. (eds) *Reading and Response*, Milton Keynes, Open University Press.

PROTHEROUGH, R. and ATKINSON, J. (1991) *The Making of English Teachers*, Milton Keynes, Open University Press.

PUGH, A.K. (1993) 'Factors affecting the growth of literacy', in BROOKS, G., PUGH, A.K. and HALL, N. (eds) *Further Studies in the History of Reading*, Wandsworth, UKRA.

PUMFREY, P. (1991) *Improving Children's Reading in the Junior School: Challenges and Responses*, London, Cassell.

ROEHAMPTON CHILDREN'S LITERATURE RESEARCH CENTRE (1994) *Contemporary Juvenile Reading Habits*, London, Roehampton Institute (British National Bibliography Research Fund, Report, 69).

ROSE, J. (1984) *The Case of Peter Pan, or, The Impossibility of Children's Fiction: Language, Discourse and Society*, London, Macmillan.

ROSENBLATT, L. (1978) *The Reader, The Text, The Poem: The Transactional Theory of the Literary Work*, Carbondale, Southern Illinois, UP.

ROWE, K. (1991) 'The influence of reading activity at home on students' attitudes toward reading, classroom attentiveness and reading achievement: An application of structural equation modelling', *British Journal of Educational Psychology*, **61**, pp. 19–35.

RUDDUCK, J. (1994) *Developing a Gender Policy in Secondary Schools*, Buckingham, Open University.

SAMPSON, G. (1921) *English for the English*, Cambridge, Cambridge University Press.

SARLAND, C. (1991) *Young People Reading: Culture and Response*, Milton Keynes, Open University Press.

SARLAND, C. (1994a) 'Attack of the teenage horrors: Theme and meaning in popular series fiction', *Signal*, **73**, pp. 49–62.

SARLAND, C. (1994b) 'Revenge of the teenage horrors: Pleasure, quality and canonicity in (and out of) popular series fiction', *Signal*, **74**, pp. 113–30.

SHAPIRO, J. (1990) 'Sex-role appropriateness of reading and reading instruction', *Reading Psychology: An International Quarterly*, **11**, 3, pp. 241–69.

SMITH, F. (1983) *Essays into Literacy: Selected Papers and Some Afterthoughts*, London, Heinemann Educational.

SMITH, F. (1984) *Reading that Helps us Teach: Joining the Literacy Club*, Reading, Reading Reading Centre.

SMITH, J. (1994) 'Thinking through our book conversations with children', in CORCORAN, B., HEYHOE, M. and PRADL, G. (eds) *Knowledge in the Making*, London, Heinemann Educational.

STABLES, A., DAVIES, S., HENDLEY, D., PARKINSON, J., STABLES, S. and TANNER, H. (1995) 'Attitudes to English at Key Stage 3', *English in Education*, **29**, 3, pp. 29–38.

ST CLAIR, W. (1989) 'William Godwin as children's bookseller', in AVERY, C. and BRIGGS, J. (ed.) *Children and their Books*, Oxford, Oxford University Press.

STEEDMAN, C. (1982) *The Tidy House: Little Girls' Writing*, London, Virago.

STENHOUSE, L. (1975) *An Introduction to Curriculum Research and Development*, London, Heinemann.

STEPHENS, J. and WATSON, K. (1994) *From Picture Book to Literary Theory*, Sydney, St Clair Press.

STONES, R. (1983) *Pour out the Cocoa, Janet: Sexism in Children's Books*, London, Longman.

STUCKEY, J.E. (1991) *The Violence of Literacy*, N.H. Boynton/Cook.

SWANN, J. (1992) *Girls, Boys and Language*, Oxford, Blackwell.

SWANN, J. and GRADDOL, D. (1988) 'Gender inequalities in classroom talk', *English in Education*, **22**, 1, pp. 48–65.

TAYLOR, D. and DORSEY-GAINES, C. (1988) *Growing-up Literate: Learning from Inner-city Families*, Portsmouth, N.H. Heinemann.

TEALE, W.H. and SULZBY, E. (eds) (1986) *Emergent Literacy, Writing and Reading*, Norwood, N.J. Ablex Publishing Corporation.

TEMPLE, C., NATHAN, R., BURRIS, N. and TEMPLE, F. (1988) *The Beginnings of Writing* (2nd edn), Boston, Allyn and Bacon.

THORNE, B. (1993) *Gender Play: Girls and Boys in School*, Buckingham, Open University Press.

TIZARD, B. and HUGHES, M. (1984) *Young Children Learning, Talking and Thinking at Home and at School*, London, Fontana.

TWEDDLE, S. (1992) 'Towards understanding a new literacy', *English in Education*, **26**, 2, pp. 46–54.

TWEDDLE, S. and MOORE, P. (1994) 'Working with a new literacy', in BRINDLEY, S. (ed.) *Teaching English*, London, Routledge.

URQUHART, I. (1996) 'Popular culture and how boys become men', in HILTON, M. (ed.) *Potent Fictions*, London, Routledge.

VAN MAANEN, J. (1988) *Tales of the Field: On Writing Ethnography*, Chicago, University of Chicago Press.

VINCENT, D. (1989) *Literacy and Popular Culture*, Cambridge, Cambridge University Press.

WALDEN, R. and WALKERDINE, V. (1982) *Girls and Mathematics: The Early Years*, Bedford Way Papers No. 8, London University Institute of Education.

WALKERDINE, V. (1981) 'Sex, power and pedagogy', *Screen Education*, **38**, pp. 14–25.

WALKERDINE, V. (1989) *Counting Girls Out*, London, Virago.

WALLBROWN, F., LEVINE, M. and ENGIN, A. (1981) 'Sex differences in reading attitudes', *Reading Improvement*, **18**, 3, pp. 226–34.

WARNER, M. (1994) *From the Beast to the Blonde*, London, Chatto & Windus.

WARWICK UNIVERSITY (1992) 'English at Key Stages 1, 2 and 3: Second Interim Report to the NCC', York, NCC.

WATT, I. (1966) *The Rise of the Novel: Studies in Defoe, Richardson and Fielding*, London, Peregrine.

WEBSTER, A., BERRIDGE, M. and REED, M. (1996) *Managing the Literacy Curriculum*, London, Routledge.

WEINBERGER, J. (1994) 'A longitudinal study of literary experiences: The role of parents and children's literacy development', Sheffield University, unpublished thesis.

WEINBERGER, J., HANNON, P. and NUTBROWN, C. (1990) *Ways of Working with Parents to Promote Early Literacy Development*, Sheffield, ERC.

WEINER, G. (1994) *Feminisms in Education: An Introduction*, Buckingham, Open University Press.

WELLS, G. (1985) *Language, Learning and Education: Selected Papers from the Bristol Study. Language at Home and at School*, Windsor, NFER/Nelson.

WELLS, G. (1987) *The Meaning Makers: Children Learning Language and Using Language to Learn*, London, Hodder and Stoughton.

WEST, A. (1986) 'The production of readers', *The English Magazine: Literature*, No. 17, Autumn, pp. 4–22.

WHEELER, M.A. (1984) 'Fourth grade boys' literacy from a mother's point of view', *Language Arts*, **61**, 6, pp. 607–14.

WHITE, J. (1987) *Pupils' Attitudes to Writing*, Walton-on-Thames, NFER/Nelson.

WHITE, J. (1990) 'On literacy and gender', in CARTER, R. (ed.) *Knowledge About Language and the Curriculum*, London, Hodder and Stoughton.

WHITEHEAD, F. (1966) *The Disappearing Dais*, London, Chatto.

WHITEHEAD, F. (1988) 'Quality revisited', *English in Education*, **22**, 2, pp. 54–60.

WHITEHEAD, F., CAPEY, A. and MADDREN, W. (1975) *Children's Reading Interests*, Schools Council Working Paper 52, London, Evans/Methuen Educational.

WHITEHEAD, F., CAPEY, A., MADDREN, W. and WELLINGS, A. (1977) *Children and Their Books: The Final Report of the Schools Council Project on Children's Reading Habits, 10–16*, Basingstoke, Evans/Methuen Educational.

WHYTE, J. (1985) 'Girl friendly science and girl friendly schools', in WHYTE, J., DEEM, R., KANT, L. and CRUIKSHANK, M. (eds) *Girl Friendly Schooling*, London, Methuen.

WILLINSKY, J. (1993) 'Lessons from the literacy before schooling 1800–50', in GREEN, B. (ed.) *The Insistence of the Letter: Literacy Studies and Curriculum Theorising*, London, Falmer Press.

WILLINSKY, J. and HUNNIFORD, M. (1993) 'Reading the romance younger: The mirrors and fears of a preparatory literacy', in CHRISTIAN-SMITH, L. (ed.) *Texts of Desire: Essays on Fiction, Femininity and Schooling*, London, Falmer Press.

WILLIS, P. (1977) *Learning to Labour*, London, Saxon House.

WINNICOTT, D.W. (1968) *The Family and Individual Development*, London, Tavistock Publications.

Index

Abbs, P., 36
action, 44, 152
action and adventure books, 53, 54
Adams, M.J., 31
adolescence, 110–11
adventure, 53, 54, 109, 161
Alcock,   112
Allen, D., 41
alphabet method, 32
1966 Anglo-American Dartmouth
    seminar, 41
Apple, M., 181
Appleyard, J.A., 109, 129–30, 179
Arnold, M., 39
Arnot, M., 9
Assessment of Performance Unit, 15, 95
authors, favourite, 54–7
Ayres, G., 13

Baines, B., 18, 40
Balzac,   125–6
Bardsley, D., 56, 152
Barnes,   124, 145
Barrs, M., 94, 168
Barthes, R., 113–14, 117, 118, 121,
    125–6
Beano, 62–3, 64, 115
beat em' up games, 71–2
Benjamin, B., 110, 124
Benjamin, W., 152–3, 154
Benton, P., 15, 50, 56, 74–5, 113, 163,
    167
Berridge, M., 176, 177
Bettelheim, B., 111
biological determinism, 18–19
Bissex, G.L., 13, 37
Blyton, E., 56, 115
Book Weeks, 169

books
    choice, 11–15, 43, 49–76, 112–13
    favourite, 53, 61
    provision, 168–9
Bordo, S., 156
bottom-up approach, 32
Bourdieu, P., 22, 30, 156
Boys and English, 15, 17, 28
Braidotti, R., 18
Brember, I., 13
Brindley, S., 162, 163
Britton, J., 35–6, 95
Bronte, E., 111
Brophy, J., 9
Brownstein, R., 13, 55
Bryant, P., 150
Bullock Report, 14, 36, 116
Byars, B., 23, 100, 107, 119

Capey, A., 14
cartoons, 63
Casualty, 68–9
Ceefax, 178
Chall, J., 31
Chambers, A., 108–9
characters
    female, 95, 109, 157
    male, 108, 109
    pupil's choice, 130–1
Cherland, M., 19–20, 21
Chodorow, N., 24–5
Christian-Smith, L., 94
Clark, M., 12–13, 37, 150
Clarricoates, K., 9, 158
class divisions, 40
class readers, 44, 112–13, 117
class reading, 163, 171
classic books, 50, 113

207